David R Bromham, Maureen E Dalton,
Jennifer C Jackson, Peter JR Millican (Eds.)

Ethics in Reproductive Medicine

Springer-Verlag
London   Berlin   Heidelberg   New York
Paris   Tokyo   Hong Kong
Barcelona   Budapest

David R. Bromham, PhD, FRCOG
University Department of Obstetrics and Gynaecology, St. James's
University Hospital, Beckett Street, Leeds LS9 7TF

Maureen E. Dalton, MB BS, MRCOG
Department of Obstetrics and Gynaecology, Sunderland District
General Hospital, Kayll Road, Sunderland SR4 7TP

Jennifer C. Jackson, MA
Department of Philosophy, University of Leeds, Leeds LS2 9JT

Peter J.R. Millican, MA, B Phil
Department of Philosophy, University of Leeds, Leeds LS2 9JT

ISBN-13:978-1-4471-1897-8   e-ISBN-13:978-1-4471-1895-4
DOI: 10.1007/978-1-4471-1895-4

British Library Cataloguing in Publication Data
International Conference on Philosophical Ethics in Reproductive Medicine
(2nd: 1991)
Ethics in reproductive medicine.
I. Title II. Bromham, David R. (David Richard)
176
ISBN-13:978-1-4471-1897-8

Library of Congress Data available

Typeset by Photo·graphics, Honiton, Devon
2128/3830-543210 Printed on acid-free paper

Preface

Medical ethics is a difficult and controversial field and that part of it dealing with reproductive medicine is no exception. Our first conference on philosophical ethics in reproductive medicine (PERM 1) in 1988 discussed many of the controversies in this field. The acclaim it received encouraged us to organise PERM 2 but choosing a relevant and topical programme was a clairvoyant challenge in its own right. Since PERM 1 we have seen a number of developments, in the UK and internationally, that have thrown the problems that society must face into sharp relief. Drawing on the expertise of contributors from science, many medical specialities, philosophy, theology and economics, we have sought to address the issues raised by these new developments, as well as a number of long-standing issues that remain as contentious as ever, but of undiminished significance.

On the scientific front, the long-predicted technique of embryo biopsy and diagnosis is now a reality. This has prompted the inclusion of some of the topics addressed by this second conference. If it is possible to identify abnormal genes in embryonic cells, how feasible and, indeed, how useful would it be to replace them with healthy ones? Should we set out down that path and if so where should we stop? Should we also ask whether the availability of such a technique would eventually have to be considered in the same light as Caesarean section: another technological advance to which a mother might be expected to feel a moral obligation to submit for the benefit of her potential child?

Against the background of the developments in embryo diagnosis *some* of the recommendations of the Warnock Report of 1984 were processed to UK law as the Human Fertilisation and Embryology Act 1990. At least one recommendation was not included, namely the greater provision of treatment facilities under the National Health Service. However, radical changes in the structure and funding of the health service in England have also come about and brought with them new problems for reproductive medicine and ethical analysis. While many people hold that the reproductive system is too important to humanity to allow medical interference, the meagre allocation of resources for both fertility control and infertility treatment seems to suggest that reproduction is regarded as an unimportant luxury.

Globally, the twin spectres of death in pregnancy of epidemic proportions and massive population crises continue to make our preoccupation with infertility and embryos seem very parochial.

Epidemics of sexually transmitted disease are upon us and call into question not just the ethics of reproductive technologies but the ethics of sexual behaviour. In this context the biological and philosophical significance of a monogamous family structure is addressed in this volume.

The problem of abortion is still with us. In the last conference we concentrated mainly on the status of the human embryo: this time we have taken a wider view and considered the implications, for society, of a legalised abortion service and the philosophical relevance of some of the arguments and other methods of persuasion employed in the debate.

All of these problems it is our joint responsibility to address; their resolution is our joint interest. More than one discipline is equipped to help make sense of them, as we hope the multidisciplinary contents of this volume demonstrate.

While we have attempted to present a spectrum of opinion on a few selected topics, we acknowledge that some may feel their views to have been under-represented. Time and space do not permit otherwise. However, we hope you enjoy and are informed by this book.

Leeds,
1991

David R. Bromham
Maureen E. Dalton
Jennifer C. Jackson
Peter J.R. Millican

Acknowledgements

There are many whom we must thank for their contributions both to the organisation of the conference and to the preparation of these volumes. Most specifically, our colleagues in the Departments of Obstetrics and Gynaecology (St. James's Hospital), of Philosophy, and of Continued Professional Education in the University of Leeds.

We would also once again like to express our thanks to those organisations who supported the conference in various ways without influencing its subject matter. These were Bayer UK Limited, The British Fertility Society, Hoechst UK Limited, The National Association of Family Planning Doctors, Organon Laboratories Limited, Roussel Laboratories Limited, Schering Healthcare, Serono Laboratories (UK) Limited, Upjohn Limited.

We are also grateful to Cambridge University Press for permission to reproduce Fig. 9.1. This originally appeared in: Short RV (1985) Species difference in reproductive mechanisms. In: *Reproduction in Mammals 4: Reproductive Fitness*. Cambridge University Press, Cambridge, p 24.

Contents

Contributors

S.L. Barron, MB BS, FRCS, FRCOG
Consultant Obstetrician and Gynaecologist, Royal Victoria Infirmary, Queen Victoria Road, Newcastle upon Tyne, NE1 4LP, UK

P.R. Braude, PhD, MRCOG
Professor of Obstetrics and Gynaecology, UMDS Department of Obstetrics & Gynaecology, 6th Floor, North Wing, St. Thomas's Hospital, Lambeth Palace Road, London, SE1 7EH, UK

D.W. Brown, MA, PhD
Van Mildert Professor of Divinity, Department of Theology, Abbey House, Palace Green, Durham, DH1 3RS, UK

P.A. Byrne, BA, B Phil
Lecturer in the Philosophy of Religion, King's College London, Strand, London, WC2R 2LS, UK

J. Hutton, BSc, B Phil
Senior Research Fellow, Centre for Health Economics, University of York, Heslington, York, YO1 5DD, UK

J.C. Jackson, MA
Lecturer, Department of Philosophy, University of Leeds, Leeds, LS2 9JT, UK

Lord Jakobovits,
Chief Rabbi, Adler House, Tavistock Square, London, WC1H 9HN, UK

M.H. King, MD, FRCP, FFPHM
Reader in Public Health Medicine, Department of Public Health Medicine, University of Leeds, 32 Hyde Terrace, Leeds, LS2 9LN, UK

A.K. Maynard, B Phil
Professor of Economics and Director, Centre of Health Economics, University of York, Heslington, York, YO1 5DD, UK

P.J.R. Millican, MA, B Phil
Lecturer in Philosophy and Computer Studies, Department of Philosophy, University of Leeds, Leeds, LS2 9JT, UK

M.E. Pembrey, BSc, MD, FRCP
Mothercare Professor of Paediatric Genetics, Institute of Child Health, 30 Guilford Street, London, WC1N 1EH, UK

D.M. Potts, MB, B Chir, PhD
President Emeritus, Family Health International, International Family Health, 15 Bateman Buildings, Soho Square, London, W1V 5TW, UK

J.G. Schenker, MD
Chairman, Department of Obstetrics & Gynaecology, Hadassah Hebrew University, Jerusalem, Israel

I.P. Senanayake, MB BS, DTPH, PhD
Assistant Secretary General, International Planned Parenthood Federation, Regent's College, Inner Circle, Regent's Park, London, NW1 4NS, UK

W.R. Sheaff, D Phil, AHSM
Lecturer, Health Services Management Unit, (Manchester University), Devonshire House, Precinct Centre, Oxford Road, Manchester, M13 9RN, UK

L. Somorjay, BSc
National Childbirth Trust, The Old Farmhouse, Bullocks Lane, Kingston Seymour, Somerset, BS21 6XA, UK

B. Steinbock, PhD
Associate Professor of Philosophy, Department of Philosophy, HU257, The University at Albany, Sunya, 1400 Washington Avenue, Albany, NY 12222, USA

J.G. Thornton, MD, MRCOG, DTM & H,
Senior Lecturer and Consultant, University Department of Obstetrics & Gynaecology, St. James's University Hospital, Beckett Street, Leeds, LS9 7TF, UK

M. Warnock, MA, B Phil
Mistress, Girton College, Cambridge, CB3 0JG, UK

CHAPTER 1

Embryo Therapy: What Can Be Done?

P.R. Braude

Genetic disease is a major cause of mortality and morbidity (Milunsky 1986). There are over 4000 diseases known to be caused by a defect in a single gene (monogenic), others which are caused by a defect in, or loss or gain of one or more chromosomes, and many thousands more diseases which are clearly inherited on a multifactorial (polygenic) basis (Stanbury et al. 1983 and Table 1.1). There has long been speculation that if the genetic sequences for these diseases could be identified precisely, then it might be possible to treat or prevent them by manipulating or replacing the genes that cause the disease (Nichols 1988).

Types of Genetic Inheritance

There are three main types of inheritance of genetic disease. Each individual normally carries two copies of each gene, one allele inherited from their father

Table 1.1. Types of genetic disorders

Multifactorial	
Heart disease	
Diabetes	
Neural tube defects	
Schizophrenia	
Chromosomal	
Autosomal abnormalities	(Trisomy 21 – Down's syndrome)
Sex chromosome abnormalities	(Monosomy X – Turner's syndrome)
Monogenic	
Haemophilia	
Sickle cell disease	
Adenine deaminase deficiency	
Lesch-Nyhan syndrome	

and one from their mother. If both copies of a normal gene are required for normal cell function, then a defective gene in just one of the alleles may cause the genetic disease to manifest (a dominant gene). Thus half the offspring from the union of an affected and non-affected individual could be afflicted with the disease (Fig. 1.1). If only one of the two copies of the gene is necessary for normal function, then a disease state will only manifest when no normal copies are present (i.e., when two copies of the defective gene are inherited). Thus in this recessive type of inheritance there are three possible phenotypic states: two copies of the normal gene present (normal individual); one normal and one abnormal copy (unaffected by the disease but a carrier for it); two copies of the abnormal gene (affected by the disease). From these combinations it will be seen that if two carriers produce children, then there is a one-in-four chance of the offspring being affected by the disease and a one-in-two chance that they will be carriers themselves. A special type of recessive inheritance occurs with genes which are carried on the X chromosome. Their inheritance is linked to the gender of the individual and their offspring. As females have two copies of the

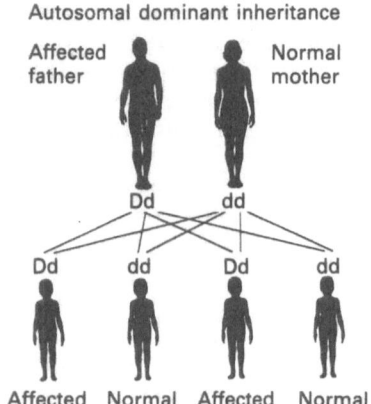

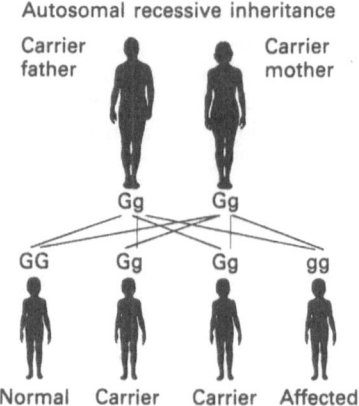

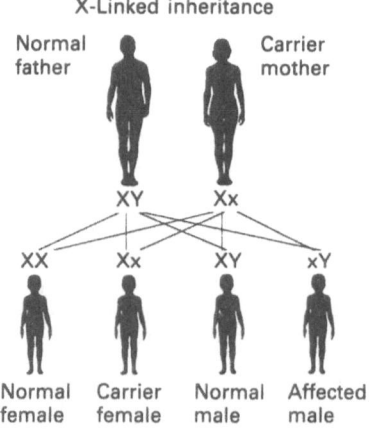

Figure 1.1. The three main types of inheritance of genetic disease.

X chromosome, if one copy gene is defective, it will be balanced by the other normal copy resulting in a carrier state only. However, males have only one copy of the X chromosome, such that a defect in the gene on this chromosome will result in the manifestation of the disease state. Thus, in sex chromosome or X-linked disorders, the female offspring of a female carrier have a 50% chance of being carriers themselves, but the male offspring have a 50% chance of being affected by the disease.

How Do Abnormal Genes Cause Disease States?

Each gene carried in the DNA of the chromosome is composed of a specific genetic sequence which codes for the production of a messenger RNA, which itself forms a template for the production of specific sequences of amino acids of which the proteins of the cell are comprised (Drlica 1984). Each protein has a precise three-dimensional structure which confers function on it. Certain proteins will function as enzymes catalysing normal intracellular chemical reactions, whereas others will be integral to the structure of the cell. Since the three-dimensional configuration of the protein is dictated by its specific amino-acid sequence, alteration or loss of even just one of the specific amino acids comprising the protein as a result of a change in the DNA sequence coding for them may result in loss of function of the protein. In those cases where the protein is an enzyme there might be an alteration to the normal chemical pathway within the cell and a build up of a noxious substrate on which the enzyme acts. Alternatively, there may be a lack of synthesis of a product which the enzyme normally would facilitate. In each of these cases, product excess or product lack, a disease state may result. For example individuals with the disease phenylketonuria have a deficiency of the enzyme phenylalanine hydroxylase and cannot convert the amino acid phenylalanine to another amino acid tyrosine. Build-up of phenylalanine damages cerebral neurones and can result in mental retardation (Stanbury et al. 1983). Similarly, congenital lack of production of the hormone thyroxin will result in abnormal thyroid function and the disease state of cretinism also associated with mental retardation.

Individuals affected by a genetic disease, or known to have a substantial chance of passing on a genetic disease, may wish to have their disease state treated or ameliorated by therapy, or to avail themselves of the opportunity of preventing transmission of the disease.

Treatment of Genetic Disease

Current modes of treatment for genetic disease rely on three main options.

Metabolic Manipulation

Where there is the possibility of build-up of a substrate due to failure or lack of specific enzyme activity, dietary restriction can be instituted to try and reduce the build-up of the toxic substrate. For example in a mild disease state such as gout (xanthine oxidase deficiency) the intake of protein in the diet may be reduced, or foods with a high phenylalanine content excluded in patients with phenylketonuria. Alternatively, attempts can be made to try and lower the level of toxic substance with chemical agents or drugs, e.g., Probenecid will increase uric acid excretion in primary gout and allopurinol will decrease the rate of formation of uric acid. Similarly, penicillamine can be used to mop up excess copper ions in Wilson's disease.

Replacement of the Gene Product

Where the product of the gene is known it can sometimes be administered exogenously to overcome a disease caused by its deficiency, e.g., insulin in diabetes, thyroxin in cretinism, clotting factors in haemophilia. Replacement of deficient enzymes is more problematic as the site of their need is very specific and is usually intracellular and often within the brain. Large amounts of the enzyme and extremely high blood levels may be needed to achieve minimal intracellular change, and in most conditions the enzyme is degraded or does not cross the blood–brain barrier where the action is most needed. However, combination of the enzymes with polyethylene glycol may be more successful and has given some cause for cautious optimism (Hershfield et al. 1987).

Tissue Transplantation

Structural defects resulting in inappropriate function of a tissue or organ may be treated successfully by whole organ or tissue transplantation. In cystic fibrosis some successes have been achieved in overcoming the deteriorating lung function by heart–lung transplantation, and by liver transplants in haemophilia. However it is still too early to judge long-term outcome for such patients. In sickle cell disease or thalassaemia, the defective red blood cells may be partially or wholly replaced by transfusion, which in essence is transplantation of blood tissue. Unfortunately normal red blood cells have a finite life span of around 120 days and thus repeated transfusions are required with all their attendant risks. Where there are defects of the white blood cells such as in severe combined immunodeficiency disease (SCID), caused by a deficiency of the enzyme adenosine deaminase (ADA) and producing a disease similar to AIDS but congenitally inherited (Thompson and Seegmiller 1980), bone marrow transplantation has been tried but is complicated by the difficulties created by rejection and graft vs host disease. If it were possible to engineer the patient's own marrow-producing cells in such a way that their white blood cells could produce the ADA, the problems of rejection would be overcome and the enzyme would be indefinitely available in the circulation. This is the basis for somatic gene therapy (Verma 1990).

Gene and Embryo Therapy

Somatic Cell Gene Therapy

The term gene therapy usually refers to methods for modifying the genetic constitution of a cell with the intention of replacing a defective gene or adding to the genetic material of the cell a sequence of DNA which will code for the product which is defective (Weatherall 1989). A number of methods have been postulated or used experimentally to alter the genetic material. In all cases the task that faces the genetic engineer is similar. First the gene responsible for the genetic defect must be isolated and cloned (multiple copies made). Secondly, an appropriate carrier cell for the gene must be selected and the required gene must be inserted into the carrier cell. Finally, once the gene has been inserted, the cells should still be capable of reproducing normally and the inserted gene should be capable of expressing normally, that is to say producing the gene product required through subsequent cell generations. Modern techniques of molecular biology have enabled the genes which are responsible for a number of important genetic diseases to be isolated and many of these have been cloned and sequenced. Methods for the insertion of genes into cells have been the subject of intense investigation (Williamson 1982; Nichols 1988). Microinjection of the sequences directly in the nuclei of cells is now commonplace in the laboratory as a means of creating specialized lines of laboratory animals for the study of cellular and genetic mechanisms (Stewart et al. 1982). Attempts to introduce sequences into cells using chemical means (transfection) or by cell fusion or electroporation have been successful but inefficient. The natural ability of viruses to insert short genetic sequences into the DNA of cells has been harnessed by the molecular biologist and viruses have been produced which will insert functional genes into cells (viral vectors) (Nichols 1988; Verma 1990). To create a viral vector, viruses are modified to contain, within their simple genome, a specific sequence which codes for the normal human protein known to be deficient or defective in the disease. The virus is also carefully modified to be unable to replicate itself after entering the cell. Thus the transformed virus is allowed to "infect" a human cell line (e.g., marrow stem cells) into whose nuclei it inserts its own genome, which now contains the required sequence. The cell with the incorporated sequence now produces messenger RNA from the new sequence which codes for the protein which has previously been deficient or defective. Although a fiendishly clever trick, there is always danger that (i) the virus may undergo spontaneous mutation and perhaps begin replicating itself thus infecting the individual with a new disease; or (ii) perhaps transform the cells in such a way that they become cancerous (Kirk and Capecchi 1986). Thus despite the technology being developed to insert genes into cells there are still many questions to be answered about efficiency and safety. Nevertheless, this has not deterred some clinicians from beginning clinical trials (Anderson 1984).

Germ Line Gene Therapy

All of the above methods involve the manipulation of the genome in somatic cells from the individual affected by the disease but not his/her gametes. Thus any advantageous or disadvantageous effects will be limited to the life of the affected individual and thus contained within that generation. Far more contentious than somatic cell gene therapy is the possibility of using the techniques described to modify the genes of the germ line of the individual such that the genetic modifications would be passed on in the gametes to subsequent generations (Editorial 1988; Weatherall 1989). Practically it would be difficult to modify the germ cells themselves since they are laid down very early in fetal life (Johnson and Everitt 1989), or to incorporate new genetic material into the unfertilized oocyte or sperm which are released in a non-replicating haploid state. However it would be possible to modify the genome of the zygote immediately following fertilization, or the embryo at the earliest stages of development. For example, special genetic constructs could be inserted by micro-injection into either the male or female pronucleus following fertilization *in vitro*. Indeed, the insertion of human genes into pronucleate stages of mouse embryos to create so-called "transgenic" mice is widely used in studying the regulation of important genes (Grosveld et al. 1988; Epstein et al. 1989), but the efficiency of successful incorporation and expression is still very low. Although the poor efficiency of expression may be acceptable in laboratory animals where large numbers of fertilized oocytes can be obtained, it would not be acceptable for humans unless the efficiency improved dramatically.

Alternatively it might be possible to modify embryos cultured *in vitro* at very early preimplantation stages. As these are diploid dividing cells it might be plausible to use viral vectors to incorporate new DNA into morulae or blastocysts, but all the caveats which applied to somatic gene therapy would still apply. The low efficiency would be accentuated with the small number of cells present in the early conceptus, and the risks of mutation would still present a significant threat. Thus it would seem that embryo therapy by insertion of new genetic material presents enormous practical difficulties and is fraught with many potentially lethal disadvantages for the fetus and subsequent generations. The alternative to germ-line gene therapy or embryo therapy by substitution or insertion of genetic material would be the elimination of genetic disease by gamete selection or by selection of embryos at either post or preimplantation stages, or by genetic selection of gametes.

Gene Therapy by Embryo or Gamete Selection

Prenatal diagnosis of genetic disease is now commonplace and is offered routinely to pregnant women who may be at risk of passing on a genetic disease or carrying a child with a chromosome abnormality (Rodeck and Morsman 1983; King 1988). Currently amniocentesis, usually performed between 14 and 16 weeks of gestation, or chorion villus biopsy, done at about 11 weeks of gestation, may be offered. Cells biopsied from the placenta, or desquamated from the fetus into the amniotic fluid, can be karyotyped for chromosomal abnormality, or used for more sophisticated molecular techniques to identify genetic disease in the fetus. If detected, the couple can consider termination of the pregnancy which will prevent the disease being passed on to subsequent generations. However, there are many people who have strong reservations about induced abortion and may not wish to avail themselves of such a "search and destroy" policy. An acceptable alternative for some may be the diagnosis of the genetic disease at a stage prior to implantation of the conceptus (preimplantation diagnosis). Embryos generated following fertilization *in vitro* can be biopsied for the purposes of genetic typing, and only those embryos shown to be unaffected by the genetic disease replaced into the individual in order to try and achieve a pregnancy (Braude et al. 1989 and Figure 1.2). Techniques have been developed to take such a biopsy by removing a single cell at the 8-cell stage of development and to amplify the DNA content from the single nucleus sufficiently to enable a genetic diagnosis to be made (Handyside et al. 1989). Although the process of biopsy might be expected to compromise development in what is already a very precarious form of assisted conception (Hardy et al. 1990), pregnancies have been achieved using this technique (Handyside et al. 1990). Preimplantation biopsy relies on the premise that the single cell removed is representative of the rest of the cells that will be replaced following diagnosis. There are now cogent reasons to suspect that in certain circumstances this may not be the case (Winston et al. 1991), and that the reliability of the technique for clinical practice is yet to be proven. Some problems could be eliminated by having larger numbers of cells on which to perform the diagnostic test. Techniques are being developed to biopsy the preimplantation embryo at the blastocyst stage, approximately 5 days in development, when about 100 cells are present (Monk et al. 1988; Summers et al. 1988; Dokras et al. 1990). Although a more reliable diagnosis could be made, there are difficulties in getting embryos to cleave *in vitro* to this stage of development (Bolton and Braude 1987; Bolton et al. 1988), or even in retrieving sufficient numbers of embryos fertilized *in vivo* by uterine lavage after superovulation (Buster et al. 1985). Furthermore, as the diagnosis may not be available within a day, the remaining blastocyst may have to be cryopreserved (Hartshorne et al. 1991), a technique which is very inefficient when the zona pellucida has been breached, as it must be in order to take the biopsy.

Selection against genetic disease prior to fertilization is an attractive option. New techniques now make it possible to biopsy the polar body from an oocyte (Gordon and Gang 1990; Verlinsky et al. 1990), perform a DNA diagnostic

Embryo biopsy on day 3 after fertilization in vitro:

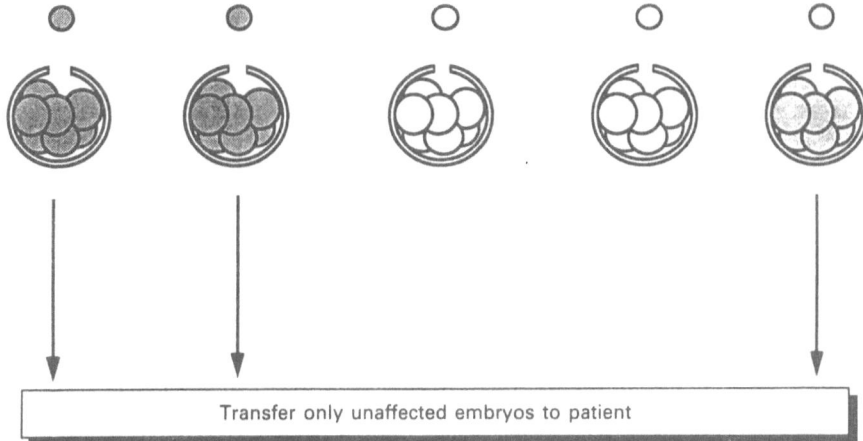

Figure 1.2. Gene therapy by selection.

technique on the chromosomes contained within it (Monk and Holding 1990), and to select only unaffected oocytes for fertilization *in vitro*. Although these techniques have been shown to be feasible, once again their diagnostic accuracy has not been tested thoroughly and use of the technique is fraught with difficulties. For example, it may be difficult to predict precisely the DNA content of the polar body because of crossing over of the genetic material during meiosis. Thus, estimating the DNA content of the oocyte by extrapolating from the DNA content of the polar body involves certain presumptions which may be too inaccurate for a clinical diagnostic technique. Furthermore, the necessary piercing of the zona pellucida prior to fertilization in order to perform the biopsy will increase the likelihood of abnormal fertilization due to polyspermy (Cohen et al. 1991) following insemination *in vitro*. Attempting to avoid this by subzonal insertion of a single spermatozoon will dramatically reduce the likelihood of fertilization.

Applying the genetic selection process to spermatozoa which could then be used for artificial insemination *in vivo* would greatly improve the likelihood of conception following the diagnostic technique. Methods have been developed to try and sex spermatozoa which would enable selection against sex-linked disorders (Amann and Seidel 1980), but so far no technique provides any more than a skewing of the sex ratio, and thus does not avoid the need for some form of confirmatory postimplantation prenatal diagnostic test. Future enhancements using chromosome painting and fluorescent activated cell sorters may enable the use of more specific genetic probes and the accuracy and specificity of selection to be improved. Nevertheless, although the efficiency of all these preimplantation and prefertilization diagnostic techniques is likely to improve, the enormous technical difficulties that they pose, and the reduced chance of pregnancy that they offer when compared with natural conception, will make them an option worth pursuing only for those with a substantial risk of passing on a genetic disease and with strong ethical objections to antenatal diagnosis and abortion (McLaren 1985).

Thus modification of the genetic material of the embryo in order to try and prevent the inheritance of genetic disease by introduction of new genes has little place in medical practice when the alternative of genetic selection can provide the same end result more accurately and with more predictable and controllable side effects.

References

Amann RP, Seidel GE (1980) Prospects for sexing mammalian sperm. Colorado Associated University Press, Boulder, Colorado

Anderson WF (1984) Prospects for human gene therapy. Science 226:401–409

Bolton VN, Braude PR (1987) Development of the human preimplantation embryo in vitro. In: Monroy A, McLaren A (ed) Current topics in developmental biology. Academic Press, New York, pp 93–114

Bolton VN, Hawes SM, Taylor CT, Parsons JH (1988) Development of spare human preimplantation embryos in vitro: an analysis of the correlations among gross morphology, cleavage rates and development to the blastocyst. J In Vitro Fert Embryo Transfer 6:30–35

Braude PR, Monk M, Pickering SJ, Cant A, Johnson MH (1989) Measurement of HPRT activity in the human unfertilized oocyte and pre-embryo. Prenatal Diagnosis 9:839–850

Buster JC, Bustillo M, Rodi IA et al. (1985) Biologic and morphologic description of donated human ova recovered by non-surgical uterine lavage. Am J Obstet Gynecol 153:211–217

Cohen J, Talansky B, Malter H et al. (1991) Microsurgical fertilization and teratozoospermia. Hum Reprod 6:118–123

Dokras A, Sargent IL, Ross C, Gardner RL, Barlow DH (1990) Trophectoderm biopsy in human blastocysts. Hum Reprod 5:821–825

Drlica K (1984) Understanding DNA cloning: a guide for the curious. John Wiley, New York

Editorial (1988) Are germlines special? Nature 331:100

Epstein H, Hardy R, May JS, Johnson MH, Holmes N (1989) Expression and function of HLA–A2.1 in transgenic mice. Eur J Immunobiol 19:1575–1583

Gordon JW, Gang I (1990) Use of zona drilling for safe and effective biopsy of murine oocytes and embryos. Biol Reprod 42:869–876

Grosveld F, van Assendelft GB, Greaves DR, Kolias G (1988) Position independent, high level expression of the human β globin gene in transgenic mice. Cell 51:975–985

Handyside AH, Kontogianni EH, Hardy K, Winston RML (1990) Pregnancies from human preimplantation embryos sexed by Y-specific DNA amplification. Nature 344:768–770

Handyside AH, Pattinson JK, Penketh RJA et al. (1989) Biopsy of human pre-implantation embryos and sexing by DNA amplification. Lancet i:347–349

Hardy K, Martin KL, Leese H, Winston RML, Handyside AH (1990) Human preimplantation development *in vitro* is not adversely affected by biopsy at the 8-cell stage. Hum Reprod 5:708–714

Hartshorne GM, Elder K, Crow J, Dyson H and Edwards G (1991) The influence of in vitro development upon post thaw survival and implantation of cryopreserved human blastocysts. Hum Reprod 6:136–141

Hershfield Ms, Buckley RH, Greenberg ML et al. (1987) Treatment of adenosine deaminase deficiency with polyethylene glycol modified adenosine deaminase. N Eng J Med 316:589–596

Johnson MH, Everitt BJ (1989) Essential Reproduction, 3rd ed. Blackwell Scientific Publications, Oxford

King CR (1988) Prenatal diagnosis of genetic disease with molecular genetic technology. Obstet Gynecol Surv 43:493–508

Kirk TR, Capecchi MR (1986) Introduction of homologous DNA sequences into mammalian cells induces mutations in the cognate gene. Nature 324:34–38

McLaren A (1985) Prenatal diagnosis before implantation: opportunities and problems. Prenatal Diagnosis 5:85–90

Milunsky A (1986) Genetic disorders and the fetus, 2nd edn. Plenum, New York

Monk M, Holding C (1990) Amplification of a β-haemoglobin sequence in individual human oocytes and polar bodies. Lancet 335:985–988

Monk M, Muggleton-Harris AL, Rawlings E, Whittingham DG (1988) Pre-implantation diagnosis of HPRT-deficient male and carrier female mouse embryos by trophectoderm biopsy. Hum Reprod 3:377–381

Nichols EK (1988) Human Gene Therapy. Harvard University Press, Cambridge, Mass.

Rodeck CH, Morsman JM ((1983) First-trimester chorion biopsy. Br Med Bull 39:338–342

Stanbury JB, Wyngaarden JB, Fredrickson DS, Goldstein JL, Brown MS (1983) The metabolic basis of inherited disease. McGraw Hill, New York

Stewart TA, Wagner EF, Mintz B (1982) Human β-globin gene sequences injected into mouse eggs, retained in adults and transmitted to progeny. Science 217:1046–1048

Summers PM, Campbell JM, Miller MW (1988) Normal in vivo development of marmoset monkey embryos after trophectoderm biopsy. Hum Reprod 1:89–94

Thompson LF, Seegmiller JE (1980) ADA deficiency and SCID. Adv Enzymol 51:167–210

Verlinsky Y, Pergament E, Strom C (1990) The preimplantation diagnosis of genetic diseases. J In Vitro Fert Embryo Transfer 7:1–5

Verma IM (1990) Gene therapy. Scientific American (November)

Weatherall DJ (1989) Gene therapy. Br Med J 298:691–693

Williamson B (1982) Gene therapy. Nature 298:416–418

Winston NJ, Braude PR, Pickering SJ et al. (1991) The incidence of abnormal morphology and nucleo-cytoplasmic ratios in 2, 3 and 5 day human pre-embryos. Hum Reprod 6:17–24

CHAPTER 2

Embryo Therapy: Is There a Clinical Need?

M.E. Pembrey

In an age when pre-implantation human embryos can be sexed to ensure transfer of only females and thereby avoid serious X-linked disease (Handyside et al. 1990), it is perhaps natural to raise the question of embryo therapy, particularly the correction of genetic defects. It is easy to assume that the therapeutic maxim "the earlier the better" holds true even at this primitive stage of development. Indeed, the Report of the Committee of Enquiry into Human Fertilisation and Embryology (Warnock 1984) commented in para 1.1 "It is now possible to observe the very earliest stages of human development and with these discoveries came the hope of remedying defects at this **very early stage**". However, examination of the clinical needs and how best to meet them now and in the future, suggests that embryo **gene** therapy, at least, has little to offer. That is not to say that other therapeutic procedures during embryonic life (i.e., between conception and eight weeks' gestation) will not have a place, but the recent decision in Britain to outlaw the transfer of a genetically manipulated embryo to a woman does little to limit the clinical application of the new advances in genetics and embryology.

This being so, why is there so much interest in embryo gene therapy? Why was it a topic of the first session of the conference that this volume records? How come so many commentators imply that there *would* be clinical benefit from embryo gene therapy (so-called germ-line gene therapy), even though it is currently outlawed on the grounds that, until the techniques are perfected, inadvertent genetic damage could be transmitted to subsequent generations?

Genetic Manipulation of Animal Embryos

I think there are two main reasons why the idea of embryo gene therapy has been promoted so strongly. First, the generation of experimental transgenic animals (in which foreign DNA or transgene has been inserted into the fertilised egg or early embryo) is often justified to the public as understanding genetic disorders in the hope of finding a treatment. This gives the impression that the same approach is being planned as therapy for patients. These animal experiments are, in fact, designed to learn more about the genetic regulation of embryonic development or to create animal models of human genetic diseases suitable for therapeutic research. Other experiments have discrete agricultural objectives or are related to the synthesis of a useful biological product.

When scientists first considered inserting a specific DNA sequence into experimental animals, they were faced with the problem of actually getting the new DNA into all or most of the relevant cells. Given that techniques existed to insert the new DNA into the host genome, so that this transgene thereafter replicated with it during normal cell division, the simplest solution was to insert the DNA into the fertilised egg or early embryo. Starting at this point meant that the transgene often ended up in all the tissues, including that special line of cells set aside early in development to become the eggs or sperm of the mature animal – the germ-line. Hence the term germ-line gene therapy does not mean a technique specifically aimed at the germ-line cells alone, but just the practice of gene insertion into the zygote or very early embryo. This technique of producing transgenic animals is now performed daily in many molecular genetics research establishments, and of course it is convenient for these laboratories if the transgene is passed on to the offspring. It allows experimental matings of various kinds and saves the time and trouble of repeated genetic manipulations of very early embryos. So it can be seen that it is in no way intended as a trial run for human embryo gene therapy. Despite this, the recent transgenic mouse experiment to test whether the Sry gene (sex-determining region of the Y chromosome) could alone direct male development in a chromosomally female mouse embryo (Koopman et al. 1991) led to the usual crop of claims in the media that "it will almost certainly provide an opportunity for human couples to decide the sex of a future offspring" (*Evening Standard*, 9 May 1991). In fact, in terms of the opportunities for human sex selection, it is absolutely no different from the knowledge that the Y chromosome determines maleness; knowledge that has already been employed for clinically relevant sex selection for 25 years.

The second reason for the assumption that there will be a clinical need for embryo gene therapy stems simply from scientists failing to think through what would actually be the situation in clinical practice. The occasional flippant writing by protagonists of gene therapy hardly helps to reduce misunderstandings. An anonymous leader in *Nature* published on 14 January 1988, questioned the consensus that genetic manipulation of the germ-line should be outlawed by arguing that "Royal families with haemophilia would no doubt have jumped at the technique". The author had completely overlooked the fact that pre-implantation diagnosis and selective embryo transfer was a simpler and safer way of achieving the same end. Before developing this point further, it is perhaps worthwhile to consider in which clinical situations embryo therapy of any kind might be contemplated, now and in the future.

Clinical Circumstances in Which Embryo Therapy Might Be Contemplated (Table 2.1)

Strictly speaking, therapy is "medical treatment of disease" (*Oxford English Dictionary*) and therefore embryo therapy assumes that we can know that the embryo is diseased or is so likely to have a disease that there is an indication

Table 2.1. Possible clinical interventions involving the embryo

---

Prior risk of genetic disease
  Pre-implantation diagnosis and embryo selection
  Embryo therapy via the mother, e.g., dexamethasone in CAH
  ?Embryonic cytoplasmic exchange in mitochondrial disease
Early recognition of maldevelopment, incidental to IVF or ultrasound scan before eight weeks
  Avoidance of embryo transfer or selective abortion
  ??Therapeutic intervention
General therapy to promote early growth and implantation
??Prophylactic gene therapy, e.g., to protect against cancer

---

to perform diagnostic tests. There are two types of clinical circumstance in which embryo disease would be discovered:

1. There is a high prior chance that the embryo will inherit a specific genetic disorder and the couple are wishing to try for a healthy family whilst avoiding the birth of an affected child
2. Early observation detects maldevelopment. This would be incidental to in vitro fertilisation (IVF) or very early ultrasound examination of the pregnancy

One can also envisage some forms of prophylactic intervention at the embryonic stage to *protect* against some future disease. These more remote possibilities will be considered later.

Treatment of the Embryo Via the Mother: Congenital Adrenal Hyperplasia as an Example

The only examples of embryo therapy known to the author that are currently under clinical trial concern drug or dietary treatment via the mother. This may be empirically based, such as periconceptional multi-vitamin supplements for couples at increased risk of neural tube defects (see Sheppard et al. 1989 for a recent discussion), or specific interventions based on our knowledge of metabolic disease in mother, embryo, or both. A good example is the case of the embryo at risk of the autosomal recessive disorder congenital adrenal hyperplasia (CAH) due to mutant or deleted 21-hydroxylase genes on the chromosome 6 pair. This example illustrates some of the issues that the families themselves address in choosing between therapy and *selective abortion*. It can, perhaps, also serve as a guide to the issues that may come up in the future when embryo selection is available as a service to families at genetic risk.

CAH occurs with a birth prevalence of about 1 in 10 000. The block in the synthetic pathway of cortisol and aldosterone leads not only to adrenal insufficiency requiring lifelong adrenocorticoid hormone replacement, but excess production of androgens. In the female embryo this causes variable virilisation of the external genitalia with enlargement of the clitoris, fusion of the labia and persistence of the urogenital sinus. As females in every other way, the clinical management usually adopted includes corrective surgery to fashion acceptable female genitalia. This is relatively easy if just the clitoris is enlarged (predominantly the effect of androgens in the second and third trimester), or a difficult multistage operation if there is persistence of the urogenital sinus (predominantly an effect of androgens in the first trimester). There are now reports of several pregnancies where maternal dexamethasone therapy (from five or six weeks gestation onwards) has fully or partially suppressed virilisation in females who have inherited a double dose of the 21 hydroxylase mutation (Pang et al. 1990; Speiser et al. 1990). This creates an additional option for couples who know they face a 1-in-4 chance of a child with CAH, typically because they have had a previously affected child, although not necessarily a female with the additional complication of ambiguous genitalia. General reproductive options include:

1. Foregoing further children
2. Trusting to luck, and postnatal medical management if the child is affected
3. Gamete donation to reduce the genetic risk
4. Adoption

Specific options include:

1. Prenatal diagnosis by DNA analysis on a chorionic villus sample obtained at 9–10 weeks, followed by selective abortion of any affected fetus
2. Selective abortion of just an affected *female* fetus
3. Maternal dexamethasone medication from four weeks' gestation if possible to be discontinued except where the prenatal tests at 10 weeks' gestation show the fetus is female and affected. In such a case maternal dexamethasone will be continued for as long as is judged to be safe
4. Alternatively, the maternal dexamethasone could be given only *after* the diagnosis of an affected female fetus at 10 weeks, but this is likely to be ineffective in preventing the most troublesome aspects of virilisation.

Putting Medical Treatment into Perspective

From my somewhat limited experience of couples offered the option of this new treatment of embryos with CAH, they find the decision between treatment and selective abortion very difficult, with the alternatives finely balanced. One couple decided one way in one pregnancy and the opposite for the next pregnancy. I am fairly certain that if offered *pre-implantation* diagnosis in the future, many couples would persist for some time in trying to establish a pregnancy with an unaffected embryo rather than rely on chance and then prenatal treatment of the virilisation if it transpired they were carrying an affected female. As medical treatments go, the treatment of CAH in general is fairly effective and does not place too great a burden on the family or patient, but nevertheless some couples still opt for selective abortion.

It is worth remembering that the treating physician tends to have a very different perspective from the parents wishing to complete their family. The physician tends to compare the patient kept alive and well by medical intervention with the untreated disease state, whilst the parent compares the treated child with a normal healthy child, who has no need to be dependent on doctors with endless visits to the hospital. I was once party to assessing a paper that reported a study of the risk of a heart defect in children born to a parent who had had surgically corrected congenital heart disease. In the discussion, the authors argued that despite a significantly increased offspring risk, prenatal diagnosis by ultrasound examination of the fetal heart was unjustified because the heart defects were treatable. They appeared to have overlooked the fact that 30% of the very same babies that constituted their study had died despite "heart defects being treatable". In addition to the different perspective that families at risk may have compared to physicians, there is the natural difficulty a mother may have in telling the treating doctor what she really thinks:

> Thank you for treating my affected child, but actually I am none too impressed with what medical science can do, and although I do not generally believe in abortion (by which statement, I mean to convey some respect for fetuses, that I do love my affected child, although I can't necessarily expect you as a saver-of-life in general and my child's doctor in particular, to understand what I am about to say), I would like to be offered prenatal diagnosis and selective abortion.

Physicians and medical scientists may well have misjudged the desire for treatment rather than selection, and therefore have overstated the case for gene therapy. One example of this, to which I took exception at the time (Pembrey 1984), comes from a News and Views on Gene Therapy in *Nature* where Weatherall (1984) concluded his comments on gene transfection with the statement "offers major encouragement to those who believe that the ultimate goal of clinical genetics is gene replacement therapy, rather than termination of pregnancy". Many families I have met over the years would strongly disagree with this statement.

Bearing in mind these points, it is clear that even in weighing up *selective abortion* versus treatment, the medical profession may be over-estimating the degree of shift away from selection that will accompany the discovery of new treatments, somatic gene therapy included. As one moves to the pre-implantation stage, the preference for selection rather than treatment is likely to be even stronger.

Highlighting this limited regard for therapeutic advance is not to imply that families are increasingly seeking "perfect babies", a term invented, as far as I can tell, by the media and people involved in the "public debate" on the philosophical ethics of reproductive medicine. In the "private debate" of families at risk making real reproductive decisions, I have never heard the term "perfect baby" and only rarely the phrase "perfectly healthy". Parents talk about their baby being "all right" or "normal" and in recent years sometimes specifically state they are *not* seeking a perfect baby, as if to counter the implied criticism in the media and by some health professionals that parents have become too demanding and choosy.

I do not wish to overstate the case and imply that there is total disregard for therapeutic advance, only, that parents may not be as impressed by medical miracles as is the medical profession.

There is some evidence that the demand for prenatal diagnosis and selective abortion by couples is modified by effective treatment and good provision for affected individuals, and influenced little by the availability of the test per se. The gene for phenylalanine hydroxylase and associated DNA polymorphisms suitable for first trimester prenatal diagnosis of phenylketonuria (PKU) was one of the first to be sequenced (Woo et al. 1983). Since that time and particularly since 1985, prenatal diagnosis has been available to couples with an affected child and therefore facing a 1-in-4 risk. As one of two centres who agreed to provide a prenatal diagnostic service for Britain, we know of only three, possibly four, requests. Only two couples actually went ahead with the test. Over roughly the same time scale this compares with about 40 British prenatal tests for CAH which has a similar birth prevalence and several hundred requests for tests for cystic fibrosis which has four times the birth prevalence. One of the two couples who went ahead with prenatal diagnosis of PKU did so partly because their children would have to spend much of their life in a country that had no provision for the special diet and regular monitoring. Obviously the factors influencing individual decisions are usually complex and cannot really be divined by crude comparisons of the rates of demand for tests, but there is nothing to suggest a tendency for these tests to be requested just because they are possible. To date, there is nothing to suggest that the availability of a prenatal test per se induces a desire for selective abortion where previously a couple would not have wanted to avoid the birth of a child with that condition.

Gene Therapy in the Embryo Versus Embryo Selection

The great majority of couples facing a genetic risk for their offspring can produce a winning combination of their own genes. For autosomal dominant inheritance, where one parent carries the mutation, the offspring risk is 50%. This means that with five pre-implantation embryos there is a 97% chance that *at least* one "unaffected" embryo will be obtained. With autosomal recessive inheritance the risk of an affected embryo is 25%, giving a 98.5% chance of getting *at least* one unaffected in a collection of three pre-implantation embryos. Given the current widely accepted practice of generating several embryos in vitro simultaneously, the option of embryo selection by pre-implantation genetic diagnosis is going to be feasible. Imagine the clinical situation in which a couple are facing a one-in-four risk of their child being born with cystic fibrosis. A clinical embryologist contemplating gene insertion/correction therapy on the preimplantation embryo will first have to diagnose whether the embryo in question is homozygous for the cystic fibrosis mutation. If that were the case, the couple would have a stark choice; to be the first to have transferred a genetically manipulated embryo in the hope that the experiment will lead to the birth of a healthy baby, or select another embryo that has a winning combination of their own normal genes. For both practical and ethical reasons, I think the choice will always be selection.

Even if embryo gene therapy were planned, most practical scenarios I can think of would require several embryos to be generated in the first place, given the two-stage procedure of first finding an affected embryo and then successfully treating it. Since the success rate of producing undamaged "corrected" embryos would be (much) less than 100% (it has to be remembered that a second diagnostic biopsy would be necessary before implantation to check that the gene insertion had worked), I believe one would have to aim for the treatment of several affected embryos. The process of finding these affected embryos in the first place is very likely to reveal unaffected embryos. If it is desirable to transfer a "corrected" embryo with less than certainty that the baby will escape cystic fibrosis, surely it is even more desirable to transfer the unaffected embryo that does not have the potential to produce a baby with cystic fibrosis? If there is a theoretical small risk of damaging the preimplantation embryo by biopsy of one of its cells, then it is clearly more risky to perform two such biopsies plus a gene insertion procedure. Thus, where the chance of a couple producing an unaffected embryo equals or is greater than that of producing an affected embryo, I have been unable to imagine any situation that would constitute a reasonable request for gene therapy rather than embryo selection.

Couples Who Cannot Produce a Winning Combination of Genes

Having, on balance, supported the current ban on pre-implantation embryo gene therapy, I am duty bound to draw attention to some rare genetic circumstances in which *all* the offspring are at risk of genetic disease. What are the options for these families and are they likely to regard the current ban as closing the door on their dream of normal healthy children?

Profound hearing loss, present at birth and therefore interfering with the easy acquisition of speech, is usually inherited in an autosomal recessive manner. This means that a proportion of couples where both are profoundly deaf (but not all, because different gene loci can be involved) will produce only deaf children. Whilst the same principle applies to all autosomal recessive disorders, the probability of similarly affected people marrying is usually extremely small. Profound hearing loss, and to a lesser extent blindness, tends to be an exception, being a disorder that draws similarly affected people together through special educational establishments. My guess is that with genetic information made available to them before their marriage, the demand in the distant future from deaf couples for a genetic correction of the gene defect by embryo therapy would be small, given much improved cochlear implants to restore a form of hearing in the baby.

A second example comes as more of a "bolt out of the blue". It concerns couples who, after their first baby is diagnosed as Down's syndrome, are told that *all* future children of theirs would be so affected. The extra 21 chromosome that causes Down's syndrome can sometimes be attached to another chromosome, and occasionally this is another chromosome 21. In a proportion of such children, it is found that one or other parent is carrying a balanced 21/21 translocation. This healthy parent has the usual two 21s, but they are attached to each other; this abnormality having arisen in the egg or sperm that led to their conception. As a consequence, that person can only produce gametes that either have two 21s (to give a baby with Down's syndrome) or no 21, which leads to early miscarriage. It is possible to imagine techniques developing in the future to add a normal 21 from a donor cell to the zygote with only one, or destroy by ultrasound one half of the 21/21 composite chromosome in the zygote that has this abnormal chromosome. The former situation overlaps somewhat with gamete donation, which might well be an acceptable option for many such couples, but one has to admit that, if legalised, there could be "takers" for ultrasonic chromosome surgery (perfected, one might imagine, for legitimate genetic research purposes in animals). Since this technique could only ever remove (excess) chromosome material, it is very difficult to see how it could be exploited for undesirable positive eugenic purposes, which may therefore make it a more acceptable technical development.

The final example poses more immediate ethical problems, and concerns the options available for women who are suffering from (or carrying in an asymptomatic fashion) mutant mitochondria. Mitochondria are organelles in the cytoplasm of cells concerned principally with energy production. In evolutionary terms, they are believed to represent bacterial cells entrapped in a symbiotic relationship within the larger cells of multicellular organisms. In keeping with this, mitochondria have their own circular chromosome with expressed genes that replicate independently of the 46 regular chromosomes that make up the human nuclear genome. A mature ovum has about 2000 mitochondria but during the passage from one generation to the next the number of mitochondria in the germ-cell lineage is thought to go through a "bottleneck" of fewer than 10 mitochondria. Whilst both eggs and sperm have mitochondria, none is transferred with the sperm pronucleus at fertilisation, so mitochondrial inheritance is exclusively maternal. What is true of normal mitochondria is true of mutant mitochondria, and exclusive maternal transmission characterises those diseases due to mutation in the mitochondrial chromosome. The mitochondria accumulate mutations at a relatively fast rate and, due to the "bottleneck" effect, some offspring of a woman carrying one or a few mutant mitochondria can end up with the majority, even all, of their mitochondria of the mutant variety. There are now several serious mitochondrial diseases described and at the severe end of the spectrum they can result in progressive neurological deterioration, stroke-like episodes, epilepsy, deafness, visual impairment, and a myopathy affecting skeletal muscle as well as the heart (see Van Hellenberg et al. 1991).

Genetic counselling can be very difficult. *All* the offspring of a mildly affected or asymptomatic carrier woman are at risk of serious disease, although only a proportion (perhaps 10%–15%) will in fact be seriously affected. In general, these are likely to be the embryos that end up with a high proportion or all the mitochondria in their cells being the mutant ones. Pre-implantation diagnosis followed by embryo selection will be problematic because the proportion of mutant mitochondria in the biopsied cell may not faithfully represent the proportion in the remaining seven or so cells and ultimately the baby.

One interesting solution worth consideration was raised in discussion at the PERM conference from which this chapter results, by Dr. Jack Cohen. It is likely to be technically possible to transfer a cell nucleus from the couple's pre-implantation embryo into an enucleated blastomere from a donor; in other words, to perform a cytoplasmic exchange. It is possible that the cytoplasm from a donated egg, rather than blastomere, will suffice. The resulting embryo would have all its regular nuclear genes from the couple concerned, but not the mutant mitochondria. My feeling is that there could well be a clinical demand for such a procedure, if it were permitted. I am afraid I did not raise this as a possible legitimate use in clinical genetics at the time of the preparation of the Human Fertilisation and Embryological Bill, and it is almost certainly outlawed under the prohibitions on "replacing a nucleus of a cell of an embryo with a nucleus taken from the cell of another person, another embryo or a subsequent development of an embryo" and "altering the genetic structure of any cell while it forms part of an embryo".

The procedure of nuclear transfer to an enucleated blastomere is normally associated with the idea of cloning where the aim would be to produce several or many individuals who have an identical (nuclear) genetic make up. It was this that the bill seeks to ban. Cytoplasmic exchange ("replacing the cytoplasm of a cell of an embryo with the cytoplasm taken from the cell of another person, another embryo or a subsequent development of an embryo") would have entirely different objectives. It would permit a woman with a mitochondrial disorder to have her own children by the partner of her choice without the considerable risk of producing a severely handicapped child. It would not result in a "genetic clone" of some existing person, just the usual combination of parental nuclear genes in a child. It is difficult to know what normal characteristics are largely determined by mitochondrial variation. It is possible that sporting abilities, such as those related to oxygen utilisation by the muscles during sprinting or the increase in mitochondrial numbers during training, fall under mitochondrial influence. If cytoplasmic exchange were permitted, there is the chance that a woman undergoing the procedure because of her own mitochondrial disease might request the cytoplasm from a cooperative Olympic athlete, hoping that her child would not only escape the muscle weakness that she has suffered, but goes one better and is particularly well endowed where muscle function is concerned. Despite this rather fanciful scenario, I do not think permitting cytoplasmic exchange for mitochondrial disease would encourage distortion of its strictly clinical objectives.

General Therapy and Prophylactic Embryo Gene Therapy

Therapeutic intervention could also be prophylactic. One can easily imagine that, whilst the preimplantation embryo might not yet be damaged, it could be given some "treatment" that protects it against inadvertent temperature change shock, or treatment that generally enhances successful implantation. The use of such procedures, once tried and tested, would probably raise few ethical problems.

More controversial would be the future possibility that we may know sufficient about some common adult disorders, such as cancer, to contemplate prophylactic genetic manipulation of the embryo. Over half of breast, lung, colon and bladder tumours have been found to carry a mutation of the gene on chromosome 17 that encodes the normal p53 protein (reviewed by Harris 1991). This protein is believed to be a tumour-suppressor molecule involved in regulating cell division. Imagine that an extra copy of this gene neither interfered with normal development, nor (as might have been expected) increased the chance of a mutant p53 protein arising, which would actually enhance tumour progression. Instead, imagine that a very small percentage of the general population is discovered to have a constitutional duplication of their p53 gene, and they are healthy, long lived and have a remarkably low incidence of cancer. In short, we have discovered that Nature has already performed the clinical trial; p53 gene duplication was not only safe, but may well be an evolutionary adaptation to the increased carcinogens and mutagens in the environment. What would be our reaction to couples who request that an extra p53 gene be inserted into their pre-implantation embryos? Do we say that presymptomatic screening and treatment for cancer will be so good by the time the embryo in question reached middle age that embryo gene therapy is unjustified? Do we say to such couples; if it is so important to you, why don't you rear embryos that are the result of donated sperm and/or eggs from people with duplication p53 genes? Or do we press for a change in the Human Fertilisation and Embryology Act to allow gene therapy in the embryo? And who are the "we" in this hypothetical dilemma?

I will leave the philosophers to dissect the issues involved. As a clinical geneticist, I have more immediate issues to discuss with families at risk of transmitting genetic disorders to their children. Embryo therapy will not be high on the list.

References

Handyside AH, Kontogianni K, Hardy K, Winston RML (1990) Pregnancies from biopsied human preimplantation embryos sexed by Y-specific DNA amplification. Nature 344:768–770

Harris AL (1991) Telling changes of base. Nature 350:377–378

Koopman P, Gubbay J, Vivian N, Goodfellow P, Lovell-Badge R (1991) Male development of chromosomally female mice transgenic for Sry. Nature 351:117–121

Pang S, Pollack MS, Marshall RN, Immken L (1990) Prenatal treatment of congenital adrenal hyperplasia due to 21-hydroxylase deficiency. N Engl J Med 322:111–115

Pembrey ME (1984) Do we need gene therapy? Nature 311:200

Sheppard S, Nevin NC, Seller MJ et al. (1989) Neural tube defect recurrence after "partial" vitamin supplementation. J Med Genet 26:326–329

Speiser PW, Laforgia N, Kato K, Pareira J, Khan R, Soo YY et al. (1990) First trimester prenatal, treatment and molecular genetic diagnosis of congenital adrenal hyperplasia (21-hydroxylase deficiency). J Clin Endocrinal Metab 70:838–848

Van Hellenberg Hubar JML, Gabreels FJM et al. (1991) Melas syndrome. Report of two patients and comparison with data of 24 patients derived from the literature. Neuroped 22:10–14

Warnock M (1984) Report of the Committee of Inquiry into Human Fertilisation and Embryology. Her Majesty's Stationery Office, London

Weatherall DJ (1984) A step nearer gene therapy. Nature 310:451

Woo SLC, Lidsky AS, Guttler F, Chandra T, Robson KJ (1983) Cloned human phenylalanine hydroxylase gene allows prenatal diagnosis and carrier detection of classical phenylketonuria. Nature 306:151–155

CHAPTER 3

Embryo Therapy: The Philosopher's Role in Ethical Debate

Mary Warnock

In the 1950s moral philosophy was generally supposed to have nothing whatever to contribute to actual moral or ethical debate. The task of philosophy was held to be the analysis of the language of morals, such words as "good", "duty", "ought" and "right" (or I suppose their opposites, though these did not get much of an innings). It was thought to be enough for philosophers to explain that such words were hidden imperatives, or were the expressions of feelings, so that people who used the words might know what they were doing in using them. For a philosopher to claim to know what to apply the words to, how to distinguish as ordinary people had to between what actually was right and wrong would have been intrusive. He had no more authority to do such a thing than a mathematician or indeed a bank-manager.

Things have changed since then. Ever since the Vietnam war when American students involved their philosophy teachers willy nilly in such questions as what counted as a just war, and the rights and wrongs of draft-dodging, philosophers have increasingly been expected to tangle with real moral problems. And now I believe that too much is expected of them. Certainly politicians are prone to think that if a philosopher chairs a committee of enquiry something positive will come of it; and they are disappointed at the tentative non-unanimous results. Yet they should understand that moral questions do not admit of straight yes or no answers. If a question is moral (or ethical, I make no distinction between these terms) then inevitably, indeed by definition, it is a matter more felt than reasoned. Therefore disagreements are likely to be deeply entrenched and to arise out of different traditions, histories and cultures. Such is the nature of morality. A philosopher, however long he thinks, cannot eliminate such differences nor is he entitled to say to people that they ought to give up their long-established views, even if he personally thinks they are mistaken.

So if philosophers can, as I believe, do more than analyse the meaning of moral terms, but cannot, as I also believe, prove or otherwise show conclusively that one view is to be preferred to another, what can they do? My argument will be that, though the philosopher will not produce proof or certainty, yet analysis itself may be, in a modest way, useful. It may lead, though slowly, both to better decisions and to the possibility of explaining a decision once it is made. Both these factors are of equal importance, especially in what is, and should be, an increasingly open society, with an increasingly open style of government.

I want to consider the philosophers' role in a bit more detail in the context of embryo manipulation, including embryo therapy. There are three main issues concerning which philosophical discussion may have a contribution to make. The first is the issue of fear. The general public has long been afraid that science is going too far, too fast and is de-humanising the world, or rendering it positively unsafe. This is not merely (though it is in part) a relic of romanticism. It is not just the spiritual descendants of Blake who are afraid. We fear not only for our green and pleasant land, but for our life and our freedom. In the 1950s it was mostly physicists who were the bogey-men. Now it is the biologists. The mad professor is a professor of medicine.

Fears may be rational or irrational, well or ill-founded. It may be possible for philosophers to help people draw this distinction. However it is important to notice that looking at what it is that people fear, and trying to ascertain whether they are right to fear it is not the same as simply trying to allay their fears. If people think that statements put out by, for example, the Department of the Environment about the disposal of toxic waste are intended primarily to allay fears, they will not believe those statements. They will be extremely cynical, often with justice. No-one likes to be treated as an ignorant child who may be comforted by myths or fairy tales. In order properly to address the question of whether or not fears are rational it is necessary first of all to try to ascertain the facts; and if there are indeed grounds for fear, then to consider what steps should be taken to render things safer. Often rational fears can be laid to rest not by Government statements, but only by legislation, by control, that is, over the outcomes of which people are afraid, or the powers to which they feel they are being subjected. I shall return to this point below.

First, however, there is a very general fear sometimes expressed about the kind of research which is leading to the mapping of the human genome, to prenatal and pre-implantation diagnosis, and the possibility of therapy by the alteration or replacement of genes. It is sometimes thought that it would be better if this kind of research did not go on, because it will in the end lead to knowledge that it would be better not to have. This knowledge is, as I have suggested, sometimes feared because of the powers it will give to those who may use it. But sometimes it is feared, it seems, almost for its own sake. We should not know too much about our own genetic inheritance. Not only may this tell us to what diseases we are prone, but what traits of character are ineliminable, whether we are likely to be good people or criminals, whether we shall succeed or fail in the things we undertake. Whether or not such detailed knowledge is in fact likely, it is often felt to be undesirable even to pursue it. For it is thought it would sap our initiative, undermine our courage, make us passive in the face of the fate we knew to await us. So let us forget about genetics and go on with our lives as we always have, believing that if we try we can succeed, if we have moral fibre we can keep out of trouble.

This kind of anxiety seems to me futile. We have always believed that there were some factors limiting our freedom but that within these constraints we can choose well or ill. An increased general knowledge of genetics will not cause us to give up the whole vocabulary in which we talk about our decisions, our likes and dislikes, the things we do as opposed to the things which simply happen to us. We are perfectly accustomed to there being a shifting boundary between those features of our lives about which we feel inclined to say "I couldn't help it" and those about which we know that we could have helped it, or could help it another time. The boundaries may be drawn differently in future, but they will not disappear. The philosophical debate about determinism, which has been going on for centuries, is a debate about how we should think of ourselves. We may come to think of ourselves somewhat differently in future (and indeed there have been radical changes of view in the past). But we shall never be in a position where we cease to think of ourselves as individuals with lives to lead in a variety of possible ways. Such vague fears of a new and worse kind of determinism could never be sufficient reason to prevent the pursuit of knowledge, even if it were imaginable that anyone could prevent it.

Turning, therefore, from the pursuit of genetic knowledge itself to the uses to which such knowledge may be put, we come upon the very prevalent fear that we shall somehow cross the line between the benign use of gene therapy for the treatment or elimination of genetic disease, to the use of gene manipulation for positively changing either individuals or the human species as a whole, in accordance with some preconceived ideal. The horror of this picture arises from the question *Who should decide?* To what lengths could on the one hand paternalism (the insistence on changing people for their own good) or on the other hand mad megalomaniac imperialism go? Could we not move imperceptibly from ensuring that no-one was born with Duchenne muscular dystrophy to ensuring that no-one was born with any aggressive inclinations, which might make them oppose whoever was in power? Could it not be possible that instead of having to rely on propaganda and control of the media, Big Brother could actually shape people genetically to the conformity he wanted?

Such a fear is in one sense irrational, in that such positive uses of the techniques of human genetic engineering are not at the present time within the bounds of possibility. Yet it is in itself a genuinely philosophical question to ask how far we ought to be constrained by present possibilities, rather than letting our imaginations have free play to range over what might be possible in the unforeseeable future. It has always been part of the stock-in-trade of philosophers to invent cases which are not actual but hypothetical, and then raise the question "What if this were so?" For example, Plato used the myth of the ring of Gyges, which would render its wearer invisible, to raise the perfectly genuine philosophical question whether there were things that were bad in themselves or whether on the other hand if we were only invisible and therefore undetectable we would all of us do whatever we liked. In other words is what is called "bad" only that which, as things now are, we would be punished for if we were caught? No-one has ever thought the worse of this kind of question simply on the grounds that the ring of Gyges was a myth. Likewise there are many philosophers of this century who try to analyse the complex notion we have of our own identity by supposing that there could be total brain transplants, and trying to see how the idea of identity survives or fails to survive such a hypothesis.

Philosophically, then, we may well be under an obligation to raise hypothetical cases and imagine the day when the human genome map was so detailed and accurate that we could trace what genetic pathways, what permutations and combinations would ensure that people were musical, amenable to discipline, good at mathematics, born leaders and so on. We could then raise the essentially political question "Who should have power to decide what sort of people there should be?" But meanwhile the people who fear the slippery slope should be given some reassurance that here and now we are not slithering down it out of control. This reassurance it seems to me can come only from legislation (though obviously legislation provides reassurance only to those people who have faith in the institutions of parliamentary democracy).

In practice, therefore, it seems to me of the utmost importance to introduce controls over what may or may not be undertaken in the way of genetic therapy whether this therapy is undertaken after the birth of a baby or prenatally or as a way of either selecting or indeed changing a pre-implantation embryo in the laboratory. As has been suggested many times by now, both in this country and elsewhere, the simplest control would be to have an agreed list of conditions to remedy which such genetic manipulation should be licensed. The criteria by which such conditions should be determined would be that they would entail the early death (or perhaps the prolonged but painful life) of anyone born with such a condition, and the absence of any cure for the condition short of genetic intervention. At present such a list would consist solely of monogenetic diseases and it would be a long enough list to be going on with, there being upwards of a thousand known monogenetic disorders whose outcome is disastrous in this sort of way. In addition to those genes the presence of which was certain to give rise to a disease that would satisfy the criteria for inclusion in the list of permitted intervention, one might well argue for intervention, if it became possible, in the case of someone who might or might not suffer from Huntington's chorea before the age of fifty; and there might well be other conditions of this sort.

The point of the list would simply be that of containment. If it were accepted, it would essentially be a list of diseases. Without entering the thorny topic of what is the definition of a disease, we may nevertheless agree that there are clear cases of disease (or perhaps better of illnesses) which are either horrible and intolerable for the patient, or lethal, or both. Where such a condition can be prevented then it is in full accordance both with the ethos of the medical profession and with the desires of all other members of society that intervention should occur. I do not myself see how a slippery slope argument can be invoked to prevent treatment, of whatever kind, so long as its aim is exactly the same as is the aim of all other medical treatment. It is to prevent a shift away from such aims and towards positive eugenics, however, that a barrier of some kind is needed. In my opinion such a barrier must necessarily be legal, or it will not command universal respect, and might be breached by unscrupulous doctors, who could intervene as the market might demand. Guidelines, or agreed codes of conduct within the profession would not be enough to prevent people coming, perhaps from abroad, to practise eugenics, or cosmetic genetic engineering for money. The comfort of legislation as a block to prevent descent down the slope is that any change in the law would have to go through the whole process of parliamentary debate, and there would most probably be extreme caution in parliament about permitting any relaxation of the law, especially if it were known that the public was anxious about it.

So perhaps it is lawyers rather than philosophers who should be looked to for aid in settling our doubts about genetic manipulation in general, and therapy practised on embryos in particular. Yet there is no question but that the issues raised in this field, especially with regard to such matters as embryo selection before implantation, or the possibilities of germ-line therapy, are widely seen to be primarily moral questions. It is held that the law should be written only after the moral questions have been settled. And so the issue becomes a familiar one. What is the relation between the law and morality? The old dispute, dating from the 1960s, about morals and the law turned on the questions raised by the Wolfenden Report on homosexual practices between consenting adult males. Lord Justice Devlin argued that such practices should remain criminal offences, since the agreed moral opinion of the country condemned them, and it was the function of the criminal law to enforce the agreed morality of a society, and indeed to reinforce it by attaching penalties to what people already believed was wrong. A shared common morality was, he argued, the cement which held society together. To act against that morality was a species of treason, since society would collapse without it. Therefore the law must enforce it.

On the other side Professor Hart, then professor of jurisprudence in the University of Oxford argued that even if a kind of action was generally believed to be wrong, before criminalising those actions one needs to ask whether the law may not have even worse consequences than the original acts. Such consequences would be an undue restriction of individual freedom, of intrusiveness if the law were to be enforced, or a general neglect of the law which might bring all law into contempt. He regarded the laws which criminalised homosexual acts between consenting adults to be damaging in all these ways, and therefore due to be abolished. He did not explicitly deny that there was a consensus morality; but he suggested that the desire to preserve it could be outweighed by the evils of enforcing it. In Hart's view, in order to decide whether or not to criminalise some kind of act (or in the case of the Wolfenden Report to continue to criminalise it) we must look at the overall consequences of the existence of such a law. And because of a respect for human freedom, there is an initial presumption against making new criminal offences, or retaining old ones where the law is unlikely to be enforced.

However, whether one feels inclined to follow Devlin or Hart in the matter of the relation of the law to morality as then understood, it is a new question altogether where there seems to be no consensus morality to enforce. And this is the case with many of the new issues arising out of the existence of living human embryos in the laboratory. In the nature of the case there can be here no long tradition on which our moral views are based, since the whole situation is new. No living embryo existed in any laboratory anywhere before 1978; and people in general did not begin seriously to think about the status that should be accorded to such entities until considerably later. It would be strange then if everyone took the same view about what it was right to do with them or whether they might be manipulated or destroyed.

The only way in which the issue could be made to seem easy was by likening these embryos to something else; human children on the one hand, human tissue on the other. It seems to me right that in such wholly novel situations the law should not go far ahead of moral thought. But to inspire moral thought, to raise it above the standard of prejudice, is something that takes time and patience. We have to start with the recognition that there are some people who will adopt an intransigent attitude, either because of what they hold to be an imperative of their religion or because they place total reliance on their own independent gut-reaction, a reaction generally impervious to argument or the presentation of the facts. Thus there will be many people who will be indifferent to any presentation of facts. And if in any country there were a majority of such people, then the laws of that country would, it seems to me inevitably, follow whatever was the majority opinion. Thus in Germany there is so strong a gut-reaction against any form of genetic manipulation that there would be no possibility of getting through any legislation which permitted it. Indeed, quite recently, wholly restrictive legislation, forbidding research using human embryos and any form of preimplantation diagnosis or therapy has been passed. This is surprising to no-one. For the German people, as they freely acknowledge themselves, are sensitive to the past, and are filled with a shared horror of the slippery slope down which they once slid, and which they believe now that they should not block, but simply never approach, never get to the top of, again.

Within countries with no such communal sense of shame, however, it may be far more difficult to ascertain what is the common view. Indeed, as I have suggested, it is likely that there genuinely is no common view. In these circumstances it is almost inevitable that we have recourse to utilitarianism, the Greatest Happiness principle. It is here that perhaps philosophers may have some role to play. For they are at least able to distinguish one theory from another, and perhaps clarify for people the basis on which their moral views are founded. There are those among the general public (and of course among members of parliament) who are prone to use as a justification of their moral views such expressions as "I just feel it's wrong" or "it is totally repugnant". There are others who rest their arguments on purely utilitarian grounds. They point out the human suffering involved in, for example, the birth of a child who is condemned to a short and painful life as a result of a genetic disorder; and they go on to show the advantages, in terms of human happiness, of selective implantation, or, ultimately, of genetic therapy applied to the embryo. They use no other criteria but those of the weighing of benefits against harms, pleasures over pains. The differences between these approaches are at least familiar to philosophers. Philosophers know them of old; they have names for them ("intuitionism", "consequentialism"); they can explain to people what sort of theory they are relying on, even when they did not know that they were relying on a theory at all. And this is a considerable service to perform. It sharpens debate, shortens it, sometimes makes it less repetitive and inconclusive. Again philosophers are quite good at distinguishing questions of science, where evidence may be conclusive, from questions of value or opinion, where further evidence will never settle the case, or not by itself. Having listened to endless declarations about when human life begins, I think my personal greatest triumph was to get the acknowledgment from someone who thought human embryos ought always to be preserved that the issue was one of value, rather than fact . . . that scientific knowledge could never solve it.

The commonplace acknowledgment that sometimes one must agree to differ is an important start in the business of moral dialogue. But it is not perhaps very helpful where the outcome of the dialogue is supposed to be legislation. Here we come upon a crucial distinction, and one which philosophers have perhaps been reluctant hitherto to acknowledge, and that is the distinction between private and public morality, between making moral decisions for oneself, and making them for society at large.

There has always been a distinction drawn between moral and political philosophy. This was the distinction between questions about the basis of judgments about duties or personal virtues or obligations, and questions about the basis of political rights or the justification of obedience or disobedience to the law. Moral philosophy could talk about justice as a personal virtue, political philosophy was concerned with justice as an institution. Such distinctions have long been familiar to philosophers. What they have not been quite so much interested in (since their interest has not until the recent past generally been practical) has been the difference in the actual processes of decision-making in the private and the public arena.

A moral person, making a moral decision for himself, can be variously described. He may be heeding his conscience, following his principles, listening to the voice of God through prayer and meditation. However he is characterised (and there would be many philosophically different ways of saying what he is doing, all with different implications for the analysis of a moral decision, or the account of its nature) we most of us recognise what he is up to. We also recognise that, if his decision is genuinely moral, as opposed to prudential or a matter of expediency, he may have to sacrifice some of his wishes in making it. Indeed if there were not the possibility of his saying "I must do this though the heavens fall" we should hardly be inclined to describe his decision as a moral one. I am not saying that whenever someone decides what it would be right to do he must take up a heroic or self-immolating stance. But, in the first place, if we are to think of him as engaged in *moral* decision-making, in making his decision he must put his own interests temporarily on one side. If he puts his own interests first or even if he puts them on an exactly equal footing with those of others, we are less inclined to think he is motivated by the desire to do what he thinks right. And this entails a second criterion: if he is sincerely trying to do what he thinks right he must see the possibility of his taking up a stand that will prove damaging to his own interests. He must be prepared for, relatively speaking, martyrdom. But martyrdom is essentially a personal fate: it cannot, or cannot normally, be the fate of someone or some body attempting to decide what is in the public interest. And this is the characteristic aim of those who are trying to make good decisions in the public as opposed to the private arena. They are trying to see what is on the whole for the best. It is difficult for them to adopt a principle and be determined to stick to it though the heavens fall. It is difficult for them to do otherwise than embark on an overtly utilitarian calculation of the balance of benefits over harms. Heroics are out of place. Self sacrifice is not on the agenda, because they are not each for themselves making their own moral commitment.

Into the arena of public moral decisions has emerged of recent years the Ethics Committee. Such committees may come in varying forms. There is the local hospital ethics committee set up to examine new procedures in research, and especially in research using patients. Sometimes such a committee also examines new procedures in treatment and often the distinction between research or experiment and new and untried treatment is hard to draw. At the other end of the spectrum there is the Government Committee of Enquiry, established to examine a particular problem and having as part of its task to give advice to Ministers with a view to legislation. There is not much in common between these different kinds of committees except that all of them are concerned with morality, and all have to make decisions or recommendations in the public sphere.

Often it must seem to doctors and those engaged in medical research that the ethics committee has taken away their own responsibility for deciding what to do and what not to do; and that it has certainly sapped their initiative. They may feel totally hedged about by restrictions, and by other people's judgments, so that they are afraid to decide anything at all, lest they fall foul of the ethics committee. I believe that this inhibition is a real hazard for doctors. It has come about partly from the American example. Because of the prevalence of litigation against doctors in the United States, it is essential for doctors there to have cleared themselves with a local ethics committee if they are to be able to prepare a defence in certain cases. In this country we have taken to the ethics committee not so much because of possible litigation (though the threat of this is increasing all the time) as because of a more general feeling that doctors must not have too much power, but must be subject to the restraining force of the "lay", those who are actual or potential patients, and who are no longer willing blindly to obey "doctor's orders". Thus Ethics Committees, of whatever kind, tend to be established in such a way that the lay, non-medical members are in the majority. Often the medical profession, though they may feel in some ways relieved of the burdens of responsibility by their subjection to such committees, may all the same feel frustrated. It is a bit as though a committee of non-historians were to be set up to decide what historians might teach. The difference is that in the case of medicine the doctor's decision may be a matter of life or death for the patient, or at least a matter of a tolerable or an intolerable life. Yet it is widely believed (and perhaps rightly) that doctors get carried away by the excitement of new treatment, and do not think enough of how it will be for the patient. So, in the case of embryo therapy, there is fairly widespread fear that the medical profession might become over-excited by the thought of what is possible, without taking enough account of either the real benefits to society, or, worse, the moral outrage that might be caused by the reckless pursuit of possible procedures.

Yet reassuring in some ways as the establishing of an ethics committee may be, such a committee cannot in fact overcome the difficulty that there is within society no obvious moral consensus, nothing that could be said to be the cement binding society together. Embryo therapy may involve research using human embryos (or human ova) and the selective destruction of defective embryos, and those that have been used for research. There are those who hold that human embryos are in effect human persons and that therefore they ought not to be used for research and not to be destroyed. Such moralists share in no consensus moral view with those who argue that the use of embryos for therapeutic or research purposes is not only defensible but actually morally obligatory, on the grounds that it reduces human suffering in the long term. An ethics committee if it is properly representative will include people who hold these views. How are they therefore to reach any satisfactory decisions?

It seems to me inevitable that committees must in the end present the views of the majority of their members. Thus if a hospital ethics committee happens to be composed mostly of people with extreme or absolutist moral views, they will prevail, and the doctors and scientists working in that hospital will have some restrictions placed on their research and therapy which they would not suffer if they happened to work in a more liberal hospital. I do not believe that we can eliminate such differences if we are to use the ethics committee system. There are ways, however, for moving towards a method for at least informing committees what their opposite number in other hospitals have decided. I believe it is imperative that this information should be disseminated, whether through some publication available to all members of committees or through some system of mandatory publication of decisions. In this way committees could at least know whether or not their own decisions were eccentric, or whether indeed in the end a kind of consensus was gradually emerging, with respect to particular procedures.

In the case of a government committee there is, again, no alternative but to present to Government the view of the majority of the committee. But such a majority view (and this is equally true of hospital ethics committees) must be founded upon proper knowledge of the facts and thorough understanding of the issues. A government committee has a certain advantage over regular civil servants, whose normal task is to advise their ministers. A committee is given time to ascertain the facts and think about them, collecting evidence from as many sources as they see fit; and they, unlike civil servants, are not anonymous. They are open to lobbying, to argument and to instruction from anyone who wishes to approach them. Their sources of information are thus not wholly chosen by themselves. Information, and, as well, contribution from the prejudiced, the dogmatic and the downright dotty, comes in from all sides. In the end such a committee has to weigh up all this vast input, and weigh up their own arguments and responses. It is of no use to have members of such a committee who do not believe in the force of evidence. If, in the end, their conclusions are not unanimous, it is because each member of the committee has had conscientiously to think what he believes right, on the basis of evidence and a genuine attempt to find agreement.

What, then, is the place of philosophy in the proceedings of such committee decisions, decisions about what is right in the public rather than the private domain? Philosophers have a role, it seems to me, simply as professional people who by training and habit are accustomed to distinguishing good evidence from bad, sound arguments from fallacies, dogma from experience. They are also professionally accustomed to setting out conclusions and preliminary lines of reasoning in an intelligible way. But there are many other people besides philosophers who are professionally accustomed to doing most of those things. Most well-educated people are educated precisely to weigh up evidence, to be cautious about jumping to conclusions, to examine their own first thoughts in the light both of second thoughts, and of other people's thoughts. They are, most of them, reasonably good at explaining what they mean, and setting it down intelligibly. I would therefore be more interested in making sure that a committee of enquiry, or indeed a hospital ethics committee, contained a fair number of well-educated people, whatever their subject of professional expertise, than that it contained specifically any philosophers. I would defend philosophy as a useful and generally applicable academic subject; but I would not defend it as uniquely useful in this kind of context. It is what used to be called the "trained mind" that is here in question. I would as soon trust an academic historian or lawyer or mathematician or linguist as a philosopher, as far as committee work goes. Any of them, and many other educated persons would be equally useful, if they had the patience to serve.

It is important, and indeed, necessary, in my view, that moral decisions perhaps to be translated into legislation should be taken by committees. This kind of public moralising is intrinsically different from private moral decision-making. In the field of embryo therapy there is no doubt that we shall need legislation, and therefore we shall need preliminary work by ethics committees.

But I do not think that it is right to look especially to philosophy to provide the necessary non-scientific elements in such committees.

It has been argued, for example by Peter Singer, the professor of medical ethics at the University of Monash in Melbourne, that we should educate up a number of "moral experts" to serve on ethical committees of the kind I have been discussing. He thinks such experts should be generally educated people who have had at least a smattering of philosophy in their education, so that they know what are the general characteristics of different moral theories (they should know, for example, what utilitarianism is, or moral realism or intuitionism). The general public should then be prepared to entrust public moral decision-making to such experts, and legislation that resulted from their expert advice would thus command general support. Professor Singer raises the question of how otherwise can such ethical committees be constructed, if not out of ethical experts. And this is indeed a difficult question to answer. Nevertheless there is a deep reluctance felt by everyone to accepting the suggestion that there exist "moral experts". Unless we live in a theocratic society where our rulers are supposed to have direct access to the will of God who will dictate what is right and wrong, we are inclined to be highly democratic about morality. Each has his own source of moral insight, his own conscience or feeling, about what is right and wrong. We are not prepared to be dictated to. Such is the protestant, independent individualist view most prevalent in this country. Committees of so-called moral experts would be suspect from the start. And yet philosophers are often appointed to such committees because there is a lurking hope that they *are* experts. I have suggested that they are not and cannot be. But they may be useful members, on account of their education, as may many other people who are not philosophers. The only advantage philosophers have is that of being accustomed to talking without embarrassment about moral problems, real or hypothetical (a thing some people find hard to embark on). They are also accustomed to discussing other people's subjects, including the sciences. Philosophers may then set the tone of an enquiry, help to ease it along. They cannot by themselves find solutions.

There is one further point to be made. I have tried to argue that insofar as philosophers have a role to play in decision-making with regard to embryo therapy or any other medical or social problems it is in virtue of their general training in philosophical method. I do not think that there should be a special branch of philosophy called Medical Ethics in which these possibly useable philosophers should be trained. Of course it is helpful if there are philosophers who are more or less acquainted in advance with some of the issues they are likely to encounter as members of hospital ethical committees or government committees of enquiry into medical problems. But even if they are not, they can soon learn; and they will always need scientists and doctors to keep them up-to-date as members of such committees. They cannot be expected to know what are the latest developments, or what is now possible that was not possible before, and what the outcomes are likely to be. So having been in a special medical ethics department may not in practice be of much use to them, since they will probably be out-of-date, as far as the facts go. But, more important, if they are educated on a diet of nothing but medical ethics, or, even worse, if they have taught nothing but this subject and have conducted all their research in it, they are likely to become as tunnel-visioned as the doctors and scientists themselves. Their broadening and *generally* analytic role in the enquiries may become diminished. A moral philosopher who deserves the name must concern himself with the nature of morality in general, and must be prepared to consider examples from all kinds of areas, private and public. He must understand the relation not only between morality and the law (or at least understand what the problems are) but also the relation between morality and politics, between individuals and the society of which they are part. I would mistrust a university department which taught moral philosophy in a context that was narrower than this. Nor do I believe that moral philosophy can be properly studied separately from all the rest of philosophy, epistemology, for example, or the philosophy of mind.

The role of philosophers, then, in future debates about the morality of embryo manipulation, is broadly the same as that of any educated and thoughtful people. They must constitute the "lay" element in the corporate decision-making that will lead where necessary to legislation. That there should be such an element and that it should be credible and worthy to be trusted by politicians, lawyers and doctors is extremely important. How to ensure that there exists such trust is partly a question of the personalities of the people involved, partly of the general academic context within which such ethics committees as I have been discussing actually operate. To improve this context, the academic climate as a whole, is a political imperative; but not one which falls within the subject matter of this paper.

CHAPTER 4

The Rights of the Pre-embryo and Fetus to In-vitro and In-vivo Therapy

Joseph G. Schenker

More than a decade has passed since the birth of Louise Brown (Steptoe and Edwards 1978). Since then, there have been many thousands of births that resulted from successful assisted reproductive technology in clinics throughout the world. The practices of in-vitro fertilization (IVF) and embryo transfer (ET) are becoming more widely available and applied, but the ultimate success rate, as judged by live births per cycle of treatment, remains low – around 10%. There exists a considerable difference between the usual fertilization rate of 70%–80% and subsequent pregnancy rates of approximately 20% (Schenker 1991). The pregnancy rate per one pre-embryo transfer is 9.8%. Chromosomal abnormalities represent the major cause of pre-embryonic loss during the pre- and peri-implantation period; 24%–30% of pre-implantation pre-embryos resulting from IVF have a chromosomal abnormality (Plachot 1989). Induction of ovulation by different protocols in the practice of IVF has provided an increasing number of pre-ovulatory oocytes, which are fertilized, and part of them transferred into the uterine cavity in the treatment cycle or subsequent cycles.

Therapeutic Approach to the Pre-embryo

Pre-embryo is defined as a period from fertilization until 14 days, the appearance of the primitive streak. Fertilization is not a single event but a process that includes the penetration of sperm through the oocyte covers, fusion of male and female pronuclei and formation of zygotes. The zygote cleaves to form two blastomeres at the second day, forming morula at the fourth day, and then the blastocysts will start the process of implantation.

In order to improve the potential of a pre-embryo created by IVF to undergo a successful implantation and development to embryonic and fetal stages, several "therapeutic" measures can be applied to pre-embryos.

The moral and legal status of the pre-embryo will determine the limits of action and omission of action regarding it, and thus the freedom that physicians and gamete donors have on actions concerning it.

The following therapeutic measures can be potentially applied to the human pre-embryo:

1. Cryopreservation
2. Assisted hatching
3. Pre-embryonic genetic diagnosis
4. Pre-embryonic genetic intervention

Human Pre-embryo Cryopreservation

Human pre-embryo freezing is a routine procedure in many IVF units. Using induction of ovulation, there is production of many oocytes, sometimes more than required for immediate transfer to the woman. In order to avoid multiple, and especially high multiple, pregnancies not more than 3 or 4 pre-embryos should be returned at one time. The excess of the pre-embryos should be cryopreserved for transfer to the woman in future cycles of treatment, or for donation. The transfer can be carried out either in spontaneous or in stimulated cycles. The stage at which human pre-embryos should be frozen and the cryoprotectant that should be used is a controversial issue. Some centres cryopreserved pre-embryos at blastocyst stage, 8-cell stage and even pronucloid oocytes, and no difference was found in the results after use of the standard cryoprotectant. Embryo survival was correlated with morphological features, but pregnancies were reported even when fewer than half of the blastomeres were intact after thawing. The world results of pre-embryo cryopreservation, presented at the VIth World Congress of IVF and Alternate Assisted Reproduction in April 1989 in Jerusalem by Van Steirteghem (Van Steirteghem and Van Abbeel 1990) revealed the following data: until 31.12.88, 106 centres froze 30 850 pre-embryos. From 18 322 pre-embryos that were frozen and thawed 10 920 (56.6%) were judged to be suitable for replacement; 6441 replacements took place resulting in 632 clinical pregnancies (9.8% pregnancy rate per pre-embryo replacement); 329 children were born, 220 pregnancies were still ongoing; the clinical abortion rate was 19%. Four cases of congenital malformations were observed. The present pregnancy rate following transfer of cryopreserved pre-embryo is around 10%. A cryopreserved embryo has a 5% chance to implant (American Fertility Society 1991).

Assisted Hatching of Pre-embryo: Improving Implantation

Implantation is defined as the process in which a pre-embryo attaches itself to the uterine wall and penetrates first the epithelium, and then the circulatory system of the mother. The lack of success of assisted reproductive technologies may be due to problems in implantation. Early pregnancy loss may be attributed to impaired implantation. Before implantation the blastocyst is released from the zona pellucida; a biological process that is defined as hatching (Makter and Cohen 1989). The emergence of the blastocyst from the zona pellucida – hatching – prior to attachment to endometrium is the result of the following processes:

1. Degradative enzyme at the surface of blastocyst
2. Degradative enzyme secreted by the uterus
3. Physical changes of the blastocele

It has been shown that lack of implantation is due to hatching failure.

Human pre-embryos that had undergone partial zona dissection (PZD) by micromanipulative techniques had higher rates of implantation than zona intact pre-embryos: Cohen et al. (1990a, b) achieved 25% of implantation rate of PZD pre-embryos when the patients were treated by corticosteroids and antibiotics following implantation. Assisted hatching is a relatively simple technique, which is not very time-consuming and does not require the use of new culture media. Application of assisted hatching may increase the rate of multiple pregnancy of high order. Therapeutic approach to pre-embryos by assisted hatching shortly before replacing blastocysts to the uterine cavity may significantly improve clinical results of assisted reproductive technologies.

Genetic Diagnosis of Pre-embryo

Diagnosis of genetic diseases requires detection of the presence or absence of the mutation in the individual under study. The pre-implantation diagnosis of genetic diseases requires the removal of one or more cells from the pre-embryo without affecting its normal development (Hardy et al. 1990). The development of polymerase chain reaction (PCR) enables the study of mutation and any polymorphism even in a single cell by a rapid and sensitive method. This may lead to selection of pre-embryos that lack the defect before they are implanted, avoiding the need for termination of pregnancy.

Information obtained by biopsy of animal pre-implantation pre-embryos at the 2–8-cell stage has made it possible to apply this technology in human pre-embryos. It has been shown that the pre-embryo, when transferred to the uterus after biopsy, may develop normally. Biopsy of cells from human pre-implantation pre-embryos would allow diagnosis of genetic abnormalities by karyotyping, DNA analysis or enzyme microassays.

One approach would be to create monozygotic twins by separating 2-cell or 4-cell stage into constituent cells (Verlinsky et al. 1990). One half would provide the cell sample for genetic analysis and the other would be maintained in culture or cryopreserved for possible transfer in another cycle, if the time to complete the genetic analysis extended beyond the normal time of implantation.

The second approach to diagnosis of pre-implantation pre-embryo involves the removal or one or more cells at the 4- or 8-cell stages for genetic analysis. Successful pre-implantation of pre-embryo after genetic diagnosis for gender determination has been applied using PCR technique (Handyside et al. 1989). The technique is of clinical importance to women who are carriers for X-linked diseases (Milayeva et al. 1990). The detection of sex of pre-embryo on the basis of the presence or absence of an amplified Y-specific fragment alone is not always ideal, since PCR is very susceptible to problems of contamination. Analysis of a single cell may sometimes lead to false-positive or false-negative results. It has been shown that implantation and development of pre-embryos which had undergone a biopsy is not adversely affected, and clinical pregnancies have been obtained.

Trophectoderm biopsy of human blastocyst can be performed by micromanipulative technique (Dokras et al. 1990). Biopsy of trophectoderm has the advantage that those cells only contribute to extra-embryonic tissue after implantation, and therefore, by this technique, the number of inner cell mass cells, from which the fetus is derived, is not affected. Since after in-vitro fertilization (IVF) only 40%–50% of normally fertilized pre-embryos reach in culture to the stage of blastocyst, this limits the above technique.

Uterine lavage allows noninvasive recovery of human blastocysts. Biopsy of a blastocyst and its analysis by PCR may be a useful technique. It was reported (Bustillo et al. 1983) that blastocysts transferred to the uterus may result in 60% pregnancies.

The Moral Status of the Pre-embryo

In order to discuss the parents' rights and duties for applying therapeutic measures to the pre-embryo, it is necessary to clarify the following issues:

1. The moral status of the pre-embryo
2. The legal status of the pre-embryo
3. When does human life begin?
4. The issue of wrongful life and birth

The central question regarding the therapeutic approach to the pre-implanted pre-embryo is its moral status. There are three options for the definition of the moral status of the pre-embryo.

1. The pre-embryo has no moral status; it is a collection of undifferentiated cells, lacking individuality, and therefore has a status which is not different from that of any other human tissue. The consequence of this assumption is that we have no obligations to treat the pre-embryo.

2. The pre-embryo has the full status of a human being. The bases for this assumption are: A new genotype is established during fertilization and some of the pre-embryos have the potential to become full-term fetuses, children and adults. The consequence of this assumption is that the pre-embryo has its own rights, the gamete donors are the guardians of the pre-embryo, the interests of the mother are irrelevant to the future of the pre-embryo. Therefore society has obligations to apply therapeutic measures to the pre-embryo.

3. The pre-embryo is a potential human being. This definition is a new philosophical entity, that compromises between the two other definitions, and is the one accepted today by most of the scientists, physicians and ethicists. Even though the pre-embryo is a potential human being it should be handled with dignity, its rights should be kept as long as they do not harm major social and maternal interests, or other interests.

A basic decision should be made as to the question of when the status of a potential human being is acquired: (a) at conception; (b) at implantation; (c) with the appearance of the primitive streak. It is almost impossible to reach a definite consensus about such an issue, since the issue of "When does human life begin" is not solved yet. The arguments on this subject are based on scientific, religious and traditional grounds, some of which will be presented.

1. The Roman Catholic Church point of view is that life begins at conception (Schenker 1990)
2. There are assumptions that state that the beginning of life is at implantation

(the regulations regarding federally funded research in the USA with pregnant women or with fetuses defined both pregnancy and fetal life as beginning with implantation) (US Court Decision 45 CFR 1982)

3. Life has been defined as being terminated when brain activity ends. Therefore, it is considered that life begins when brain activity starts (Schenker 1983)

4. The beginning of life is at the second of eight weeks after conception, at the point that the embryo is responsive to stimuli (Horan 1976–77)

5. Human life begins when human conception becomes a "person", has some degree of sentience or even an active volition (Grobstein 1981)

According to the above assumptions, except the one supported by the Catholic Church that human life begins at conception, human life cannot be attributed to the pre-embryo in the in-vitro status. Therefore, the question of whether the gametes donors and the medical staff have obligations to apply medical measures, arises.

The Legal Status of the Pre-implanted Pre-embryo

The legal status of the pre-embryo is difficult to establish. If one suggests it is a person, or even a potential person, it has no legal status according to the law in most countries. There is a suggestion that the pre-embryo is property; and by this definition it offends ethical principles. The above suggestions leave open the legal question of the right to use, to dispose, to sell and to purchase a pre-embryo. A pre-embryo seems not to be a human being for the purpose of criminal law. Deliberate destruction of a pre-embryo is not a criminal abortion act. The legislation regarding storage of pre-embryos in the UK and Australia and regulations in other countries give the right to the gamete donors to decide about its fate (United Kingdom Human Fertilization and Embryology Bill 1990; Western Australia Human Reproductive Technology Bill 1990). According to the wish and consent of the gamete donors it can be disposed of, donated to other couples or given for research (this differs from country to country).

Juridical protection to a pre-embryo may be difficult to achieve, except through specific legislation. The present consensus on the status of the pre-embryo is documented by several ethical committees. The USA Ethical Advisory Board (1979) states: "The pre-embryo is entitled to profound respect, but this respect does not necessarily encompass the full legal and moral rights attributed to persons" (Medical Research Council 1982). The Warnock Committee (Warnock 1984) states: "The human embryo is not under the present law of the United Kingdom accorded the same status as the living child or an adult, nor do we necessarily wish it to be accorded the same status. Nevertheless, we were agreed that the pre-embryo ought to have a special status." The same views were accepted by the Ontario Law Reform Commission (1985) and ethical committees in different countries (Schenker and Frenkel 1987). The pre-embryo is not yet a legal subject in its own right and is not protected by laws against homicide and wrongful death.

The proposed Federal Human Life Bill in the USA would give all the legal rights of personhood to the pre-embryo from the moment of conception. The legislation in Illinois, USA, applied to the pre-embryo's legal status, in-vitro, is that of the 1877 Child Abuse Act (Illinois Ann Stat ch 38 1983–84). The physician is criminally liable if he endangers the life or health of the pre-embryo. This may lead to the condition that physicians can be prosecuted when the in-vitro fertilized pre-embryo is damaged during its growth in-vitro by changing the growth medium or temperature or after application of manipulation techniques. The question is whether the physician commits a crime if he discards a pre-embryo that is not dividing properly or is damaged by the procedure of in-vitro fertilization (IVF) or in storage.

A fundamental question is whether the pre-embryo represents property or is a "person" in the eyes of the law. There are no laws on the rights of the pre-embryo in the in-vitro stage, but there are laws on the rights of the unborn, both before kicking and before it achieves viability (before it was changed by the Supreme Court of the USA) (Roe v Wade 1973; Doe v Bolton 1973). Even following the change in the Abortion Law in the USA an unborn child is considered to be living from the moment of conception for the purpose of taking under a will or trust, provided the child is born alive. The State of California law recognizes the legal rights of the unborn (California Civil code 29 1971): "A child conceived but not yet born is to be considered an existing person, so far as may be necessary for its interests in the event of its subsequent birth. The unborn also enjoys certain protection at criminal law".

Since there is a widespread consensus that the pre-implanted pre-embryo is not a person, it does not have its own legal rights, but is to be treated with special respect since it may become a person. Therefore, any intervention with the pre-embryo that is transferred to the uterus creates obligations not only not to hurt it or injure it, but even to apply therapeutic measures, since following transfer it may be born. This viewpoint imposes the traditional duty of reasonable prenatal care, and raises the question: If therapy is not applied, could the physicians and the parents – the donors of the gametes – be sued for wrongful life? There are several cases reported, initiated by parents, suits known as wrongful life, that have been brought in the name of the affected child. In those cases, the argument is essentially that the child would rather not have been born at all, than have been born with substantial defect. Most such suits failed. In the Israeli case, the Supreme Court of the State of Israel decided on the issue of wrongful life (Carmi 1990). The Supreme Court of Appeal decided it has the power to deal with the matter of the right not to be born, and that the minor had a valid course of action against the doctor, and the doctor owns a duty of care toward the unborn. Therefore, the doctor was found guilty and had to pay damages in the case of wrongful life. It seems that, according to the above decision, the right of the minor is to sue his negligent parents if antenatal care, even at the pre-embryo stage, is not applied.

Therapeutic Approach to the Fetus (Table 4.1)

Modern diagnostic tools, especially ultrasound imaging, have made possible early detection of fetal diseases. The fetus, regarded as an independent patient, has introduced new responsibilities to obstetricians. As a natural consequence of this situation, attempts are being made to treat the fetus in need. Medical and surgical methods can be applied for fetal therapy. Intrauterine transfusion for Rh isoimmunization had been a tremendous breakthrough in therapeutic approach to the fetus. In the early 1980s, waves of enthusiasm surrounded the attempts at fetal surgical interventions. This enthusiasm is now balanced by accumulated clinical experience which points to the difficulties and limitations of surgical intervention in the fetus. Consideration for in-utero surgical intervention should be based on the rationale that the malformation detected will interfere with fetal organ development, and that, if alleviated, will allow normal fetal development. Most of the correctable malformations that can be diagnosed in utero can be treated after delivery at term, or after induction of labour on a pre-term viable fetus.

There are perspectives for treatment of genetic disorders, and the reduction of the incidence of congenital malformations. Efforts to treat disorders by stem-cell transplantation and gene therapy should be attempted.

Surgical Treatment of the Fetus

Surgical treatment of the fetus may be employed in treating obstructive uropathies, obstructive hydrocephalus, diaphragmatic hernia and in aspirating an ovarian cyst.

Obstructive Uropathies Unrelieved obstruction of the fetal urinary tract causes ongoing damage to the developing kidneys and lungs. Optimal management depends on proper understanding of the different pathophysiological processes involved and their sequelae in the developing fetus. It is now clear that only a small proportion of fetuses with dilated urinary tract should be treated. Three types of obstruction may be distinguished according to the level at which they occur:

1. Collecting tubal obstruction; produces gross renal enlargement and multiple renal microcysts. The disease is fatal and no treatment is possible
2. Proximal ureteral obstruction at uretero-pelvic junction is a common renal anomaly observed. Ureteral narrowing causes renal, pelvic and calyceal dilatation. In these cases corrective surgery can be performed following birth

Table 4.1. Fetal therapy

Intra-uterine blood transfusion
Surgical repair of obstructive uropathies
Surgical approach to hydrocephalus
Repair of diaphragmatic hernia
Aspiration of ovarian cysts
Intra-uterine bone marrow transplantation
Conversion of fetal arrhythmias
Correction of congenital adrenal hyperplasia
Pharmaceutic approach to biochemical defects

3. Obstruction at the level of the bladder neck or proximal urethra is a
    condition which may benefit from intrauterine surgery (Yarkoni and
    Schenker 1984). Ultrasound scanning shows distended bladder and dilatation
    of ureters. Total obstruction is associated with oligohydramnios. Partial or
    intermittent obstruction, as occurs in some cases of posterior urethral valve
    syndrome, is associated with normal urine production and normal volume
    of amniotic fluid

An intra-uterine intervention for urinary tract obstruction should be reserved
for cases below 32 weeks of gestation that demonstrate isolated bilateral
hydronephrosis, secondary to obstruction, associated with oligohydramnios, in
which renal function appears intact. The following tests should be performed
prior to the attempt to bypass the obstruction:

Ultrasonography to confirm the diagnosis of obstruction (Golbus et al. 1985)
and rule out additional malformation
Renal function should be evaluated for electrolyte content by examination of
urine aspirated from the kidney of the fetus
Urine electrolytes, which appear to be a relatively sensitive indicator, to measure
fetal renal function

The surgical technique most commonly employed for correction of urine
obstruction is shunting of the fetal urine into the amniotic cavity by placement
of a double pig-tail fetal bladder catheter. In cases of gestation below 28 weeks
an open procedure may be applied. Under general anaesthesia hysterotomy is
performed, the lower abdominal wall of the fetus is exposed and marsupialization
of the fetal bladder is done. This surgical procedure allows a continuous drainage
that bypasses the obstruction of posterior urethral valve syndrome. This surgical
approach poses a fetal and maternal risk.

Obstructive Hydrocephalus Congenital hydrocephalus occurs in 0.5–1.8/1000
births. The causes are multiple; a minority may be inherited as X-linked or
autosomal recessive traits, or associated with fetal infections. The majority have
no clear-cut aetiology, and multifactorial inheritance is probably involved
(Golbus et al. 1985). Complete or partial obstruction of the cerebral aqueduct
is the most common obstructive type of hydrocephalus. It results in lateral and
third ventricle dilatation. While spontaneous arrest of the disease is possible,
intellectual development is frequently diminished. The prognosis of congenital
hydrocephalus is variable and depends on the aetiology, as well as the time of
onset and severity of the process. Best intellectual development occurs among
infants with hydrocephalus due to Arnold Chiary syndrome, whereas normal
intellectual development is less frequent with aqueduct stenosis and is unusual
with the Dandy Walker syndrome (Ohel and Schenker 1986).
   A high incidence of additional major malformations has been shown to be
associated with hydrocephalus. The advent of ultrasonography, which made
possible the diagnosis of hydrocephalus before the end of the second trimester,
prompted intrauterine treatment of this condition. Technically, such treatment
is possible today. Sonography can be used to guide the application of a shunt
that drains the fetal ventricles and communicates with the amniotic fluid. Such
a shunt contains a one-way valve to prevent back flow of the ventricles and
fixation flanges to prevent its dislodgement. The efficacy of ventriculoamniotic

shunting is uncertain at present, and will not be determined until controlled trials are performed and long-term follow-up is available (Manning et al. 1986). Early enthusiasm for intrauterine placement of ventriculoamniotic shunts has been replaced by a more conservative approach. At present, if such intrauterine treatment is considered, it should be limited to cases with isolated hydrocephalus, with a documented progressive ventriculomegaly and immaturity which does not allow delivery for postnatal shunting. For most cases it is probably best to manage fetal hydrocephalus with repeated ultrasound examinations and early delivery when the lesion is progressive, followed by shunting in the neonatal period when indicated (Clawell et al. 1986).

Diaphragmatic Hernia Congenital diaphragmatic hernia occurs in approximately 1 in 5000 births. Over 60% of affected newborns die within a few hours of birth. Despite today's early neonatal diagnosis and early operative procedures, the mortality remains high. The mortality is attributed to pulmonary hypoplasia, which is explained by in-utero compression, caused by the herniated viscera; this resulting in pulmonary insufficiency. Antenatal repair of the defect would, therefore, seem to offer the best approach to cure (Harrison et al. 1981).

Aspiration of Ovarian Cyst Ovarian cyst in the fetus can be detected by ultrasound. The aetiology of these cysts is different, and they can be managed in different ways, depending upon the clinical course. In cases of large cysts detected antenatally, and affecting the ongoing pregnancy, in-utero transabdominal puncture can be undertaken without increased risk to the fetus (Giorlandino et al. 1990).

Medical Fetal Therapy

Successful medical fetal therapy can be documented in several conditions.

1. *Fetal arrhythmias* (Kleinman et al. 1985). Fetal cardiac structure malformations can now be diagnosed with reasonable access using echocardiography. Fetal cardiac arrythmias, such as paroxysmal superventricular tachycardia, atrial flutter and fibrillation have been observed. An attempt to cardiovert the fetus has been made via oral maternal digoxin administration alone or in combination with other agents. Recently, fetal blood sampling by umbilical cord puncture has been used for administration of drugs directly to the fetus, and by this technique to diminish the side-effects to the mother.

2. *Congenital adrenal hyperplasia*. This condition of 21-hydroxylase deficiency can be diagnosed in utero and can be treated prenatally by maternal administration of dexamethazone (Pang et al. 1990).

3. *Biochemical defects*. Biochemical defects like methylmalonic acidemia and multiple carboxylase can be diagnosed and treated prenatally.

4. *Fetal bone marrow transplantation for genetic disorders (IBMT)*. A large number of life-threatening genetic disorders involving deficiency of normal stem-cell products and enzymes are potentially correctable by allogenic bone-marrow transplantation. This technique is feasible and can be applied to the fetus in

utero. We have carried out IBMT in order to test the feasibility of this procedure and to attempt to correct lysosomal deficiency of prenatally diagnosed metachromatic leukodystrophy (MLD). The technique can be successful only if it is applied at early stages of gestation before development of the fetal immunocompetent T-cell system (Slavin et al. 1989). It can be applied when graft versus host disease (GVHD) can be prevented, since this condition may result in intrauterine fetal death or may affect the newborn following delivery.

We have shown in our primary clinical experience that GVHD can be easily prevented if there is adequate T lymphocytes depletion prior to IBMT. In order to be successful in treatment of genetic disorders the technique of IBMT must be improved so that it can be applied in early stages of gestation.

In modern obstetrics the fetus has rightfully achieved the status of a second patient to be cared for by obstetricians as they care for the pregnant woman. The fetus as a patient usually faces much greater risk of serious morbidity and mortality than the mother.

Introduction of fetal therapy raises several fundamental questions about the rights of the mother and the fetus as patients. To whom is the physician ultimately responsible, to the mother or to the fetus, especially in cases in which there is a conflict of interest? How can the risk of fetal surgical intervention be weighed against the burden of malformation itself? What is society's obligation in protecting the unviable human fetus? Will fetal therapy significantly preserve more handicapped individuals in the population and add to the burden of suffering and to the financial burden on society?

Fetal intrauterine intervention poses risks to the mother: infection due to transabdominal punction, hysterotomy which may endanger the mother's reproductive capability and delivery by caesarean section. Therefore, from the mother's point of view, she may accept the fetal surgical therapeutic approach when the medical risks are minimal and when the therapeutic results are of proven benefit to the fetus.

In cases where the fetal therapy is unproven, experimental, and there are some calculated risks to the mother's health, there is no moral duty to accept this therapeutic approach (Robertson 1985).

Questions which arise in the practice of modern perinatology include whether a pregnant woman has moral duties toward the fetus, whether society and the physician are obligated to intervene on behalf of a fetus threatened by a woman's neglect of her health during pregnancy or her refusal to apply fetal therapy in cases where the risk to her is minimal.

The welfare of the fetus is of the utmost importance to the majority of women. There are only occasional instances where there will be a conflict between the interests of the mother and the fetus. Examples of when a pregnant woman's behaviour with respect to her health or way of life may harm the fetus are: the woman may not co-operate in medical care designed for the benefit of the fetus or she may create a potential hazardous environment for the fetus by addiction to drugs, heavy smoking, alcoholism, not controlling her diabetes, etc. The pregnant woman may refuse a diagnostic procedure, medical therapy or a surgical procedure that may preserve fetal well-being, prevent morbidity or mortality. Examples of these may be the administration of tocolytic agents to prevent delivery, intrauterine fetal transfusion for isoimmunization, intrauterine surgical intervention for correction of congenital defects and caesarean section delivery in cases of fetal defects. From the legal point of view, a viable fetus (from 24 weeks of age) has the right not to be subjected to unreasonable risk of injury by the mother, the physician or a third party. If the parties mentioned above violate those prenatal obligations by negligence, a criminal or civil legal action is possible. On the other hand, there may be a conflict between the perceived interest of the fetus with a congenital defect and the parents, especially the mother, who must give her consent for therapy. As long as the fetus is not separated from the mother, her body is the site of the treatment, and the choice of fetal therapy ought to be made only after she has given informed consent. The treatment of the mother against her wish would constitute an assault. There are reasons for a mother to refuse fetal therapy; fears about the normality of the child that will be born, or the nature of the treatment and its outcome. She may not understand the reasons for the medical advice offered due to a poor command of the language, low intellectual level or because of anxiety. Cultural and religious backgrounds may also determine her attitude to fetal therapy. In some cases she may be so psychologically or mentally subnormal that she is not able to give consent to the therapy. Sometimes the mother does not believe that the medical advice for the therapy is solely based on the patient's best interest; the advice given for experimental therapy may be potentially based on the enthusiasms of the medical team to apply new technology. The President's Commission for the Study of Ethical Problems in Medicine and Biomedical Behavior Research asserted that the informed consent doctrine in health care decisions is an ethical imperative. Therefore, fetal therapy may be done only after the mother has given her consent and efforts should be made to obtain it by detailed explanation, involvement of other family members, especially the husband, consultation with other physicians and even ethics consultations.

According to a survey reported in the literature, there have been at least 21 reported cases in the last few years in which obstetricians have already sought court orders to override the wishes of pregnant women to perform caesarean section or fetal therapy against the mother's will. In all but three cases the courts granted the order. Most directors of perinatology units supported the idea of court orders in cases where pregnant women's behaviours endangered their fetus. If a woman refuses medical therapy and her child is born damaged, the mother should be punished. Fetal rights groups expressed the idea that the unborn child deserves as much legal protection as a pregnant woman. Some feminists argued that compelled treatment is never justified because it violates a pregnant woman's basic rights of privacy, body integrity and self-determination. Reasonable efforts should be made to protect the fetus, but the pregnant woman's autonomy should be protected. Some physicians and lawyers argue that when a woman endangers the fetus by refusing treatment, society must act. The opinion expressed by the American College of Obstetricians and Gynecologists is that physicians should refrain from performing procedures unwanted by pregnant women. The search for juridical authority to implement regimens in order to protect the fetus violates the pregnant woman's autonomy. The role of the obstetrician should be one of educator and counsellor. The use of the courts to resolve fetal-maternal conflicts is never warranted. Going to court should be the last resort, since it destroys the physician–patient relationship, and the obstetrician transfers himself into an agent of state authority.

Furthermore, inappropriate reliance on juridical authority may lead to undesirable social consequences, such as the criminalization of non-compliance with medical recommendations. On the other hand, in most Western countries, in cases of diagnosis of severe congenital malformation the woman has the right to an abortion. Once she decides not to abort, she has an obligation to be submitted to an established and proved medical treatment, if it exists, to ensure the birth of a healthy child. When conflict arises and the mother refuses an established medical procedure, civil action for damages could be brought against her on behalf of the newborn for wrongful life (when she denies an abortion) and wrongful birth. If the obstetrician follows the mother's refusal without taking all the measures mentioned above, and the fetus dies or is born defective, the physician can be criminally liable.

Conclusion

The choice between maternal liberty and fetal health is difficult and filled with ethical problems. Doctors facing these problems should try to achieve the best outcome for both mother and child, recognizing that differing and sometimes conflicting values must be weighed against each other and taking into consideration that individualism and patient autonomy are not necessarily universally accepted.

It is unethical to force a competent, fully informed patient to undergo any therapy against her will. The rights of the mother prevail over the rights of the fetus, and the pregnant wife's wishes prevail over her husband's. It is her body and her health which above all bear the risks.

With the development of the field of fetal therapy it is urgently required to draw moral and legal lines, even though it is legally and ethically complicated to define the status of the fetus.

References

Bustillo M, Thorney Croft I, Simon J, Cohen S, Buster J (1983) Non-surgical transfer of ova fertilized in vivo donated to infertile patients. Fertil Steril 40:411

Cal Civil Code #29 (1971) The fetus as legal entity. San Diego Law Rev 8:126

Carmi A (1990) Wrongful life: An Israel case. Med Law 9:777–781

Clawell WH, Manco-Johnson ML, Manchester DK (1986) Diagnosis and management of fetal hydrocephalus. Clin Obstet Gynecol 29:514–522

Cohen J, Elsner C, Kort H, Malter H, Massey J, Mayer MP (1990a) Immunosuppression and antimicrobia propholaxis support implantation of zona drilled human embryos. Fertil Steril 53:662

Cohen J, Elsner C, Kort H, Malter H, Massey J, Mayer MP, Wiemer K (1990b) Impairment of the hatching process following IVF in the human and improvement of implantation by assisting hatching using micromanipulation. Human Reprod 5:7–13

Dokras A, Sargent IL, Ross C, Gardner RL, Barlow DH (1990) Trophectoderm biopsy in human blastocysts. Human Reprod 5:821–825

Giorlandino C, Rivosecchi M, Bilancioni E, Bagolan P, Zaccara A, Taramanni C, Vizzone A (1990) Successful intrauterine therapy of a large fetal ovarian cyst. Prenatal Diagnosis 10:473–475

Golbus MS, Filly RA, Callen PW et al. (1985) Fetal urinary tract obstruction, management and selection for treatment. Semin Perinatol 9:91

Grobstein C (1981) From chance to purpose: An appraisal of external human fertilization. Addison-Wesley, Reading, Mass.

Handyside AH, Pattinson JK, Penketh RJA, Delhanty JDA, Winston RML, Tudenham EGD (1989) Biopsy of human preimplantation embryos and sexing by DNA amplification. Lancet i:347–349

Hardy K, Martin KL, Leese HJ, Winston RMI, Handyside AH (1990) Human preimplantation development in vitro is not adversely affected by biopsy at the 8-cell stage. Human Reprod 5:708–714

Harrison MR, Ross NA, deLorimier AA (1981) Correction of congenital diaphragmatic hernia in utero. III. Development of a successful surgical technique using abdominoplasty to avoid compromise of umbilical blood flow. J Pediatr Surg 16:934

Horan DJ (1976–77) Fetal experimentation and federal regulation. Villanova Law Rev 22:325

Illinois Ann Stat ch 38 # 81–26(6)(7) (Smith-Hurd Supp. 1983–84)

Kleinman CS, Copel JA, Weinstein EM et al. (1985) In utero diagnosis and treatment of fetal supraventricular tachycardia. Semin Perinatol 9:113–129

Makter HE, Cohen J (1989) Blastocyst formation and hatching in vitro following zona drilling of mouse and human embryos. Gamete Res 24:67–80

Manning FA, Harrison MR, Rodeck CH (1986) Catheter shunts for fetal hydronephrosis and hydrocephalus: Report of the International Fetal Surgery Registry; N Engl J Med 315:336

Medical Research Council (1982) Statement on research related to human fertilization and embryology. Br Med J 385:1980

Medical Research International Society for Assisted Reproductive Technology. The American Fertility Society (1991) In vitro fertilization embryo transfer (IVF-ET) in the United States: 1989 results from the IVF-ET registry. Fertil Steril 55:14–23

Milayeva S, Verlinsky Y, Enriquez G, Ginsberg N, Lifchez A, Valle J, Moise J, Strom C (1990) Successful preimplantation diagnosis for gender determination (Abstract). J IVF/ET 7:27

Ohel G, Schenker JG (1986) Fetal surgery. In: Schenker JG, Weinstein D (eds) The intrauterine life: management and therapy. Excerpta Medica, Amsterdam, pp 244–249

Ontario Law Reform Commission (1985) Report on human artificial reproduction and related matters. Ministry of the Attorney General, Ontario, Canada

Pang S, Pollack M, Marshall R, Immken L (1990) Fetal treatment of congenital adrenal hyperplasia due to 21-hydroxylase deficiency. N Engl J Med 322:111–115

Plachot M (1989) Chromosome analysis of spontaneous abortions after IVF. A European survey. Human Reprod 4:425–429

Robertson JA (1985) Legal issues in fetal therapy. Semin Perinatol 9:140–145

Roe v Wade, 410 US 113, 1973; Doe v Bolton, 410 US 179, 1973

Schenker JG (1983) IVF and ET: legal and religious aspects in Israel. Isr J Med Sci 19:218

Schenker JG (1990) Research on human embryos. Eur J Obstet Gynecol and Reprod Biol 36:267–273

Schenker JG (1991) World clinical results of assisted reproductive technology. WHO Publication, in press

Schenker JG, Frenkel D (1987) Medico-legal aspects of in vitro fertilization and embryo transfer practice. Obstet Gynecol Survey 41:405–413

Slavin S, Naparstek B, Ziegler M, Bach G, Schenker JG, Lewin A (1989) Intrauterine bone marrow transplantation as a means for correction of genetic disorders through induction of prenatal transplantation tolerance. In: Hobbs JR (ed) Correction of certain genetic diseases by transplantation. COGNET, London, pp 54–63

Steptoe PC, Edwards RG (1978) Birth after the reimplantation of human embryo. Lancet ii:366

United Kingdom Human Fertilization and Embryology Bill, July 1990

Van Steirteghem AC, Van Abbeel E (1990) World results of human embryo cryopreservation. In: Mashiach S, Ben-Rafael Z, Laufer N, Schenker JG (eds) Proceedings of the VIth World Congress of IVF and Alternate Assisted Reproduction. Plenum Press, New York, pp 601–610

Verlinsky Y, Pergament E, Storm C (1990) The preimplantation genetic diagnosis of genetic diseases. J IVF/ET 7:1–5

Warnock M (1984) Report of the committee inquiring into human fertilization and embryology. Her Majesty's Stationery Office, London

Western Australia Human Reproductive Technology Bill 1990

Yarkoni S, Schenker JG (1984) Surgical interventions in the uterus. In: Schenker JG, Rippmann ET, Weinstein D (eds) Recent advances in pathophysiological conditions in pregnancy. Excerpta Medica, Amsterdam, pp 289–294

CHAPTER 5

Respect for Life: Embryonic Considerations

Lord (Immanuel) Jakobovits

In the Jewish view, full human status is not reached until birth. The destruction of an unborn child does not, therefore, constitute murder as listed in the Ten Commandments.

This is derived primarily from two biblical sources, as interpreted by the Jewish tradition (Oral Law). Homicide is defined in the verse: "He who smites a man so that he dies shall surely be put to death" (Exodus 21: 12). "A man – that is, to exclude a foetus", according to the authentic Rabbinic exegesis. Again, "And if men strive together, and hurt a woman with child, so that her fruit depart, and yet no harm follow, he shall be surely fined . . ." (Exodus 21: 22). The words "and yet no harm follow" are interpreted to mean if the mother survives the assault; in that case, a monetary fine is payable. This clearly indicates that causing the loss and therefore death of the unborn child is not deemed a capital crime.

Nevertheless, feticide is considered a very grave offence. Even the destruction of potential life is strictly forbidden as a grave offence against a fundamental moral value.

Even before fertilisation occurs, "wasting the seed" (by masturbation or other means) is regarded as a serious infringement of the moral law. Once an embryo is brought into existence, its destruction becomes correspondingly more objectionable. The gravity of this offence grows at various stages, such as the first 40 days of gestation, the "quickening with life" in about the seventh month, the viability of the child in the eighth month, and finally the start of the birth process. At each of these stages the objection to killing the human fruit becomes correspondingly more severe as "an appurtenance of murder".

There are only exceptional circumstances in which Jewish law would countenance the premature termination of a pregnancy involving the deliberate or inevitable destruction of the unborn life. This applies notably when there is a risk to the mother's life. In that case, her life – being certain and established – has priority over the unborn child whose life is as yet only potential and uncertain. Where the mother's life is at stake by allowing the pregnancy to continue, Jewish opinion is unanimous in sanctioning, or indeed mandating, an abortion.

But where there is a grave threat that the child will be born with serious physical or mental handicaps, rabbinic views on aborting such a foetus are still widely divided. As previously indicated, the objections become stronger with the growth of the unborn human fruit, being most insistent when the pregnancy has entered its seventh month.

While some modern rabbinic verdicts would countenance preventing a gravely deformed birth even then, others object to terminating the pregnancy even at an earlier stage if the mother's life is not at stake. But even a grave psychological risk to the mother would be considered as a major factor, especially if this could even remotely lead to mental instability jeopardising the life of herself (by suicide) or of others (by homicide).

All Jewish authorities are agreed that only strictly medical considerations could possibly justify an abortion. Social or economic factors by themselves would under no circumstances ever be deemed sufficient to justify the destruction of potential human life. The enjoyment of marital pleasures must be balanced by corresponding moral responsibilities.

Where serious congenital deformities are suspected or established (such as by amniocentesis or other foetal tests), a further consideration should also be given due weight. The birth of a badly handicapped child is invariably an immense misfortune. Yet it is by no means always an unmitigated curse. Pastoral and social workers will confirm that even seriously disabled children can often be a source of much joy and human fulfilment. But leaving this subjective judgment aside, the intrinsic human value of any child is surely not diminished by its handicap.

Even if we were to measure such value by the contributions made to society, who is to tell us whether a child rendered completely helpless by its abnormality does not often make a more potent contribution to the betterment and refinement of society than the most gifted normal child? Could it not be that tenderly caring for such a child ennobles the parents and their assistants by cultivating moral qualities of compassion and loving kindness which renders them into superior human beings? Maybe such service to human ennoblement has a quality which the finest contributions to science, commerce or leadership cannot rival.

Of no lesser importance than the claim to life, whenever this begins in absolute terms, is the inalienable right to be born to identifiable fathers and mothers. Jewish law cannot therefore sanction artificial insemination or *in vitro* fertilisation by donor, or by any circumstances other than within marriage. On the certain knowledge of a child's paternity and maternity depends the observance of all the laws of incest. It has happened that a man was about to marry his own daughter when he discovered that his bride had been conceived by artificial insemination 20 years earlier, and reminding himself that he had been a semen donor, followed up the trail of the date and place where the insemination occurred until he ascertained that she was in fact the product of his donation.

Altogether, the mechanisation of human life, reducing the generation of children to stud-farming methods, is utterly abhorrent to Judaism. It deprives the supreme human act of creation, in partnership with man's Creator, of the infinite dignity and sanctity which alone can serve to raise a morally healthy progeny, and in turn provide the human constituents out of which a decent society is bred.

Humans can no more be produced on assembly lines than they can be discarded like disposable goods. The highest quality of life may well depend on the reverence with which it is generated and treasured.

CHAPTER 6

Maternal–Fetal Conflict: Pregnant Drug Addicts

Bonnie Steinbock

Hardly a day goes by, it seems, in which one does not read an article about the impact of the crack epidemic on babies. Here is a description of the neonatal intensive care unit of Bronx-Lebanon hospital: "filled with baby misery: babies born months too soon; babies born weighing little more than a hardcover book; babies that look like wizened old men in the last stages of a terminal illness, wrinkled skin clinging to chicken bones; babies who do not cry because their mouths and noses are full of tubes".[1] According to one commentator, "If cocaine use during pregnancy were a disease, its impact on children would be considered a national health care crisis".[2]

Two factors in particular have contributed to the crisis: the increase in cocaine addiction, particularly among young women, and the devastating effects cocaine can have on a developing fetus. Between 1985 and 1990, the number of babies born to cocaine-addicted mothers in New York City more than quadrupled.[3] This trend appears to have slowed down somewhat. Recently, *The New York Times* reported that a decline in the use of cocaine by pregnant women, combined with improved prenatal care, helped significantly reduce infant mortality in New York City in 1990 for the first time in 4 years.[4] The crack epidemic appears to have peaked in 1988, though it continues to ravage many families.

The problem of drug use during pregnancy is not confined to large urban areas like New York City. A 1988 survey of 36 hospitals across America indicated that 11% of women were using drugs during pregnancy, resulting in 375 000 drug-exposed infants annually. Other surveys placed the number as high as 15%. Use is not confined to particular racial or socio-economic groups, although most women *prosecuted* for using illegal drugs while pregnant have been poor members of racial minorities.[5]

New evidence is emerging about the danger that cocaine can pose to fetal health. As recently as 1982, medical texts on high-risk obstetrics maintained that cocaine had no deleterious effects upon fetuses.[6] More recent studies indicate that the effects of fetal exposure to cocaine include retarded growth in the womb and subtle neurological abnormalities, leading to extraordinary irritability during infancy, and learning disorders later. In more extreme cases, cocaine can cause loss of the small intestine and brain-damaging strokes. Cocaine-exposed babies face a tenfold increase in the risk of cot (crib) death. Some of the worst effects occur during the first 3 months of pregnancy, when the woman may not even know she is pregnant. Some researchers think that even a single cocaine "hit" during pregnancy can cause lasting fetal damage.[7]

Not all researchers have found such clear evidence of harmful effects on the fetus from cocaine use.[8] It is often difficult to tell whether the symptoms in the child are specifically due to cocaine use, or other features of poverty, such as poor nutrition, poor maternal health, and little or no prenatal care. Some experts have expressed the concern that the media focus on "crack babies" enables society to blame the terrible women who impose such awful consequences on their children, while ignoring all the other factors that cause babies to be born damaged. This is certainly an important concern. Nevertheless, the evidence so far indicates that crack use during pregnancy poses special dangers to unborn babies, over and above the risks stemming from poverty.

We desperately need a framework to think about maternal and fetal rights. Typically, and unfortunately, the framework is derived from the abortion debate. Those who oppose abortion favor fetal rights, on the ground that fetuses – indeed, even pre-implantation embryos – are "pre-born children" with all the rights of born children. Pro-choice advocates, on the other hand, deny that fetuses have rights. They regard the ascription of rights to fetuses as the first step in a campaign to make abortion illegal. This has led some feminists and civil libertarians to maintain that whatever a woman does during her pregnancy is her own business. For example, the New York State chapter of the National Organization for Women (New York NOW) has joined liquor sellers in lobbying against a bill that would require restaurants, taverns, and off-licences (package-stores) to post signs warning pregnant women of the dangers of alcohol consumption. New York NOW view the warning-sign legislation as an attack on a woman's right to choose. They argue that it sends a message that the rights of the fetus exceed those of the woman carrying it.[9]

I consider both of these approaches to be mistaken. The mistake of right-to-lifers is to ignore important and morally relevant differences between embryos and children. What one does to a child *matters* to that child. If children are mistreated or neglected, they suffer. If killed, even painlessly, they are deprived of something that has value to them, namely, their lives. Even a newborn can enjoy his or her life, and so is harmed by being killed. The same is not true of embryos or early gestation fetuses. A fetus which cannot experience anything can neither suffer from being killed, nor is it deprived of anything it values or wants. Precisely when fetuses become sentient is a matter of some debate, but it is likely this does not occur until some time in the second trimester, and perhaps later.[10] Until they have the capacity to experience, to feel pain and pleasure, it does not matter to an embryo or fetus what is done to it. For this reason, I maintain that embryos and early fetuses have no interests at all, and so no interest in continued existence. Without an interest in continued existence, they cannot be harmed by being killed.[11] By contrast, babies and late gestation fetuses are sentient. They have lives that are (ordinarily) a good to them, and so they can be harmed by death. The mistake of pro-lifers is to treat fetuses, throughout gestation, as if they were experiencing, sentient babies.

Pro-choicers do not make this mistake. However, some of them ignore the fact that if a woman decides not to abort, but to carry to term, it is not the welfare of the fetus that is at stake, but rather the welfare of the *future child*. The question that must then be addressed is: What moral obligations do women have to protect the welfare of their future children, the children they intend to bear? To address this question is not to exalt the rights of *fetuses* over those of women, but rather to emphasize that *children* have the right not to be injured prior to their birth. Most women who are expecting a child will voluntarily adapt at least some of their behaviour to protect their babies. They drink alcoholic beverages only moderately or not at all. They try to eat regular nutritious meals and take daily vitamins. A few even manage to stop smoking.[12] They do all this because they want more than anything else a healthy baby. But what if the woman is an alcoholic or a crack addict? What if she is ignorant or indifferent to the health of her baby? Does society have the right – indeed, the responsibility – to coerce the mother to protect the not-yet born child?

Society clearly has a legitimate interest in the welfare of its children, both those existing today and those that will exist in the future. The mere fact that people do not now exist is no reason to discount the interests they will have, when they come into existence. If we do nothing about the national debt, if we allow the ozone layer to be depleted, if we do not solve our waste disposal problem, then actual people will suffer. We have a responsibility to these actual, future people not to destroy the world they will live in, even though they do not now exist.

The primary responsibility for protecting the interests of children belongs to their parents. Yet although parents have a great deal of discretion in deciding how to care for and raise their children, they do not have absolute freedom. They are morally and legally obliged not to inflict injury on their children, to feed and clothe them, to provide them with necessary medical care. Parents who fail in these obligations may have their children taken from them; they may even be criminally charged. If the coercive power of the state is justifiably used to protect children, why can it not be used against a woman whose behaviour injures her child before it is born?

Again, I stress that it is the future *child*, not the fetus, who would be the intended beneficiary of such protective legislation. Because of this, law professor John Robertson, who has argued in favour of some coercive measures to protect not-yet born children, once said to me, "I hope you're not planning to title your talk "Maternal–Fetal Conflict". The conflict, he said, is not between mother and *fetus*, but between mother and surviving *child*.

In fact, the term "maternal–fetal conflict" is disliked by virtually everyone, regardless of philosophical standpoint. Janet Gallagher, a feminist lawyer who has argued against intervention into pregnancies, maintains that the term "maternal-*fetal* conflict" misrepresents the situation in the obstetrical cases (e.g., forced caesareans), because the conflict is typically not between mother and fetus. Rather, it is between mother and *doctor*, who disagree about what is best for both mother and child.[13] Still others object to the word *conflict*, on the ground that it opposes mother and fetus when, in most cases, their interests are inseparably intertwined.

All the above points are good ones. However, in some cases, the interests of the woman and the not-yet born child are not the same, as when a pregnant woman chooses to behave in ways likely to harm the future child. In many cases, the behaviour also endangers *her* health, but it is wishful thinking to pretend that this prevents the possibility of conflict. The unfortunate reality is that some women want to use drugs, despite the risks to their own health and that of their unborn children. In such cases, the term "maternal–fetal conflict" is accurate.

As for Robertson's point, that it is not the fetus whose interests are protected, but the surviving child's, I entirely agree. However, the reason for speaking of maternal–*fetal* conflict is that the behaviour likely to harm the child occurs while the woman is pregnant, and the child still a fetus. We cannot remove the fetus from the woman, as a child can be put in protective custody. We can protect the future child only through the body of the pregnant woman or by controlling the woman's behaviour during pregnancy. This raises concerns about privacy and bodily autonomy that simply do not exist in ordinary child welfare cases.

Thus, the issue of maternal–fetal conflict is both like and unlike the abortion issue. It is like abortion in raising the question of how much control the state should have over the bodies and lives of its citizens. It differs from abortion in that it is not the fetus *per se* who is the object of moral concern, but rather the future child. Whatever one's position on the morality of abortion, one can and should recognize moral obligations to the children one intends to bring into the world.

Moral Obligations to the Not-Yet Born

How shall we characterize moral obligations to not-yet born children? It is useful to think about these obligations in the context of general parental obligations to children.[14] This prevents us from imposing especially stringent obligations on pregnant women, or thinking that pregnant women are morally required to subordinate all their interests to their fetuses. No one requires this of parents generally. Parents are supposed to take reasonable steps to protect their children's health and well-being. They are not morally required to avoid any and all risks to their children's health. If they were, they could not allow their children to ride in cars or learn to rollerskate. They could not even inoculate them against disease. So the obligation is rather to avoid *unreasonable* risks of *substantial* harm.

But which risks are unreasonable? How much harm is substantial? Consider, for example, drinking during pregnancy. We now know that alcohol is a potent teratogen, which can cause irreversible damage to the body and brain of the developing fetus. Heavy drinking during pregnancy – especially binge drinking – is particularly risky. It can cause fetal alcohol syndrome (FAS), which is often marked by severe facial deformities and mental retardation. One study showed that even moderate drinking – defined as one to three drinks daily – during early pregnancy can result in a lowering of as much as five IQ points.[15] Perhaps most important, there is no established "safe" level of alcohol consumption. While there is no evidence that a rare single drink during pregnancy does damage, there is no guarantee that it does not. The safest course is, therefore, total abstention. But is the safest course the morally obligatory one? We do not require this standard of parents regarding their already born children. If we did, we could not justify leaving children with babysitters while we go out to dinner. What if something should happen? It seems to me that having a single drink occasionally in pregnancy falls into the area of individual discretion, both because the risk of causing harm is very low (perhaps non-existent) and the nature of the harm (loss of a few IQ points) hardly devastating.

The attitudes toward pregnant women drinking contrast sharply in America and Britain. Judging from the play "It's a Girl!" the idea of a pregnant woman drinking is still considered quite humorous in Britain; I doubt it would get a laugh in America, where there has been considerable media attention paid to the risks of drinking alcohol during pregnancy. In fact, Americans seem to have gone to the opposite extreme. In March 1991, a bartender and a waitress attempted to dissuade a pregnant woman in Seattle from ordering a rum daiquiri. First they asked her whether she would prefer a nonalcoholic drink. When she said she would not, the bartender removed the warning label from a bottle of beer, which says that the Surgeon General has determined that pregnant women should not drink alcohol because of the risk of birth defects, and placed it on her table. She was understandably upset, and complained to the management. As it turned out, the woman was past her due date and had been very careful to avoid liquor throughout her pregnancy. She had decided that one drink was unlikely to do any harm. In my view, this was a perfectly reasonable decision, and it was appalling that she should have been harassed. It is one thing to *inform* pregnant women of the risks posed by alcohol, quite another for bartenders and waitresses to assume the role of enforcers. Ironically, the greatest risk for the unborn occurs during the first trimester, when the pregnancy is unlikely to be evident and outside intervention therefore impractical. If the occasional drink should be considered a matter of individual discretion, binge drinking, which has a 35% chance of subjecting one's baby to full-blown FAS,[16] clearly qualifies as unreasonably risking the health of one's baby. So does smoking crack. The difficulty with saying that women have a moral obligation not to drink heavily or smoke crack during pregnancy is that these behaviours are often the product of addiction. They are less than fully voluntary – some would say not voluntary at all. If a woman *cannot* modify her behaviour, then she cannot have a moral obligation to do so.

However, I think we should distinguish between being able to stop doing something *at will*, and not being able to stop at all. Although it is difficult to get over addictions, many smokers, alcoholics, and drug users do manage to change their behaviours. In a study done by the Boston University Fetal Alcohol Education Program, two-thirds of heavy drinkers who received counselling were able to cut down considerably or stop altogether.[17] We can recognize that it may be very difficult for some women to fulfil their moral obligations to the babies they intend to bear, and acknowledge that they will need to do so, without denying that they have such obligations. Unfortunately, such help is often not forthcoming. Many in-patient alcohol rehabilitation programmes exclude pregnant women. The situation is even worse for pregnant drug addicts. Two-thirds of the hospitals surveyed by the House Select Committee on Children, Youth and Families reported that they had *no* drug treatment programmes to which their pregnant patients could be referred; *none* had special programmes providing comprehensive drug treatment and prenatal care. Dr. Wendy Chavkin, of the Columbia University School of Public Health, surveyed 78 drug treatment programmes in New York City (95% of the city's programmes). She found that 54% categorically excluded pregnant women, 67% excluded pregnant women on Medicaid and 87% had no services for crack-addicted pregnant women.[18] And even in areas where there are treatment programmes for pregnant addicts, there are not nearly enough spaces for everyone who wants help. In 1988 the waiting list for a bed in Los Angeles

County's rehabilitation programme for pregnant women was 7 months long.[19] The absence of treatment programmes makes it virtually impossible for substance abusers to fulfil their moral obligations to the children they intend to bear, even with the best will in the world.

Some may object that often women do not "intend to bear" children. Drug addicts, in particular, may regard pregnancy as something that "happens" to them, often as a result of bartering their bodies for drugs, rather than something they intend. Nor do they necessarily choose to give birth: they may not be able to afford an abortion or it may not be available in a particular geographical area. For some women, abortion is not a morally or culturally acceptable option. Do restrictions on the choice whether to bear a child affect the woman's moral obligations to the child she bears? It seems to me that these restrictions do not affect how the woman ought to act, but they may affect how much she is to be blamed if she acts wrongly. Consider a woman who deliberately gets pregnant, intending to have a baby. If she goes on drinking and smoking and using recreational drugs, knowing of the possible effects on her baby's health, and making no effort to stop, she acts very wrongly indeed. She is selfishly indifferent to the health of her not-yet born child, and she deserves harsh criticism. By contrast, consider a woman who has no responsibility for becoming pregnant (she was raped), in a jurisdiction that prohibits abortion. She is the victim of two grave injustices, first in being raped, second in being denied an abortion. Still, that would not justify behaviour likely to inflict severe damage on the child she will perforce bear. Ideally, she should behave as if the pregnancy were chosen, since she is prevented from terminating the pregnancy. That is, she should stop smoking, drink moderately or not at all, etc. However, her failure to do so is certainly less blameworthy than the failure of a woman who has chosen to conceive and bear a child. Obviously, most cases will fall somewhere between the extremes of deliberate conception and forced childbirth. In general, the fewer options a woman has regarding pregnancy and childbirth, the less she deserves blame for failing to fulfil her obligations to her future child. At the same time, women are not relieved of moral responsibility simply because they do not "see" pregnancy as a choice.

Legal Obligations to the Not-Yet Born

The next question is whether the moral obligations women have to their not-yet born children should be made legal. In particular, should there be criminal prosecutions of women whose babies have been harmed, or exposed to the risk of harm, because they used illegal drugs during pregnancy? Since 1987, about 60 criminal proceedings against women for drug use during pregnancy have been instigated in 19 States and the District of Columbia.[20] The charges include criminal child abuse, assault with a deadly weapon, manslaughter, and criminal delivery of drugs. In most, the charges were ultimately dismissed or dropped, sometimes before indictment.[21]

Whereas drug use itself is typically a misdemeanour punishable by probation, especially in a first-offence case, delivering drugs is a felony in most jurisdictions in the United States, which can be punished with a hefty jail term. Drug dealers in Florida face a possible sentence of 30 years.[22] In July 1989, Jennifer Johnson of Florida became the first woman to be convicted of delivering cocaine to her newborn child through the umbilical cord. She was sentenced to 1 year in a rehabilitation programme and 14 years probation. The conviction was upheld by a Florida appeals court. The American Civil Liberties Union (ACLU), which represents Ms. Johnson, plans to appeal the case to the State Supreme Court.[23]

By charging Johnson with delivering a drug to her newborn, not her fetus, the prosecution avoided the issue of the legal status of the unborn. Many experts regard as dubious the theory that cocaine is passed through the umbilical cord just before it is clamped. Even if the scientific basis were more solid, the legal basis for these prosecutions is shaky. Applying existing drug laws to the prenatal cases ignores very real differences between the two situations. For one thing, the intent ordinarily necessary for a criminal charge is missing. A woman who uses drugs during pregnancy does not intend to give her child drugs. It is absurd to treat her like a pusher in a schoolyard. The absence of criminal intent is seen in the case of Kimberly Hardy, a Michigan woman who smoked crack the night before her baby was born. Reportedly, Ms. Hardy thought that smoking crack would help her relax and go into labour. She was quoted as saying, "The baby was so far along that a couple of hits couldn't possibly hurt."[24] As it turned out, she was wrong. The baby weighed five pounds, was jaundiced, and kept regurgitating his feeds. Ms. Hardy was charged with criminal delivery of drugs, a charge usually reserved for drug dealers, and ordered to stand trial. On 2 April 1991 a Michigan appeals court ruled that Ms. Hardy should not stand trial. The court unanimously rejected the state's argument that Ms. Hardy passed cocaine to her baby in a way that constituted criminal delivery of drugs. The prosecutor plans to appeal to the Michigan Supreme Court.[25]

Another possibility is to charge mothers of babies who are born addicted with child abuse. This is a less serious offence than the drug-delivery charge; in Florida, it generally carries a sentence of no more than 60 days.[26] So far, about 12 States have expanded their definitions of child abuse to include fetal drug exposure. A bill that is currently pending in Louisiana would make drug use during pregnancy a felony.[27] Laws that make it a crime for pregnant women to use illegal drugs and hold them criminally responsible for the effects of such drug use on their offspring are probably constitutional. They do not discriminate against pregnant women, since no-one is allowed to use these drugs. If no-one has a right to use cocaine, then a statute that imposes additional penalties on pregnant women who use cocaine is not invasive of their privacy.

Nevertheless, such laws can be criticized on policy grounds. It seems unlikely that such laws would have a significant deterrent effect. If a woman is willing to risk criminal prosecution for drug use, why will she be deterred by additional penalties for harming her unborn child? It may be objected that the same could be said of prosecuting women for postnatal child abuse. It is unlikely that laws prohibiting child abuse can have much deterrent effect, because most abuse is not deliberate or planned, but stems from inability to control frustration or anger. So, it might be said, why punish any child abusers? And if we do think that some abusers deserve to be punished, regardless of deterrent effect, why can the same not be said of some women who inflict prenatal abuse? This may not be the only or the best way to protect babies, but nevertheless, it might be argued that some prosecutions are justified. They are justified, on this view, when a woman is aware that her voluntary and non-compulsive behaviour poses serious risks to the health of her not-yet born child, yet disregards these risks, causing her baby to be born seriously damaged. Perhaps a yuppie recreational cocaine user would come into this category. Her behaviour is immoral; why should she not be prosecuted?

However, even if we concede that prosecution in such a case might be justified, there are good reasons not to embark on this path. It is unlikely that prosecution would be confined to such cases – if they exist at all. There is a real danger that fetal abuse statutes, even constitutionally acceptable ones, would be used primarily to prosecute uneducated and low-income addicts, who are, as I have argued, less than fully responsible for their harmful behaviour.

Another rationale for prosecution is that it is a way to pressure women to get into treatment. Tony Tague, a prosecutor in Muskegon County, Michigan, who has prosecuted a number of women whose newborns tested positive for crack cocaine, says, "When physicians make suggestions, it doesn't appear that's enough for them to seek treatment. The possibility of prosecution is a strong incentive."[28] However, seeking treatment may not help a woman avoid prosecution. One woman who was indicted after she tried to get help with her drug problem says, "I feel betrayed. Everyone I talked to about my drug problem has been subpoenaed."[29]

Moreover, as I noted earlier, many pregnant addicts who want help have found that there are no treatment programmes for them. Dr. Chavkin says, "The important thing to remember about the Jennifer Johnson case is that this is a woman who tried to get treatment and was turned away."[30] It makes no sense to spend resources prosecuting women in order to force them into treatment, when there are not adequate programmes for women who will voluntarily undergo treatment. Kary Moss of the ACLU asks: "Why is it that we have to make women criminals before we can get them drug treatment?"[31]

It might be argued that laws criminalizing drug use in pregnancy have an important symbolic function, even if they do not directly protect babies. They express society's outrage and convey the message that drug use during pregnancy is totally unacceptable. This is a legitimate function of law, but the social costs must be considered. The threat of prosecution may cause women to lie to their doctors about their drug use, preventing doctors from having information necessary to safeguard the baby's health during labour and delivery, and after birth. Kimberly Hardy, who admitted crack use to her doctor, says, "If I had known things would have turned out this way I would have taken the easier, softer way out and not told anybody. What woman wouldn't be afraid to tell her doctor if she had the threat of prosecution hanging over her?"[32] This threat may lead pregnant drug users to avoid hospitals and doctors altogether, for fear of being turned in to the authorities. In that case, the very purpose of such laws – to protect infants – would be subverted.

We cannot solve the problem of damaged babies with a "win the war on drugs" mentality. Instead, the problem must be treated with a comprehensive approach that includes funding drug treatment programmes for pregnant women, and by ensuring that all pregnant women have adequate prenatal care. Such care must include a close personal relationship with a caring and non-judgmental obstetrician. In my view, such care, which most middle-class women take for granted, would do more toward ending substance abuse, legal and non-legal, in pregnancy than any number of prosecutions or fetal abuse laws.

Notes

1. Anna Quindlen, Hearing the cries of crack. *The New York Times*, 7 October 1990, E19.

2. A. Revkin, Crack in the cradle. *Discover*, September 1989, pp 63–69.

3. Ibid.

4. Celia W. Dugger, Infant mortality in New York City declines for first time in 4 years. *The New York Times*, 20 April 1991, p 1.

5. A study done by the National Center for Perinatal Addiction Research and Education assessed the prevalence of drug use in pregnancy by collecting urine samples from all pregnant women who visited public health clinics or private obstetricians' offices in Pinellas County, Florida for one month in 1989. In Florida, all drug use during pregnancy must be reported to health departments. The researchers found that about 15% of both the white and the black women used drugs, but black women were 10 times as likely to be reported to the authorities, and poor women were more likely to be reported than middle-class women (Racial bias seen on pregnant addicts. *The New York Times*, Friday 20 July 1990 A13).

6. Revkin (see note 2).

7. Jane E. Brody, Cocaine: litany of fetal risks grows. *The New York Times*, 6 September 1988, C8.

8. See, for example, Doberczak TM, Shanzer S, Senie RT, Kandall SR, Neonatal neurologic and electroencephalographic effects of intrauterine cocaine exposure. *J Pediatr* 1988; 113:354–358.

9. Kevin Sack, Unlikely union in Albany: feminists and liquor sellers. *The New York Times*, 5 April 1991, B1.

10. It seems likely that third trimester fetuses can feel pain. After examining the anatomical, neurochemical, and behavioural evidence, K.J.S. Anand and P.R. Hickey, researchers at Children's Hospital in Boston, conclude, "Numerous lines of evidence suggest that even in the human fetus, pain pathways as well as cortical and subcortical centers necessary for pain perception are well developed *late in gestation*, and the neurochemical systems now known to be associated with pain transmission and modulation are intact and functional." (Anand KJS, Hickey PR (1987). Pain and its effects in the human neonate and fetus. *N Eng J Med* 317:1326. Emphasis added.
   It is very unlikely that a fetus can feel pain prior to the end of the second trimester, because the nervous system is insufficiently developed. Most sensory pathways to the neocortex, where pain and other experiences are registered, have synapses in the thalamus. The synaptic connections between the thalamus and neocortex are not completed until between 20 and 24 weeks of gestation.

11. This view is based on Joel Feinberg's theory of harm as a setback to interests, elaborated in his book *Harm to Others* (Oxford University Press, 1984). I defend sentience as the basis of moral status in my forthcoming book, *Life Before Birth: The Moral and Legal Status of Embryos and Fetuses*, to be published by Oxford University Press.

12. Only a tiny fraction stop smoking when pregnant. *JAMA*, 6 January 1989.

13. Janet Gallagher, Compelled medical treatment of pregnant and birthing women: legal and policy considerations and alternatives. Delivered to London '89, The Second International Conference on Health Law and Ethics, 21 July 1989.

14. This point is made in Murray TH (1987) Moral obligations to the not-yet born: the fetus as patient. *Perinatol* 14:329–343.

15. Streissguth AP, Barr HM, Sampson PD, Darby BL, Martin DC (1989) IQ at age 4 in relation to maternal alcohol use and smoking during pregnancy, *Dev Psychol* 25:7–8.

16. Ibid.

17. Ibid.

18. Chavkin W (1990) Drug addiction and pregnancy: policy crossroads. *Am J Public Health* 80:485.

19. Rorie Sherman, Keeping baby safe from Mom. *National Law Review*, 3 October 1988, p 25.

20. Isabel Wilkerson, Court backs woman in pregnancy drug case. *The New York Times*, 3 April 1991, A15.

21. Tamar Lewin, Drug use in pregnancy: new issue for the courts. *The New York Times*, 5 February 1990, A14.

22. Mother who gives birth to drug addict faces felony charge. *The New York Times*, 17 December 1988, p 9.

23. Tamar Lewin, Appeals court in Florida backs guilt for drug delivery by umbilical cord. *The New York Times*, 20 April 1991.

24. Jan Hoffman, Pregnant, addicted – and guilty? *The New York Times Magazine*, 19 August 1990, p 53.

25. Wilkerson (see note 20).

26. Mother who gives birth to drug addict faces felony charge (see note 22).

27. Women's Rights Project, American Civil Liberties Union, Memorandum: Update of state legislation regarding drug use during pregnancy, 22 May 1990.

28. Hoffman (see note 24), p 55.

29. Ibid.

30. Lewin (see note 21).

31. Hoffman (see note 24), p 57.

32. Wilkerson (see note 20).

CHAPTER 7

Expanding Human Populations and Their Ecosystems

Maurice King and James Thornton

Last year the Lancet published one of the most controversial papers that has ever appeared in that journal (King 1990). Although the controversy centred round the ethical dilemmas of the demographic trap, its main purpose was to break the taboo on discussing the trap at all, and to encourage aid agencies to adapt their policies to it. The resolution of ethical dilemmas is a social process of balancing competing premises, and unless the taboo is broken, this cannot be done for the trap. An accompanying editorial quoted the paper as saying that, for communities deep in the demographic trap "such . . . measures as oral rehydration should not be introduced on a public health scale since they increase the man-years of human misery, ultimately from starvation". Subsequently this has sometimes been misinterpreted as meaning all health measures rather than particular ones. *The Times* carried a headline "Doctor says let sick children die", but although there was no popular debate in the United Kingdom, nor yet any significant academic one, this was not so in Sweden or the Netherlands.

The Demographic Trap is a Disorder of "(Eco)sustainability"

Sustainability has several meanings, two of which are commonly confused. It can mean "able to be maintained or continued", for example, "the sustainability of a health programme after the donor agency has left . . .". The important new meaning of sustainability is "able to support life in quantity and variety", for example, "a community has exceeded the (eco)sustainability of its agricultural land so that it will no longer support them and the community starves". To avoid confusion this new meaning should be distinguished as "ecosustainability". Theoretically, both meanings ultimately converge, because if something is to be continued for long enough, it has to be ecosustainable.

"The trap" may be considered as it affects an isolated community and the global community.

An Isolated Community

All communities in the process of modernising start their demographic transitions with high death rates and high birth rates, and low and more-or-less stable populations – they are in the "trap open" stage; few such communities now remain. As soon as the death rate in a community starts to fall and its population starts to rise, the "trap is set". If it is lucky its birth rate eventually falls to match its death rate, it escapes out of the trap, and it is left with a stable but now much larger population. It has successfully completed its demographic transition, as have all communities in the industrial world.

Unfortunately, a community can only remain in the "trap set" stage for a limited time. If it stays there too long because its birth rate does not drop to match its death rate, its rising population eventually outgrows and destroys its biological support system (ecosystem), and its death rate starts rising; it has entered the "trap closing" stage. As the trap shuts people either die where they are from starvation, or flee as ecological refugees, as has happened recently in parts of Ethiopia and the Sahel, where communities have exceeded the ecosustainability of their farm land.

The critical point in this model is that which divides the "trap set" from the "trap closing" stages, since this determines whether a community will progress towards a demographic transition or towards starvation. It is the point at which "ordinary family planning" is too late to prevent death from starvation; from then on this can only be prevented by the "extraordinary family planning" of one-child families. This point has been shown here as that at which the death rate starts to rise, as is already happening in several developing countries. There is presumably also a point (not shown) at which, due to the demographic momentum of a community, even one-child families are too late.

The Global Community

The opposite extreme to an isolated community is the whole world and the global food supply. UNFPA (1991) reports that the world's present population of 5.4 billion will probably double and could triple. Future projections are continually being revised upwards, so that it is now following the United Nations "high variant" and is expected to reach 8.5 billion by 2025.

Unfortunately, Brown (1991) reports that the world's farmers are already having increasing difficulty in feeding us. Global per capita grain production, having risen for many years, has now started to fall. Most of the land that could usefully be cultivated has been; the cultivated area per head is steadily falling and will only be a tenth of a hectare by the year 2000. The main hope for more food lies in increased yields, and although the global average grain yield is only about 2.5 tonnes per hectare, whereas the most productive countries produce about 7 tonnes, there are major constraints on increased productivity, particularly a shortage of water and the deterioration of the soil. A further threat is that global warming is more likely to impair than to improve productivity.

If there is little hope for much more food, and there are certainly going to be many more people, those who eat the most are going to have to eat less. An intake of 2000 kcal per day requires about 200 kg of grain per year. The UN Subcommittee on Nutrition (1991) reports that the world now produces about 300 kg of grain per person per year, the balance being fed to cattle. So on present production, a largely vegetarian diet and completely equitable distribution, the world could feed half as many people again, or about 8 billion, but it could not feed a population that will double and may triple. Unfortunately, it is unlikely that everyone will become vegetarian, or that food will be distributed with perfect equity.

Between the extremes of those local communities who rely on subsistence agriculture and the entire global community lie the majority of communities who produce, import and export in varying combinations. As people increase and food becomes scarcer, the unjust realities of politics and economics promise to make starvation tragically unequal, both between communities and within them. Subsistence farmers already starve as they exceed the ecosustainability of their farms, so do huge cities as their poorer citizens fail to be able to buy grain on the national and international market. UNFPA (1991) reports an impending food crisis in many developing countries with governments already having great difficulties feeding their cities. Meanwhile, droughts and wars trigger starvation in particular places.

Neomalthusian?

The demographic trap is a new term and a good one. It is more than merely neomalthusian because Malthus did not foresee the demographic transition, or the need to pass through its second stage quickly, nor did he see that negative feedback could destroy biological support systems and cause ecological collapse. To be accused of being neomalthusian is to be wrong by accusation, because neomalthusians have so often been wrong before. However, although the data predicting the trap may be imperfect, they are better than any we have had hitherto. The key indicator, global per capita grain consumption, is the product of so many others that it is difficult to see an improvement in any one of these making much difference. Cold nuclear fusion producing enough cheap safe energy to desalinate sea-water is perhaps the only technical break through which might relieve entrapment, but we cannot rely on it.

Which Communities are Trapped?

When I asked John Seaman, Director of the British Save the Children Fund, which communities are in the "trap closing" stage, in that they are likely to starve before they undergo a demographic transition, he replied "much of the Indian subcontinent (particularly Bangladesh), Kenya, and Nigeria". Malcolm Potts, of Family Health International, and the Director of another major family planning agency agree (1991). This then is the opinion of three experienced and independent observers. UNFPA (1991) confirm this by reporting 580 million people living in absolute poverty on such marginal or fragile land that they are migrating to the cities as ecological refugees.

One Child Families

Besides starvation, the only other escapes from the trap closing stage are: (a) very bloody war: (b) disease, such as a particularly lethal strain of influenza: (c) emigration which is impossible on the necessary scale: (d) one-child families.

Of the possible alternatives to starvation, one-child families are the least undesirable. Even to suggest them when conventional family planning is proving so difficult is to risk ridicule. Be that as it may, *the alternative is starvation*. One-child families are generally considered unworkable outside China, because only China has the mechanisms of social control that make them possible, and even China has difficulty. But they should at least be considered if the only alternative is to starve. One authority has argued that people should be made to see the necessity for them, but should not be coerced, and that if they fail to adopt them, then at least everything possible has been done. At present it is not being done.

Why Family Planning Agencies Refuse to Admit the Trap – Officially

The realities of the trap, and the difficulty of one-child families, puts the directors of family planning agencies into the illogical position of pronouncing publicly that, if the world does its utmost, ordinary family planning will be just in time, while privately at least two of them will admit that for trapped communities ordinary family planning is already too late. They refuse to admit the trap publicly on the grounds that to do so would be to "write off" some communities. Their reports give the success stories (Thailand, Indonesia) but not the impending disasters (Bangladesh, Pakistan, Kenya, Nigeria and the northern states of India).

Not to mention the trap is to write off trapped communities by default, because the need for one-child families is never even mentioned. Tragically, by refusing to admit the trap the agencies also deprive governments of the stimulus the trap would have in promoting ordinary family planning; this would not prevent starvation, but it would have some mitigating effect. Family planning agencies must therefore admit the trap. This requires that when they make population projections they should link these with food and the environment, and when entrapment looks likely they should say so.

Why Unicef Refuses to Admit the Trap

The trap is the result of the gap between fertility and mortality in the second stage of the demographic transition persisting too long, and so threatening the agencies concerned with both. In trying to narrow this gap, reducing fertility has fewer ethical problems than not doing everything possible to reduce mortality, which is to "set levels of mortality control".

Family planners seek to reduce fertility, and their ethical problems (especially whether or not to admit entrapment) are dwarfed by those agencies whose task it is to reduce child mortality. Unicef will be taken as an example, since it is the only agency with global, centrally planned vertical programmes of technical fixes for child survival (ORT and EPI, see over), with the possibilities these have for making the pressures of the trap worse. For Unicef everything hinges on what lowering the child death rate does to the birth rate.

If lowering the child death rate immediately lowers the birth rate Unicef (1990) would be correct in saying: "It may come as a surprise that by saving so many young lives we [Unicef] also reduce the population growth rate".

If, however, lowering the child death rate does not immediately lower the birth rate, it increases the population growth rate. There are then two possible situations depending upon where a community is in relation to the trap: (1) If it is still in the "trap set" stage, this causes no problems, because the community can still progress to a demographic transition. (2) If however it has progressed to the trap closing stage, an increase in the population growth rate makes the pressures of the trap worse, so that the community will starve sooner. This puts Unicef in an intolerable dilemma because it then faces a conflict between the interests of: (a) the present child; this is the Hippocratic ethical premiss, and it is also Unicef's premiss since it is Unicef's charter; (b) that child saved for the moment, but condemned to a malnourished future and an early death. Scheper-Hughes (1991) has provided a particularly vivid description of just such a child; (c) the community which will become progressively more entrapped and will starve sooner. A further instance of the complexity of these relationships is that the good of the community is ultimately the good of future children.

Unicef escapes from this dilemma in two ways:

1. It refuses to admit the existence of the trap, as does WHO and all the other international agencies, although privately many of their officers have no illusions about its reality
2. Unicef insists that lowering the child death rate *always* lowers the birth rate

The Limits of Contemporary Demography

Unfortunately, although there are many clues, there is no adequate general theory as to what does exactly determine fertility: it is the ultimate demographic unknown (Hohn and Mackensen 1982). One item of data which is almost completely missing in the mysteries of the human bedroom, is the frequency and pattern of sexual intercourse in particular communities, especially in the past. Demography also handles cultural factors inadequately.

Potentially, child mortality can affect fertility in at least three ways: (1) By its interval effect; which is the death of one child leaving less time in a mother's reproductive life for the conception of other children, especially if she breast feeds. (2) By replacement effects; a family replacing a dead child by another one. (3) Through insurance effects in a which a family expects some children to die and deliberately has some "spares". These effects can be investigated at the level of the family, but it is not possible to investigate them rigorously at the level of society.

I follow Preston (1978) who concluded that: "The picture is not attractive for those who look to mortality reduction as a means of reducing fertility through familial effects, let alone those who advocate such measures as a means to reduce growth rates. Nor does it lend much support to models of fertility decision making that view couples as proceeding . . . deliberately towards some target number of surviving children".

When trying to make the most of why lowering the child death rate lowers the birth rate, Unicef (1991) stresses the alleged synergism between its programmes in that ORT (oral rehydration treatment) and EPI (expanded programme of immunisation) promote the uptake of family planning. However for this synergism to take place, the mother of a child receiving ORT or EPI must also be able to get family planning, so that it is also highly desirable and perhaps even necessary that workers providing ORT or EPI actively promote family planning. Hellberg (1991) observes that "for a long time it has been totally irresponsible to provide health care and medical services without family planning". Unicef is doing this by "going to scale" globally with EPI and ORT without at the same time making sure that some agency or other does the same with family planning.

This synergism is held to be important at another level, in that without health services there can be no family planning services. This is one reason why a consortium of aid agencies is supporting the peripheral health services in

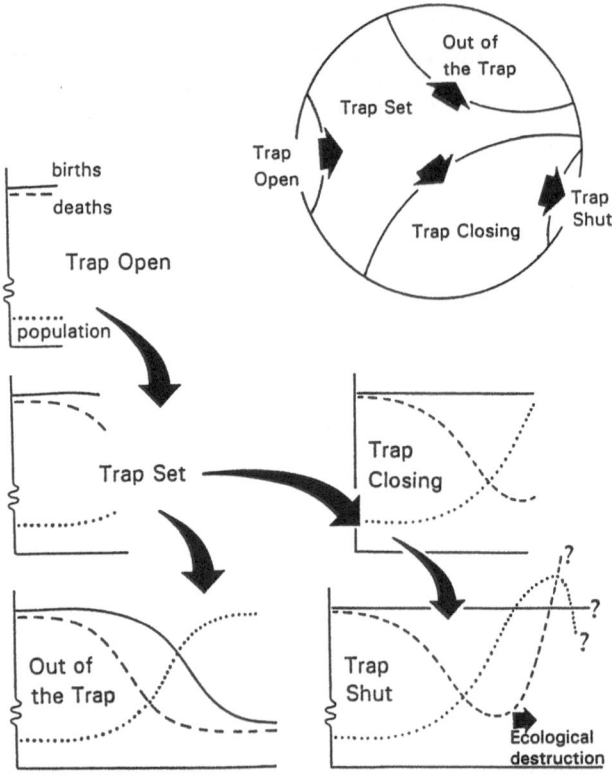

Figure 7.1. The world, according to the demographic trap. For simplicity the birth rate is shown as constant; the important variable is the difference between the birth rate and the death rate.

Bangladesh. However, CBD (the community based distribution of family planning supplies in ordinary shops) implies that even this synergism is not always necessary.

The Demographic Consensus

The demographic consensus appears to be that the major effect is not a falling death rate lowering the birth rate, but that both are lowered independently by various "socio-economic gains". Unfortunately there are severe physical constraints (especially lack of arable land and water) which prevent these gains operating adequately on the birth rates of the world's poorest billion before this billion is trapped.

Those demographers who maintain that lowering the birth rate lowers the death rate to do so, not because there is proof, but because they say the arguments are strong: the main one being that when parents see that their children do not die they will have fewer of them. There are, however, many exceptions, particularly the Arab countries, such as Syria and Yemen, where childhood mortality has fallen but fertility has not and where families with eight children are not uncommon. Even if there is an effect, these demographers admit that there is a time lag, which might allow a community to be trapped before the effect has had time to operate.

Amid this confusion the one certainty is that communities differ, that they have to be assessed individually and that Unicef cannot always assume, as it presently does, that lowering the child death rate will always lower the birth rate, especially fast enough to avoid the entrapment which it presently does not recognise.

Ethics

If lowering the child death rate does not lower the birth rate fast enough to avoid entrapment how should Unicef solve the dilemma of the three conflicting premisses? I follow Macintyre (1987) who points out that "western liberalism" has inherited an assortment of conflicting ethical premisses from its cultural past. These include equity, the greatest good of the greatest number, the sanctity of human life and many more. Although the logic of arguments from many of these premisses can be monitored, there is no way of determining that one premiss is preferable to another when they conflict, as they often do. This is unsatisfactory, but at least we know where we are. The social purpose of (often heated) ethical argument is to improve the reconciliation of these conflicting premisses in a given society at a given time.

Among the assortment of conflicting premisses which particularly concern Unicef are the interests of (a), (b) and (c) above, with no logical method of deciding between them. At present Unicef decides entirely in favour of (a), the present child; it does this by default in New York, by refusing to admit that the trap exists, and by insisting that lowering the death rate lowers the birth rate.

What Should Unicef Do?

Unicef and the other agencies concerned with family planning should:

1. Accept the reality of the demographic trap and discuss its implications frankly. This applies the premiss that the truth should be generally known, however unpleasant.

2. Encourage local communities to understand the trap and to find out where they are in relation to it. This applies the premiss of local autonomy.

3. Promote family planning with every dollar it can usefully absorb. For communities in the trap set stage it can be "ordinary family planning", both precoital and postcoital. For communities in the trap closing stage it will have to be "extraordinary family planning" with one-child families. This applies the premisses that access to family planning is a universal human right.

4. Admit that technological fixes for child survival (EPI and ORT) do not, alas, reduce fertility, especially when Unicef goes to scale with them without making sure that some agency does the same with family planning (this is a technical rather than an ethical issue).

5. Let local communities in the trap closing stage look first at what can be done to reduce fertility (one-child families), and then if necessary decide on the unhappy compromises to be made in the interests of (a) the present child, (b) the future child, and (c) the community. This applies the premiss of local autonomy; in practice these decisions may be better made by ministries of health.

6. Adapt all their programmes to the demographic realities of particular communities. Unicef and other aid agencies may need to apply the different components of their programmes with different vigour in different places, instead of applying the same components uniformly in all of them (this is another technical issue).

7. Match their ecosustainability campaign in the developing world with a complementary one in the industrial world (the premiss of equity). This should come first, since the industrial world consumes at least ten times as much of the world's resources per capita as does the developing world, and in doing so does most to pollute the globe, particularly with carbon dioxide.

Premisses (a), (b) and (c) and the Status of the Child in Western Liberalism

This is the common culture of contemporary "western civilisation", and is the culture in which the aid agencies operate. It goes back at least to the Greeks, and although it is now atheist, it has been powerfully influenced by Christianity. Deeply embedded in this culture are certain values and ethical premisses, one of which, at least in theory, is the enormous importance of the child, which reached a pinnacle in the recent "Summit for Children".

The status of the child presently stands so high that:

1. Even the most marginal dissent from it is considered an outrage

2. Ethical conflicts involving the child, such as those between premises (a), (b) and (c) above cause acute psychological tension. In extreme cases, as shown by Taylor (1992), it can end in the denial of the reality of the trap and the refusal even to debate the issue

3. "The child is always right" so that even to criticise Unicef is considered malicious (Jolly 1991)

4. The dilemma and the tragedy that by his own very numbers "the child is his own worst enemy" and that "the child is destroying himself" is not even thinkable

The present high status of the child in western liberalism is comparatively recent; it is hardly more than 100 years old and its extreme pre-eminence is even more recent. Other cultures both today and at other times have rated the child quite differently; thus, the British sent their children down the mines 150 years ago and the Greeks exposed their unwanted children to the elements. Other societies are encouraged to examine western liberalism from the perspective of their own culture, and not to take it for granted in the critical act of escaping from the trap.

The Ultimate Anathema?

The trap presents appalling dilemmas for the Western liberal conscience and particularly for the Christian, although it is said that there is no specifically Christian response to it. Are the following statements anathema?

> . . . Mother Theresa has reminded us that the world's poorest need our love and compassion – tragically, such programmes may not be part of that love.

> Macintyre observes that ethical premises are influenced by the metaphysical position of the contestant. So what has Christianity to say about all this? It is no less than the problem of evil and suffering in the world. It is part of the Christian mystery that the Almighty enters his world and suffers with it. We are required to care for (love) our fellow men. Excruciatingly, restriction of public health programmes may be part of that love.

A Philosophical Note

Much of this paper has been concerned with the practical problems and dilemmas of trying to reduce suffering by population control. Philosophers should first address the logically prior question of what population should we prefer. Utilitarians need to make some calculations, but even if they disregard the problem that there is no generally agreed scale of utility, there are at least three different defensible utilitarian formulae:

1. Maximin utilitarianism. We should act to maximise the utility of the least well-off group of the population

2. Average utilitarianism. We should aim to maximise the average utility of the individuals involved

3. Classical or total utilitarianism. We should act in a way to maximise total utility

The first solution, the policy of maximising the welfare of the least well-off group, was advocated by Rawls (1971). Many people find it an attractive way of allocating resources among a fixed population. However, when faced with the decision as to whether to cause more people to exist, the consequences seem unjust. It appears to commit us to preventing the birth of people who would be in the worst-off group in society, even if such people's lives were well worth living, since in this way we should increase the happiness of the worst-off group that exists. The repeated application of the principle would lead us to the elitist view that utility would be maximised if only the best-off reproduced.

The second solution is probably the unspoken assumption of most non-philosophers who advocate population control. At first sight it accords with our intuition that a moderate population of happy people is preferable to an enormous population of people whose lives are only just worth living, even if the total utility of the enormous population were greater. Unfortunately, it appears to commit us to the view that extra worthwhile lives which happen to be of less than average happiness are of negative utility, since they reduce mean utility. The reasons for this have been described in detail by Parfit (1986).

The third solution is that suggested by classical or total utility. Any new people with worthwhile lives who come into existence will increase total utility, unless their existence reduces another individual's quality of life by more than their own. It has been argued that this view commits us to the repugnant conclusion that a society of a huge number of people with lives barely worth living would be preferable to a smaller society, so long as the total utility was greater. If this is so, total utilitarians could hardly support population control in the world as it is, since even the poorest groups regard their lives as worth living, and more of them would increase total utility. Average and maximin utilitarians can advocate population control, but they must be able to stomach the injustices to which their theory appears to commit them.

It is the duty of philosophers to answer these problems before tackling the practical issues raised in the present paper. There is not space to go into the arguments here, but those philosophers who have recently addressed this question have come to the tentative support of the total utilitarians. Parfit (1986) argued that the repugnant conclusion resulted from using faulty utility scales and Hare (1988) from failing to take the practical problems and disutility of population expansion sufficiently into account. If they are right and our demographic conclusions are correct (admittedly an uncertainty) then the correct course of action is clear. We should apply some principle of universalizability (for example, the golden rule, Kant's categorical imperative, or Hare's universal prescriptivism) and then act to maximise total utility. It follows that vigorous population control should take precedence over such measures as oral rehydration and food aid which reduce ecosustainability in countries in the demographic trap.

References

Brown L (1991) The state of the world 1990. Worldwatch/WW Norton New York

Hare RM (1988) Possible people. Bioethics 2:279–293

Hellberg H (1991) Maurice King is right. An anomaly in the paradigm. Nu-nytt om u-landshalsovard 1:17. International Child Health Unit, Uppsala University, Sweden

Hohn C, Mackensen R (1982) Determinants of fertility trends: theories re-examined. International Union for the Study of Population. Ordina Editions, Liège, 3

Jolly (1991) Unicef's real concerns with child health, population growth and ecological sustainability. Nu-nytt om u-landshalsovard 1:10. International Child Health Unit, Uppsala University, Sweden

King MH (1990) Health is a sustainable state. Lancet 336:664–667

King MH (1992) Hitting the nail on the head. Nu-nytt om u-landshalsovard 1. International Child Health Unit, Uppsala University, Sweden

Macintyre A (1987) After virtue. London, Duckworth

Parfit D (1986) Overpopulation and the quality of life. In: Singer P (ed.) Applied ethics. Oxford University Press, Oxford.

Preston S (1978) The effects of infant and child mortality on fertility. Population Division, United Nations. Academic Press, New York

Rawls J (1971) A theory of justice. Oxford University Press, Oxford

Scheper-Hughes N (1991) Social indifference to child health. Lancet 337:1144–1147

Taylor C (1992) Nu-nytt om u-landshalsovard 1:92. International Child Health Unit, Uppsala University, Sweden

UNFPA (United Nations Population Fund) (1991) The state of world population

Unicef (1990) *Guardian* 22–23 Sept, p 48

Unicef (1991) State of the world's children

United Nations Subcommittee on Nutrition (1991), SCN News

Postscript

The most recent comprehensive summary of the evidence relating to whether lowering the child death rate lowers the birth rate, and therefore to Unicef's dilemmas, has recently been prepared by the UN. It is anonymous, it makes no reference to entrapment, and has been " . . . edited and consolidated in accordance with United Nations practice and requirements". Referring to the observation that " . . . improvements in child survival typically precede sustained fertility decline . . . " the report continues that this observation " . . . cannot lead to the automatic conclusion that policy interventions to improve the health of children will be *immediately* (emphasis inserted) followed by a decline in the birth rate. The actual consequences of such interventions depend not only on the type of intervention, but also on the prevalent family building strategy, and the nature and scope of family planning programmes in the particular location where the intervention takes place". This statement of the situation allows plenty of opportunity for ill-advised child survival programmes to promote entrapment. *Immediately* is particularly significant, since delay can on occasion be a generation or more.

United Nations (1987) Family Building by Fate or Design. United Nations Department of Economic and Social Affairs, New York.

CHAPTER 8

Maternal Mortality in Developing Countries

Pramilla Senanayake

When a woman dies from complications related to pregnancy or childbirth she often dies unnecessarily. But more than half a million women in the developing world die each year under such circumstances and millions more suffer temporary and permanent disability and illness.

On the face of it, this tragedy may appear to be a matter for resolution by health personnel and departments of health. However, the underlying causes that subscribe to this tragedy have philosophical and ethical aspects that go far beyond the confines of the health services.

Although millions of women have died and are still dying from pregnancy-related causes, it was not until the middle of the 1980s that the world's attention was drawn to this tragedy. In July 1985, an article in *The Lancet* (Rosenfield and Maine 1985) entitled "Where is the 'M' in MCH" claimed "It is difficult to understand why maternal mortality receives so little serious attention from health professionals, policy makers, and politicians. The world's obstetricians are particularly neglectful of their duty in this regard. Instead of drawing attention to the problem and lobbying for major programmes and changes in priorities, most obstetricians concentrate on subspecialties that put emphasis on high technology."

Later in 1985, the First Inter-Regional Meeting on Prevention of Maternal Mortality was held at WHO in Geneva when the extent of the tragedy was vividly described.

> Every four hours, day-in, day-out, a jumbo-jet crashes and all on board are killed. The 250 passengers are women, most in the prime of life, some still in their teens. They are all either pregnant or have just delivered a baby. Most of them have growing children at home, and families that depend on them. (WHO 1985)

It is clear that if more is not done to present maternal deaths during the 1990s, this decade will see the largest number of women dying from maternal causes than in any previous decade. This number will be even greater than the number of men and women who will die from AIDS during the same period.

Incidence of Maternal Mortality

Today, the rates of maternal mortality in rich and poor countries show a greater disparity than any other public health indicator – including the infant mortality rate, which is most often taken as the measure of comparative disadvantage. Thus, for a woman in the developing world, the average lifetime risk of dying of a pregnancy-related cause is between one in 15 and one in 50, compared with an average lifetime risk of between one in 4000 and one in 10 000 for a woman in the developed world (Royston and Armstrong 1989).

Data currently available do not provide a true picture of the burden of maternal morbidity or mortality on women, their families and their communities. The mortality associated with pregnancy is the primary killer of women in many developing countries. A quarter of all maternal deaths in these countries are due to obstetric causes, resulting directly from pregnancy, labour or the puerperium. The immediate causes of these deaths can be from intervention, omissions, incorrect treatment or from a chain of events resulting from any of these.

The proportion of maternal deaths can be even higher when it is taken into account that in some poor rural areas, overall mortality from infectious diseases, accidents, etc. is already very high. Therefore, maternal mortality should be viewed as a chronic disease developing over a long period, as the outcome of a pregnancy is profoundly influenced by the circumstances of a woman's life, by the economic and environmental conditions in which she lives, as well as by her social status. These factors have a profound ethical and philosophical background.

Worldwide, the incidence of maternal mortality is estimated at more than 500 000 per year. Of these women, 99% live in developing countries (WHO 1988). Between sunset yesterday and sunrise this morning 800 families lost their mother, the pivot round which the life of the family revolves. Her death disrupts the life of the entire family. A mother dying at childbirth is often fatal to the newborn. In Bangladesh, for example, the infant she leaves behind has a 95% chance of dying in the first year (Chen et al. 1974).

If the maternal mortality rates in developing countries were the same as in the developed countries, 460 000 women's lives would be saved each year! (WHO 1988). These figures may still be a gross underestimate. In studies carried out in some countries, it has been shown that 40%–50% of maternal deaths are wrongly attributed to other causes. Yet in other countries data are not collected at all.

Other studies have demonstrated significant under-reporting of maternal deaths, particularly in developing countries. For example, studies in Egypt and Jamaica show that maternal mortality rates are twice as high as government statistics. Even in the United States, it has been shown that civil registration data underestimate the number of maternal deaths by at least 25% (Fathalla et al. 1990).

In the developing world, the primary reason for under-reporting is that a majority of maternal deaths occur outside hospitals or are not attended by trained health personnel. Of all deliveries in developing countries 30%–90% are attended by a Traditional Birth Attendant (TBA), a relative or no-one.

A maternal death is dramatic and unambiguous. Morbidity often is not. As such, data on maternal morbidity are even more difficult to obtain. Pregnancy-related morbidity places a heavy burden on women, yet it is largely ignored.

Causes of Maternal Mortality

Definition

A maternal death is defined as the death of any woman while pregnant or within 42 days of termination of pregnancy, irrespective of the duration or site of pregnancy, from any cause related to or aggravated by the pregnancy itself or its management (Fathalla et al. 1990).

Maternal deaths can result from many causes: these include obstetric factors, health service factors, low rates of contraceptive use, and low socio-economic status. Obstetric deaths result from complications of pregnancy, delivery or their management. In developing countries, a majority of maternal deaths are direct obstetric deaths resulting primarily from haemorrhage, infection, toxaemia, obstructed labour and induced abortion. Anaemia is a serious underlying factor in maternal mortality. A recent study in Bangladesh concluded that anaemia was a factor in nearly all of the maternal deaths that occurred there (Alauddin 1986) and a recent workshop in Lusaka identified anaemia as the most important complication of pregnancy in tropical Africa (Mwanza 1986).

Health service factors include lack of treatment for complications, shortage of staff and supplies, and improper management and treatment.

Low socio-economic status can have an important part to play in maternal mortality. Women who have a low socio-economic status are more likely to be malnourished, to lack access to health care and to have a low status in society.

In developing countries, millions of women are malnourished and suffer from chronic anaemia, malaria and intestinal diseases, all of which weaken a woman's chances of surviving childbirth.

Selected Case Histories

Let me share with you some case histories from the types of women that my paper is all about.

> *Bola, 17,* and her husband were farmers living in a remote village. They had their own little house with no electricity, and the open field served for refuse and excreta disposal. The couple had no formal education, and Bola was married at 13. Her first child was born dead after 4 days of labour. The prolonged and obstructed labour caused a hole between Bola's bladder and her vagina. The consequences of this fistula are incontinence and a persistent smell of stale urine, which makes many women suffering from this injury into virtual outcasts. However, Bola had undergone reconstructive surgery, and became pregnant again two years later. Living far from a health centre she had no prenatal care. In the seventh month of her pregnancy Bola started to bleed from the vagina while carrying water home from the river. Later that day her membranes ruptured and labour started. After three days of labour without progress, Bola was taken to hospital in a state of distress, with a high temperature and pulse rate. Though the baby was small, rigid

scar tissue from the fistula repair was obstructing its delivery. The baby was dead and was delivered by destructive operation in hospital. On the third day after delivery Bola was very ill. Infection of a ruptured uterus was diagnosed, but her poor condition due to undernourishment and anaemia militated against her survival. Bola realized she was going to die and communicated her fear and misery to the hospital staff. In spite of surgery to remove her infected uterus, Bola died in hospital. (WHO 1987)

Fatima, *27*, lived in Yemen, in a remote village on the top of a steep hill. Her husband Mohammed worked as a labourer in Saudi Arabia. Fatima had five girls which she had delivered safely in the village, and since the nearest health station was a long walk away she received no prenatal care during her sixth pregnancy. At full term one day in the late afternoon, her membranes ruptured. Within 7 minutes she had three strong contractions and gave birth to a baby boy. The afterbirth did not come away and initially there was no bleeding. However, about an hour later Fatima felt weak, had difficulty breathing and was bleeding quite heavily from the birth canal. The family agreed that it would be best to take Fatima to hospital in Sanaa. However, a woman needed permission from her husband for transfer to hospital. In Mohammed's absence another male relative had to give permission. More than 2 hours elapsed before her uncle was located in a neighbouring village. A stretcher was then prepared and several men took Fatima, by the light of a lantern, down the track to the bottom of the hill. From there they continued for another 15 km along the rough road, at the end of which they reached an asphalt road. The hospital was another 40 km away. At that point, dawn breaking, they noticed that the stretcher was soaked with blood. Fatima had groaned at the beginning of the bumpy journey but as she became quiet later on, she was presumed to have fallen asleep. One of the men felt her forehead and thought it unnaturally cold. It was clear that Fatima had passed away during the night while haemorrhaging massively. Sorrowfully, but resigned, they began the weary climb back to the village with the deceased woman. It was ironic that in gaining a son, they lost the mother. (WHO 1987)

Esperanza, *30*, lived in Colombia. She had already borne five children, one of which had died at the age of 10 months, and neither she nor her husband was happy when she became pregnant again. The health centres accessible to her provided MCH care but not family planning service. Esperanza did not know about the Family Planning Association clinic in the capital city of the province. Esperanza had recently found work as a housemaid in the city and her wages were much needed by the family. She took the decision alone to visit an abortionist in town. She was frightened and unsure what was actually done to her. After 3 days of bleeding Esperanza developed severe abdominal pain and began to vomit. Her husband took her to hospital where the diagnosis was incomplete septic abortion. She was treated and sent home after 48 hours. The pain returned, but Esperanza did nothing about it at first, fearing she would lose her job if she took any more time off. When she developed a high fever and started vomiting, she was admitted to the Intensive Care Unit of the hospital. Abdominal surgery was performed for peritonitis. But her condition deteriorated, her heart-beat became irregular and she died five days later. (WHO 1987)

Negisti, *18*, lived in Ethiopia. She was not married. She lived with her parents just outside the city, and was in her last year at school. Negisti became pregnant unintentionally and, afraid of her parents, she left home to conceal her pregnancy. At the end of the 9 months she returned home and confided in her mother, who tried to conceal the situation from Negisti's father. The girl had headaches and vomiting for a while before she went into labour. Then, very early one morning she complained to her mother of abdominal pains, and contractions subsequently began. Eight hours later Negisti started to have convulsions, and at that point her mother hid her in a shed in the garden to keep the situation from the father. However, when the convulsions grew worse and more frequent, Negisti's mother became really afraid and decided to tell her husband. He immediately arranged transport to take his daughter to hospital in the city, where they arrived 16 hours after labour had begun.

Negisti was unconscious; her breathing was loud and her tongue bleeding where she had bitten it during her fits. Her parents were told that Negisti's headaches before delivery had probably been caused by toxaemia – high blood pressure associated with pregnancy – and at hospital eclampsia was diagnosed: her blood pressure had become catastrophically high, causing her convulsions. The girl was sedated and delivered of twins, both dead. But treatment came too late. She went into an irreversible coma, probably due to a brain haemorrhage following 9 hours of severe convulsions, and died. (WHO 1987)

As shown above, causes of maternal mortality include obstetric factors, health service factors, low rates of contraceptive use and low socio-economic status.

The Obstetric Factors

Obstetric factors include haemorrhage, infection, toxaemia, obstructed labour, unsafe abortion.

Unsafe abortion

One of the major causes of maternal mortality in the developing world is unsafe abortion. WHO studies in various settings indicate that the share of maternal deaths caused by induced abortion range from 7% to more than 50%. For example, in Latin America complications of illegal abortion are thought to be the main cause of death in women between ages 15 and 39 (Sai and Nassim 1989).

The number of abortion deaths is a direct reflection of access to safe services. Thus it is not difficult to understand the high rates of abortion-related maternal mortality in Ceausescu's Romania. In the mid 1980s 86% of maternal mortalities in Romania were abortion-related (Royston and Armstrong 1989). Of the preventable causes of maternal mortality the one that possibly poses the most philosophical and ethical dimensions is the issue of abortion.

To a large extent the debates on abortion have been governed by issues of moral philosophy and legislative definitions centring on the rights of the unborn child and the rights of women to determine their own and their families' futures.

It is now being suggested by many writers that these arguments provide an effective smoke-screen on the real underlying issues surrounding the cultural socio-economic conditions under which women take the decision to terminate pregnancy. To address truly the issue of abortion in its complete context, discussion needs to move beyond the confines of "the narrow concept of maternal health, to a more inclusive concept that recognises the role of much more fundamental issues, such as women's rights and status in society, the physical and mental humiliations that are women's lot in many societies and the overt and covert violence meted out to women. All these conditions substantially influence women's sexual development, their health and their patterns of child bearing." (Sai and Nassim 1989).

The repercussions of unwanted pregnancy and unsafe abortions reach far beyond the main indication of women's health, i.e., maternal mortality.

It is clear that high levels of unwanted pregnancies are the major reason for the incidence of abortion. Recent estimates of unwanted pregnancies have been obtained in some countries through the Demographic and Health surveys (Institute for Resource Development 1988, 1989).

These estimates include:

Kenya 1989 – over 50% of births in the 12 months prior to the survey were unwanted

Egypt 1988 – 22% of births in the 5-year-period prior to the survey were not wanted, and 27% of third or higher order births were unwanted

Botswana 1988 – 48% of births were not wanted at the time they occurred

The surveys caution that there is a likelihood of a net underestimation in these statistics due to many women's reluctance to admit to an unwanted birth or pregnancy.

The estimated worldwide total number of abortions is between 36 and 53 million, yielding an annual rate of 32–46 abortions per 1000 women of reproductive age (Henshaw 1990). Other estimates put the total figure even higher at between 40 and 60 million (Jacobson 1990).

Estimating clandestine abortion rates are clearly more problematic and unreliable. Rough figures for illegal abortion rates have been estimated as follows: "500 000 in Bangladesh, 600 000 in the rest of South Asia, 1.5 million in the rest of Asia, 400 000 in Romania, 1.5 million in Africa and approximately 2 million in the Soviet Union and 4 million each in India and Latin America." This totals 15 million estimated clandestine abortions, however, the true number could be as low as 10 million or as high as 22 million (Henshaw 1990).

Causes of Unwanted Pregnancy

Major reasons for unwanted pregnancy have been outlined as:

Lack of information on which to base family planning decision making

The shortcomings of contraceptives and family planning delivery systems

Poor standards of service provision such as inadequate counselling

Lack of woman's decision making power

High rates of adolescent fertility due to lack of knowledge of sexuality and contraception

Expectation that married adolescents should commence and continue reproduction

A husband often has control over the practice of contraception by mature married women who wish to space the births of their children

Lack of male involvement in family planning programmes

Illegal abortion can be one hundred times more dangerous than a legal termination of pregnancy and little has been written about the inhuman conditions that women suffer as a result of health policies that deny them access to safe abortion. This has serious ethical and philosophical dilemmas for health care workers, policy makers and women themselves.

Barriers to the Provision of Legal Services

Despite the legalisation of abortion in many areas, women are still denied access to safe abortion services through various forms of restriction:

Legal abortion services are often confined to specified institutions, which may be unable to accommodate the demand for services

Lack of commitment on the part of policy makers or health authorities to provide funds for the provision of adequate abortion services

Regulations, such as the requirement of approval by 3 doctors in Zambia which means that in areas where there is only one physician (and many are unsympathetic) lengthy delays may deny women access to safe services

In rural areas particularly, women may be denied access through facilities being geographically or economically inaccessible

Hospital regulations may also present a major barrier, with many hospitals being unwilling to treat women suffering from the complications of incomplete abortions

Some regulations mandate a delay for reflection by the woman, as in France, which could delay access to an early safe abortion

Authorisation may be required by the husband (as in Turkish law), and parental consent for minors is often required.

Administrative Barriers

Administrative barriers include:

Lack of information on the availability and location of abortion services

Lack of trained personnel, and limits on the types of personnel allowed to be trained as abortion providers

Negative attitudes of abortion providers

Poor referral systems, including lack of emergency transportation

Limited availability of the most appropriate techniques and equipment.

So it is apparent that even in circumstances where abortion is legal, there are serious ethical and philosophical aspects to the problem. Circumstances where women are denied access to safe abortion, invariably point women in the direction of back-street abortionists, with the risk of death or life-long suffering.

Social, Cultural and Economic Causes

Maternal mortality could be greatly reduced if more attention were paid to the health, education and general welfare of women.

Under increasing economic pressures in the past 5 years, 37 of the poorest countries have cut health spending by 50% and education by 25%. Poverty, malnutrition and ill-health are advancing again, and all these are affecting women first. Half of the world's annual expenditure goes to defence and the servicing of debts, while the number of persons living in abject poverty increases (WHO 1990).

> A woman's status and her health are intricately entwined. Any serious attempt to improve the health of women – if it is to succeed – must deal first with those ways in which a woman's health is harmed by social customs and cultural traditions simply because she was born female. (Lyons 1985)

The status of women involves a complex set of inter-related factors. A woman's status is often described in terms of her income, employment, education, health and fertility, as well as the roles she plays within the family, the community and society.

The status of women implies a comparison with the status of men and is, therefore, a significant reflection of the level of social justice/injustice in a society.

Where maternal mortality rates are high, the social status of women is low and their needs since childhood have been ignored or taken second place to those of men. This is reflected in several social and cultural practices, giving rise to philosophical and ethical issues.

Nutrition

In many societies, when resources are severely limited, poverty, disease and malnutrition affect girls more than boys. Traditionally many cultures prefer male children, the reasons for this being economic, cultural or religious. Sons, for example, are perceived as an economic asset to the family, contributing productive labour. Girls, on the other hand, are seen as a burden who often have to be provided with a costly dowry and whose economic productivity will benefit their husband's family rather than that of their parents.

When resources are scarce, son preference may entail a whole range of discriminatory practices that affect the health and well-being of girls. Although the nutritional requirements of young boys and girls are the same, in many societies boys, and later men, are being fed first and given better and more food.

Studies in some countries have revealed that mothers suckle boys longer than girls and that medical care is more often sought for a sick boy than for a sick girl. Evidence of such practices shows that they lead to poorer health status of girls than boys, fewer girls than boys are immunized, there is higher case fatality among girls brought to hospital and higher mortality overall (United Nations 1986).

Studies by the World Health Organization show that women of reproductive age require a daily absorption of iron approximately three times that of adult man. But poor diets and lack of access to dietary supplements result in very high prevalence of anaemia among women in developing countries. This is a contributing factor to maternal mortality (Royston and Armstrong 1989).

Education

Low levels of education constraints women's ability to care for their own and their children's health. In Southern Asia, the percentage of girls who attend primary school ranges from 17% in Bhutan to 100% in Sri Lanka (1986 figures). The illiteracy rates for women remain high. In every developing region of the world adult literacy rates are higher for males than females. For example, in

North America literacy rates are 57% for males and 29% for females while in Southern Asia the corresponding values are 56% for males and 31% for females.

In all regions, educated women tend to marry later, delay childbearing and practise more family planning than those without education. They generally have fewer and more widely-spaced births. Women with no schooling have almost twice as many children on average as those with 7 or more years' schooling. A study by UNESCO in 1988 indicates that illiteracy rates among females between 15 and 19 in Bangladesh and Pakistan is still higher than 70% and in India about 55% (WHO 1989).

Education of girls can act as a brake on their fertility as it tends to raise the average age at marriage and encourages the use of reliable family planning methods. Education benefits the whole family. Educated mothers are more likely to demand education for their daughters, thus multiplying the benefits of education for future generations.

Traditional Cultural Practices

There are various traditional practices still being carried out in developing countries which contribute directly or indirectly towards maternal mortality.

Son Preference

Son preference is the preference of parents for male children which often manifests itself in neglect, deprivation or discriminatory treatment of girls to the detriment of their mental and physical health. In countries where the social status of women is very low, the lack of care received by girls and women is so great that this environmental disadvantage far outweighs their genetic advantages of lower susceptibility to infections and malnutrition.

The preference for male children has multiple repercussions in a number of socio-cultural areas. As a result this practice, linked to an important formative stage of the psychology of the child, will determine the image the girl child has of herself. This image is reinforced by society and serves as the root cause of the development of the idea of the inferiority of the female in relation to the male. The image of superiority of the young males over the girls will be internalized by the female child who in her adult life will, in turn, recreate this hierarchy. It is often the women themselves who perpetuate the practice and it can even be said that the regeneration and fostering of it depends on the woman to the extent that of the two parents, it is she who has the closer relationship and greater responsibility during this period of motherhood.

Female Circumcision

Female circumcision refers to traditional practices which consist of cutting away all or part of the external female genital organs. Although in most countries where it is practised female circumcision is an integral part of the initiation rite, the operation has been shown to involve significant risks of damage to the mental and physical health of girls and women.

Over 100 million women and girls living today have undergone female circumcision (often now referred to as female genital mutilation). The practice affects millions of girls in the Arab world, sub-Saharan Africa, Malaysia, Indonesia and migrant populations in Europe, Australia and the United States.

Many reasons are given to justify these practices which reflect the ideological and historical situation of the societies in which they develop. They generally derive from the role and status of women in society. There are beliefs that female circumcision maintains cleanliness, increases a girl's chances of marriage, protects her virginity, discourages promiscuity, improves fertility, or prevents stillbirth. These have no scientific, logical or religious bases. Many philosophical and ethical issues come to the forefront when attempts are made to eradicate this practice.

Early Marriage

In many populations there has traditionally been a link between age at menarche and age at marriage, where the timing of marriage has been determined primarily by the onset or expected onset of menstruation. In countries where women marry young, such as Bangladesh, fertility rates among women aged 15–19 are high – over 200 per 1000 women in the age group (United Nations 1987).

Early childbearing among women has health, social and economic consequences for the young woman and her children and these consequences, like fertility levels and levels of premarital sexual activity, vary considerably between regions and countries. These negative consequences have implications not only at the individual level but for the society at large as well. Curtailment of educational and employment opportunities for women who become mothers during their adolescent years lowers the rate of economic growth and development. In addition, the potential of their children to contribute to economic development may be limited by the inability of the mothers to provide for their basic health and education. Parents must realize that providing for girls includes protecting them from the often considerable health risks of pregnancy and childbearing before they are fully grown.

Strategies for Reducing Maternal Mortality

There are a number of specific strategies that can be implemented to reduce maternal mortality. These include preventive approaches such as family planning and prenatal care with a referral system; improvement of emergency care; improvement in the existing health care infrastructure; and village transport and community education efforts. Long-term approaches to the problem are also needed.

Increasing Availability of Family Planning Services

A large proportion of maternal deaths take place each year because women are having more pregnancies than they want. In many countries, including Bangladesh, Cameroon, Colombia and Egypt, 40%–60% of all married women say that they do not want any more children. Many of the women, from about

50% in Egypt and Indonesia to more than 75% in Bangladesh and Cameroon, are not using any contraceptives (United Nations 1989). If all women who want to limit their families were able to do so, maternal mortality could be reduced substantially. Firstly, there could be fewer deaths from induced abortions, which account for a large proportion of maternal mortality. Secondly, women who want no more children tend to be older and have a higher parity, giving them a higher than average risk of maternal mortality.

Family planning services should be made widely accessible at the community level. Particular attention should be given to high-risk groups, including high-parity women, women under the age of 18 and over the age of 35, as well as all women who say that they want to avoid or postpone pregnancy.

Improving family planning programmes in developing countries, where women still suffer sexual and reproductive dependence, requires strengthening women's capacity to make their own decisions. The "users" perspective in family planning recognizes the needs of individual clients and calls for alternatives and choice for women, discrediting "blanket policies" by governments that attempt to control fertility without sensitivity to individual choice. Feminist ethics examine the nature of the relationships of women in family planning programmes as well as their role in society. This is an important point of the feminist philosophy as there are highly distinguishable differences between the roles and dynamics of family planning among women from industrialized societies and those of developing nations.

Prenatal Care

Many maternal deaths in the developing world could be prevented if women received adequate health care during pregnancy. All women should be provided with prenatal care in order to prevent medical problems and to ensure the detection and rapid treatment of complications which do arise. The risk of maternal death is up to 15 times higher for women who do not receive prenatal care than it is for those who do.

The effectiveness of prenatal services depends on the skills and competence of the care givers; their access to necessary equipment and supplies; women's motivation to seek care and their utilization of existing prenatal facilities; and the existence of a referral and back-up system, including adequate transport.

Education of Health Care Workers

A successful screening programme depends on educating providers of health care, women and the public about the importance of referring women at high risk for the safety of both mother and child. It is also necessary to provide health workers with adequate training and supervision to ensure that they can indeed recognize high-risk symptoms and make proper referrals, and to install and maintain adequate transportation and referral facilities.

Programmes should focus on a combination of indicators that are easily detected by the care giver; appropriate to local health and cultural conditions; and effective in maximizing the number of emergency referral cases without overloading the health care system.

Home-Based Maternal Cards

These are used in family planning and primary health care programmes to record information about a pregnant woman's health. They include information on her health status between pregnancies, the number of children she has borne, and any complications she experienced during previous pregnancies and deliveries. Maternal cards promote continuity of care and early recognition of women at risk, and present a convenient opportunity to provide health education. They also provide health workers with a complete record of a woman's health history and are useful for statistical and record-keeping purposes.

Maternal records have been used in many countries, including Kenya, Tanzania, Botswana, Papua New Guinea, Zambia and India. Many variations, adapted to suit local conditions, exist. Colour-coded cards with symbols have been developed for use by illiterate women and health workers.

Community Education

It is particularly important to educate the general public and community leaders about warning signs, especially in areas where a substantial number of births are not attended by trained traditional birth attendants (TBAs) or health workers. Nigeria offers useful examples of the types of information programmes that can be undertaken:

> A successful radio campaign in Nigeria reaches women in a 200-kilometre radius of the local hospital. The programme, which started in 1973, emphasizes that if women are in labour for more than 24 hours they should be taken to the nearest hospital without delay. In populations that keep time by the sun, not by timepiece, the community can be educated that a woman should not be in labour for more than one sunrise or sunset. (Family Care International 1990)

About 75% of all maternal deaths in developing countries are caused by haemorrhage, sepsis, toxaemia, obstructed labour and abortion-related complications. Programmes which identify women at high risk of these obstetric problems and refer them for appropriate health care can greatly reduce maternal mortality.

Early Warning and Referral System

Unfortunately, many pregnancy-related complications cannot be predicted. Even with adequate prenatal care, as many as 15% of all deliveries will result in serious complications. An effective early warning and referral system, accessible emergency services and trained personnel must be available to detect and treat complications as quickly as possible.

Maternal Waiting Homes

These are a common, lost-cost method of improving obstetric care and reducing the time it takes for a woman to receive emergency treatment when complications arise. These "homes" are established next to hospitals or health centres or at a halfway point between a village and a major health care referral facility. Pregnant women, particularly those considered at high risk, can move to the homes prior to the onset of labour (Family Care International 1990).

Training Programmes

Many countries have training and certification programmes for private or government midwives who practise out of clinics or their own homes. Professional midwives typically receive 4–5 years of training, acquiring skills equivalent to those of many doctors, except in surgery and the use of drugs. Auxiliary midwives receive less training, usually under two years. Midwives are trained in prenatal care and safe delivery practices as well as in family planning and related maternal and child health activities; many are also fully trained nurses. Some programmes have experimented with training nurses and midwives to perform surgical sterilization and caesarean sections. Such programmes may meet with opposition from the medical profession and community, and also require intensive training and back-up supervision.

To provide better maternal health care to a larger proportion of their populations, many governments and private agencies have established training programmes for TBAs. At present, 85% of all countries offer some form of TBA training. Most of these programmes concentrate on teaching TBAs the "three cleans": clean hands, clean cutting of the umbilical cord and clean surfaces for delivery. Other components include risk detection and referral and basic modern obstetric techniques. TBA training programmes are a low-cost, effective means to provide better obstetric care to a larger proportion of the population in the absence of accessible modern health care.

A wide variety of innovative methods are used to train TBAs, many of whom are illiterate or have had little education. Local materials that are easy to make or obtain and familiar to the community can often be used to convey health care concepts; plastic or locally made wooden models of the birth canal and dolls representing the infant, for example, are widely used in TBA training programmes (Family Care International 1990).

Conclusion

In conclusion, women need not die in pregnancy and childbirth. It is now well-recognized that most of the maternal deaths that occur in the developing world are preventable. Although the causes of death and solutions for prevention may vary from region to region, the common denominator for all involves improving access to health care for women. The impact that national policy on abortion and family planning has on the health status of women has also been well-documented. It appears quite clear that restrictive policies on access to these services adversely affect the health of women.

The essential elements of obstetric care must be brought much nearer to the women living in developing countries than they are today. All women in childbirth, at home and in the hospital, should have the assistance of a trained person. Improving the skills of community health workers and TBAs, providing them with equipment and enlisting their assistance and support in disseminating information to women and their families are critical steps toward improving health care for pregnant women at the community level.

Although the net effects of education, employment and income on fertility are difficult to measure in isolation, their combined effects can be assumed to have a very considerable bearing on fertility, and consequently on a woman's health and status.

If there is one single factor above all others which is responsible for the low status of women it is probably uncontrolled fertility. The status of women is both a determinant and consequence of variation of reproductive behaviour: for example, a woman's educational opportunities, employment possibilities and role in the family all affect, and in turn are affected by, the timing and the number of her children and by her knowledge of how to plan her family.

Acknowledgement

The research assistance of Ms Janet Turner in the preparation of this paper is gratefully acknowledged.

References

Alauddin M (1986) Maternal mortality in rural Bangladesh: the Tangail District. Studies in Family Planning 17:13–21
Chen LC et al. (1974) Maternal mortality in rural Bangladesh. Studies in Family Planning 5:334–341
Family Care International (1990) Safe motherhood in action. FCI, New York
Fathalla MF, Rosenfield A, Indriso C (eds) (1990) Reproductive health: global issues. Parthenon, Carnforth (FIGO Manual of Reproduction vol 3)
Henshaw SK (1990) Induced abortion: a world review, 1990. International Family Planning Perspectives 16:59–65
Institute for Resource Development/Macro Systems, Inc. (1988, 1989) Demographic and health surveys (1988) Botswana; (1988) Egypt; (1989) Kenya. IRD, Columbia, Maryland
Jacobson JL (1990) The global politics of abortion. Worldwatch Institute, Washington, DC (Worldwatch Paper 97)
Lyons C (1985) More than a medical issue. Women's World 6:30–32
Mwanza F (1986) African countries team up to tackle anaemia. People 13:33
Rosenfield A, Maine D (1985) Maternal mortality – a neglected tragedy: where is the M in MCH? Lancet ii:83–85.
Royston E, Armstrong A (eds) (1989) Preventing maternal deaths. WHO, Geneva
Sai F, Nassim J (1989) The need for a reproductive health approach. Int J Gynecol Obstet [Suppl 3]:103–113
United Nations (1986) Report of the working group on traditional practices affecting the health of women and children. Commission on Human Rights. Forty-second session. Item 19 of the provisional agenda
United Nations (1987) Population trends and policies: monitoring report. United Nations, New York, pp 335–345
United Nations (1989) Levels and trends of contraceptive use as assessed in 1988. UN, New York
WHO (1985) Report of first inter-regional meeting on prevention of maternal mortality. Geneva, Nov 1985. WHO, Geneva

WHO (1987) Safe motherhood: an information kit. Safe Motherhood Conference, Nairobi, Feb 1987

WHO (1988) World health statistics annual 1988. WHO, Geneva

WHO (1989) The health of youth – youth, a resource for today and tomorrow. A42/Technical Discussions/6, Geneva 1989

CHAPTER 9

The Nature of Love

Malcolm Potts

We test our medicines on monkeys, practise heart transplants on dogs, but separate ourselves from other animals when it comes to love and marriage. Yet, in reality, the forces of evolution, which have tailored the physiology and anatomy that we share with other species, have also honed our sexuality and reproductive system – after all, the number of our progeny is the criterion by which Darwinian evolution judges the success of any species (Fisher 1930).

The thesis of this chapter is that the evolutionary paradigm is a rational and useful one for looking at human sexuality and reproductive behaviour – and ultimately love. Unlike religious or psychological paradigms, it is open to the same tests that have convinced thinking people that our bodies are the product of a long, slow process of biological evolution and that, to a greater or lesser extent, we have a common ancestry with all other living things. This chapter will look at the biological foundations of mating and sexual behaviour and then focus on incest, rape, monogamy and contraception, using a biological perspective to illuminate ethical assertions.

It is self-evident that the most complex and interesting of human behaviours are a mixture of genetic drives and learned skills. For example, there appear to be a number of structural similarities underlying most or all languages, which presumably relate to genetically determined patterns of neuroanatomy, and there also appears to be a "window" during childhood development when certain aspects of language are acquired rapidly even though the language itself is culturally determined. The balance of genetic and cultural determinants in our sexual and reproductive behaviour may always be impossible to disentangle completely, but, as with certain aspects of speech, sexual behaviour has a genetic as well as a cultural basis. Laura Betzig (1988) of Michigan University has written "The question, it seems to us, that should be asked at this point is not whether evolution has shaped our behaviour but how."

The Biological Foundations of Sexual Behaviour

In recent decades, there has been an explosion of interest in the evolutionary aspects of reproductive behaviour. This has resulted in a set of generalizations which apply to most sexually reproducing animals and certainly to all mammals

(Symonds 1979; Trivers 1985; Masie-Taylor and Boyce 1988; Rasa et al. 1989), as well as a subset of insights relating to the behaviour of human beings and the other higher primates (Jolly 1985).

The rich and fascinating variety of living things is the outcome of competition between "selfish" genes and there are powerful reasons for assuming that the two sexes will behave differently in their mating practices. Eggs are bigger than sperm and, in practically all animal species, the female makes greater investment in reproduction than the male. Amongst mammals, where females bear live young and expend additional energy breast-feeding, the differences between the sexes in the effort they put into producing the next generation are particularly marked. Trivers (1972) has proposed that sexual selection is driven by the relative "investment [made] by the parent in an individual offspring that increases the offspring's chance of surviving (and hence reproductive success) at the cost of the parents' ability to invest in other offspring".

Biology would predict that the female will be selective in whom she chooses as a mate and coy and cautious in her courtships. She must secure the best opportunity for the survival of her offspring and select the best male available to fertilize her eggs. If possible, she wants a mate to stay with her to help provide for and protect her offspring.

Virtually all females are likely to reproduce, although none will have extremely high numbers of offspring. The male strategy most likely to leave the greatest number of offspring in the next generation is to mate with as many females as possible. There is less incentive for the male to be selective in his mating, particularly if he is going to make little or no investment in his offspring, other than the brief moments of copulation. Predictably, most mammalian species are polygamous and the males compete amongst themselves. As Darwin observed, "the female has to spend much organic matter in the formation of her ova, whereas the male expends much force in fierce contest with his rivals".

In biology, it is often exceptions that prove the rules and the sea-horse is a species of bony fish where the male carries the brood pouch and the female has a penis for inserting the eggs into his "uterus". In the case of the sea-horse, it is the males who are coy and courted and the females who are brightly coloured, aggressive and competitive.

Many birds and a few mammalian species are monogamous. When following this strategy, the male, instead of spending time competing with other males and attempting to impregnate as many females as possible (relatively few of whose offspring may survive to maturity), opts for quality rather than quantity and by assisting the female in the heavy burden of bringing up her offspring, increases the probability that a few well-cared-for individuals will be more likely to survive.

Careful field observations, however, of many monogamous birds and mammals demonstrate that the "monogamous" male, given an opportunity, often behaves polygynously. Male pigeons may leave the nest where they are caring for their young and attempt to mate with any female that will accept them. Biologically, this type of infidelity differs from that of cuckoldry, where the female mates with a male whom perhaps she "judges" to be a more vigorous father of her offspring and yet attempts to "deceive" her regular partner into caring for the "cuckoo" in the nest. It has also been suggested that female infidelity may expose women to "good-quality" sperm (Bellis and Baker 1990).

Chimpanzee Sexuality

Genetically, we are more closely related to chimpanzees than they are to gorillas. Chimpanzees live in troops where adult males defend a territory, sometimes with great viciousness and occasionally with "murderous" attacks on neighbouring troops. Males are sexually promiscuous and mate with the females as they ovulate and become sexually receptive. The members of the troop recognize one another as individuals, and children remain in a close relationship to their mothers even after weaning. Adult males are often related and commonly remain in the troop of their birth. Females, as they reach puberty, usually migrate outside their natal troop. In most mammalian species which live in a herd or troop, it is related females who form the basis of the breeding group (e.g., lions, langur, baboons, elephants). Human society, like that of the chimpanzee, is unusual in that it is based upon groups of males, who sometimes co-operate and sometimes compete with one another and who make shifting alliances within the group in order to gain power (de Waal 1982). Like chimpanzees, men are all too often prepared to kill to defend their territory. In many human societies, females leave the clan of their birth at marriage and in many patriarchal societies, elder males determine the mating patterns of the next generation. Young chimpanzees, like some brides, may end up quarrelling with the older females of the troop they join – they compete with their mothers-in-law.

Tragically, we are only beginning to understand the social and sexual life of primates at the very moment that many species are in danger of extinction. The bonobo, or pygmy chimps (*Pan panisus*), live in remote areas of Zaire and have only been studied recently and even then, knowledge is incomplete (McGinnis 1977). They appear to be distinguished from *Pan troglodytes* by engaging, like human beings, in ventral–ventral sex moderately frequently, by mutual rubbing of the genitals in females to orgasm, and by frequent hetero- and homosexual manual and oral manipulations of the genitalia.

Human Mating

Building on these biological foundations, it is possible to turn to the analysis of some specific human mating behaviours and, after analyzing each from a Darwinian perspective, add some ethical speculations.

Incest

We all carry a load of recessive genes which do little harm unless both of our parents carry the same gene, in which case there may be manifest abnormalities. Mating with near-relatives is genetically unwise because relatives are more likely to carry the same damaging recessive genes.

Most animals become widely dispersed before they reach sexual maturity. But amongst animals that live in groups, patterns of behaviour have evolved where kin (a) recognize one another (for example, by smell) and (b) do not mate with one another. Amongst 1000 matings recorded in a troop of Japanese macaque monkeys, where males remain in their natal group, Fedigan (1982) "never observed a mother–son copulation, only one brother–sister mating, and one grandmother–grandson mating".

When children of the opposite sex grow up together for a critical time before puberty, they seem not to be sexually interested in one another after they become mature. Amongst our hunter-gatherer ancestors, all the children who grew up together were also genetically related and our behaviour evolved based on the proximate fact that recognizing a person with whom we grew up was a reasonable predictor of genetic relationships. Hence in an interesting study of young children who were brought up together in an Israeli kibbutz, Shepher (1971) found that adults never married partners from their own kibbutz. A man from the Tallensi tribe of Northern Ghana explained the same inbuilt response to an anthropologist

> look . . . my sister, is she not marriageable? And here am I, however attractive she is, I do not even notice it. I am never aware that she has a vagina; she is just my sister and someone will one day come and marry her and I will give her to him and get my cows. You and your sister grow up together, you quarrel and make it up, how can you desire to have intercourse with her? (Fortes 1969)

Van den Berghe (1987) has suggested that in societies where children of both sexes play together, nudity is common and sexuality is not repressed (as is, indeed, the case in the Tallensi), then there is no need for strong incest taboos. Conversely, where the sexes are separated after weaning, or where there are sexually repressive attitudes toward prepubertal sexuality (as amongst the Ibo of Nigeria or Ashanti of Ghana), strong incest taboos will arise. Amongst the Ibo "in the old days the offenders would have been buried alive in the central Agbaja market place".

Societies sometimes go on to invent extensive (although biologically meaningless) patterns of incest restriction, between remote and often genetically unrelated individuals, as well as other arbitrary restraints on sex. St Gregory of Tours (d. 596) claimed that intercourse on a Sunday caused abnormalities in children, "leave this day unsullied to the glory of God, else the children born to you will be crippled, or epileptic, or lepers", and 500 years later Odo of Paris said if a woman sought intercourse on a Sunday her husband should "quell her impudence with fasting and beating" (Ranke-Heinemann 1990).

The same principle of familiarity also seems to be the basis of the barrier against incest between different generations in the same family. It is notable that most father/daughter incest and other abuse reported in the contemporary world is really between a *step-parent* and child (Daly and Wilson 1988). When incest does not involve a step-parent, it sometimes involves a father who brought up his daughter in a puritanical and fundamentalist religious atmosphere and never changed her nappies, bathed her or cuddled her.

As an aside, Freud's theory (republished 1950) of strong sexual attraction between children and parents is the reverse of the biological. Freudian psychology, like theology, is a series of unprovable and sometimes mistaken assertions.

In summary, from the point of view of ethics, we can conclude that laws and social standards condemning incest are biologically appropriate and should be universal. Incest between first degree relatives is condemned by virtually all societies. Amongst the two rare and special exceptions are the ancient Egyptians and the Azonde of nineteenth century Sudan (Evans-Pritchard 1971) who practised incest amongst small, restricted groups of the aristocracy and where the male drive for power and wealth seems to have overcome the biological barrier to incest. If young children grow up in a loving, non-sexually-repressive atmosphere, however, then cruelly harsh or unnecessarily complex restraints on incest are unnecessary. Some other arbitrary restraints on sexual behaviour may come from the same basic drive yet have no biological meaning whatsoever.

Rape

Behaviours that can be called "rape" have been observed amongst orang-utans, where young males sometimes use their strength and size to compel females to have intercourse, although adult males have not been seen to engage in this behaviour. Amongst human beings, rape appears to be a strategy adopted by men who have been relatively unsuccessful in the competition for resources which might normally be expected to attract women free to make their own choice of mate (Thornhill and Thornhill 1979; Shields and Shields 1987). It is also men who have least resources who are most likely to be involved in homicide (Daly and Wilson 1988).

Biology predicts, and observation appears to confirm, that societies with an unequal distribution of wealth, especially some sort of economic underclass (such as Brazil), will have a higher prevalence of rape than a more equalitarian society (such as Sri Lanka).

Monogamy

In all species where males compete for access to the females, such as elephant seals, the males are bigger than the female. The bigger the difference in size between the two sexes, the larger the harem the male tends to accumulate. Conversely, in a truly monogamous species, such as the marmoset monkey or penguins, the two sexes are the same size, or the male may even be smaller than the female. Male chimpanzees, gorillas and men are all larger than the female; in the case of men, about 10% – 15% larger and heavier. Our testis/body ratio (which has evolved to conform with frequency of copulation) is also unequivocally that of a polygynous or promiscuous animal (Fig. 9.1).

The majority of anthropologically distinct societies are polygamous, although nearly all societies also recognize that male/female relationships, at least for an interval of time, can be characterized by extraordinary passion and desire for monogamous exclusivity: in other words, we fall in love. Such love is the basis of the western (and in historical terms recent) ideal of romantic, partner choice in marriage, but it also arises in polygamous situations.

The sex lives and mating practices of rulers and aristocrats are interesting because they are not constrained by economic circumstances. Shah Jahan built the Taj Mahal to commemorate the death of his wife, Mumtaz, in childbirth in 1631. He clearly loved this one woman greatly, even though he had other wives and a harem of concubines. King Solomon had "60 queens and 80 concubines and virgins without number". Louis XIV had 17 children divided between his queen, mistresses and paramours. In the recent history of the British royal family, Queen Victoria and Prince Albert appear to have been passionately monogamous, while Victoria's father and all her uncles had numerous mistresses.

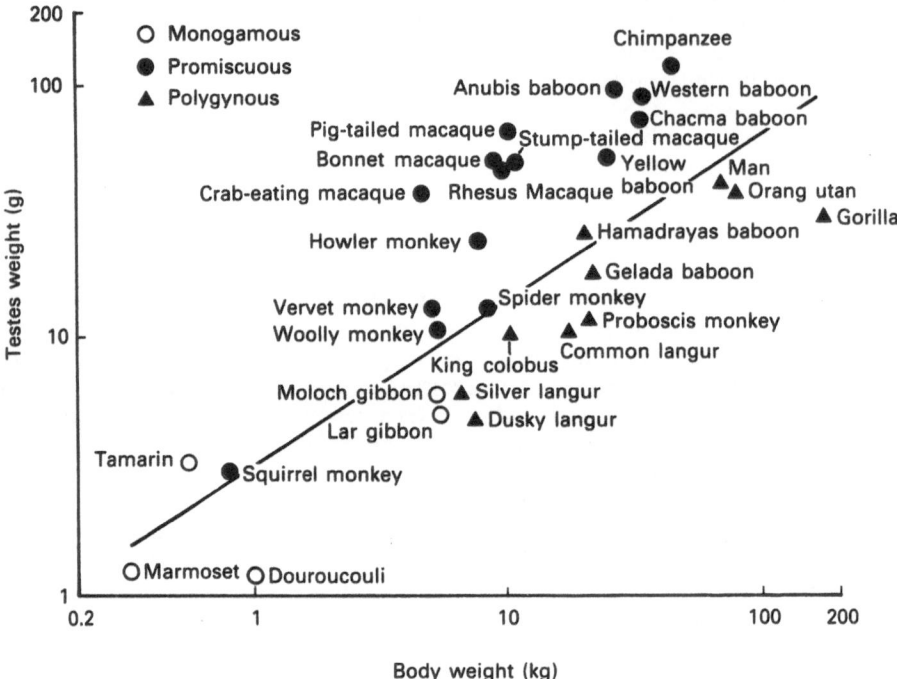

Figure 9.1. Testicular weight and body weight in promiscuous, polygynous and monogamous mammals (Short 1985).

Her uncle Leopold forced his attentions on his brother's mistress and Albert's brother had a violent sex life and suffered from gonorrhoea. Victoria's son Edward VII had several deeply emotional and long-term relationships, such as those with Lillie Langtry, Alice Keppel and Daisy Warwick, as well as numerous one-night-stands when his equerries brought pretty women from the theatre or race course who found it difficult to say "no" to a King (Aronson 1988). In a sentence, we appear to be a polygamous animal that half wants to be monogamous but where males with wealth and power commonly use their opportunity to mate widely. It is this difficult and passionate process which defines the nature of human love.

Some societies, such as Puritan England and New England, have used the force of law and custom to enforce monogamy, physically punish extra-marital and premarital relations and forbid divorce (Quaife 1979). Conversely, in the classical world, even the gods were polygamous (Pomeroy 1975) and prostitutes were a major source of tax revenue (McGinn 1989). Perhaps the contemporary compromise of a societal norm of monogamy, with legal divorce and no physical punishments of extra- or premarital relations is about the most rational and human set of ethics a society can devise.

Love

By what steps did love evolve? We can get some clues by looking at chimpanzees. Most educated people would say that human beings are distinguished from chimpanzees by language and the use of tools. In reality, chimpanzees can be taught language – albeit a sign language – and can acquire a vocabulary of several hundred words, and they use tools in the wild, for such purposes as probing ants' nests for food. What really distinguishes us from chimpanzees is a series of important reproductive behaviours.

The human female is the only mammal where neither she nor her partner knows when ovulation is occurring. Secondly, we engage in sexual intercourse throughout the ovarian cycle and not just at the time of maximum fertility, as do all other animals. Thirdly, practically all human intercourse is conducted in private, away from the rest of the troop and often at night. Lastly, again unlike any other animals, we have a sense of embarrassment and consistently cover up the genitalia of sexually adult individuals – witness the distress of a man who finds he has left his fly undone! After eating of the tree of knowledge, says the Biblical creation myth, "the eyes of [Adam and Eve] were opened, and they knew that they were naked; and they sewed fig leaves together, and made aprons" (Genesis 3 v.7).

These behavioural characteristics all appear to have arisen relatively recently (perhaps the last several hundred thousand years) in human evolution. They are the basis of our family life, of adult sexual love, and of the love and care of children by their parents.

Bonobo chimps are characterized by a more extended period of sexual receptivity at the time of ovulation than *Pan troglodytes*. Chimpanzee females of both subspecies usually mate with several males within a short time of one another and in daylight in front of the rest of the troop. Sometimes, however, a male, who may have taken a particular interest in a female and may have spent more time grooming her earlier in the sexual cycle, appears to try and lead her away from the rest of the troop at around the time of ovulation (McGinnis 1977). A behaviour which deliberately takes a pair away from scrutiny by the rest of the troop is also difficult for human observers to follow, but it is assumed that these "courtships" are associated with sexual activity and they are perhaps the closest chimpanzees come to human sexual love.

Even more than the bonobos, women are sexually receptive throughout the menstrual cycle and, even more than chimpanzees, we appear to be driven to engage in sexual activity out of the sight of the rest of the troop and in our case, commonly at the time of least diurnal activity. Male chimpanzees copulate with females who advertise ovulation by impressive, technicolour swellings of the vulva. In turn, they can also "know" when not to "waste their time" copulating with potentially infertile females. The human male does not have the benefit of such foreknowledge. If he wishes to father children by a particular female, then he is compelled to stay close by her and to copulate with moderate frequency, even though the majority of his copulations are going to be infertile. A close relationship between a man and a woman, associated with sexual activity (most of which is infertile) is a reasonable, if somewhat unromantic, description of human love.

The two sexes reveal their reproductive agendas in their fantasies and what, when it takes a physical expression, some people call pornography. Men are

erotically driven by explicit visual stimuli and physical stimulation, hence
Playboy centrefolds and sexy videos (Symonds 1979): the women are nubile and
physically perfect, while their personalities are as thin as the glossy sheet of
paper which holds their picture. The biological drive to prove paternity may be
part of the explanation of bondage and spanking fantasies. (Interestingly,
women's sexual fantasies also sometimes include restraint.)

Maternal Love

In Christian theology a perfect creation was corrupted by an original sin, which
was sexual in nature. In biology, sex is a driving force in evolution and the
problem is not to account for sin but to explain how nature "red in tooth and
claw" can also evolve altruistic behaviours. In one of the most important insights
of twentieth-century evolutionary biology, Hamilton (1964) suggested parental
care is reproductively selfish because it maximizes the survival of the parents'
genes. Amongst genetically related animals, their *inclusive fitness* can also be
enhanced by altruistic or nepotistic behaviour. The closer the genetic relationship,
the stronger the effect: some older birds will feed younger siblings, vampire
bats will regurgitate blood to prevent a relative from dying of starvation and
social insects (who as a result of their partially parthenogenetic reproduction
share many genes) may give their lives to defend the hive. Trivers (1972) has
also suggested that acts of reciprocal altruism are possible between unrelated
members of the same species, for example when one member of the herd accepts
a small risk of predation to warn others of possible attack, on the principle he
or she will benefit from similar warnings on future occasions.

   A female mammal shares 50% of her genes with her offspring; if children come
from her uterus (scientifically manipulated reproduction excepted), there can be
no doubt they are her offspring and, therefore, worth the investment of "mother
love".

Paternal Love

For a male to invest in his offspring, he must "know" who are his children.
Where one male lives with a harem of females, as amongst the gorillas, then he
can be pretty certain that the youngsters in his group come from his sperm. He
is their leader, protector, and when threats arise young gorillas look to their
father for guidance. Chimpanzees are promiscuous and there is no way of
identifying which child belongs to which father. The males will defend a troop
as a unit. They are tolerant of the playfulness of the youngsters but, if a danger
threatens, the young chimps look to their mothers for reassurance. We live in
large mixed-sex troops just like chimpanzees, yet we have taken the step of
males investing in their offspring. In practically all human cultures, men have
a sense of paternity and invest in their children, although the amount of time
and energy they spend with their children varies greatly between cultures and
between families.

   Homo sapiens' paternal drive follows from the frequent mating and closeness
between men and women. At the same time the drive to secure paternity is also
probably the foundation of a number of cruel aberrations of male power over
women. As agricultural societies became richer, so some of them sequestered

women. Purdah is still common in many parts of Islam. The cruel mutilation of female circumcision, still common in parts of Africa (Atiya 1982), and of foot binding amongst the Chinese are, or were, physical ways of controlling women and therefore of assuring paternity.

Preliterate, hunter-gatherer societies appear to provide relative sexual equality; women have latitude to move and to choose their partners while men provide parental support without excessive control. Sexual relationships can often be interrupted and new alliances formed with relatively little social pain (Shostak 1981). Agricultural societies with strict land-inheritance laws and often a caste system, sometimes link paternal responsibility with strict control of women. A humane society would encourage sufficient stability in husband/wife relationships that men invest love and substance in their children, but not so much that men dominate and exploit women. The Western legal and ethical system strives to protect a woman's autonomy, but when sexual partnerships break up, she is often left impoverished.

Marriage and Mate Selection

The differing agenda of the two sexes leads in turn to differing criteria for selecting sexual partners. Women tend to choose husbands on the basis of their ability to provide care and protection, valuing attributes that signify the acquisition of resources and power. Men use criteria of reproductive value, or the life-long probability of reproduction. The criteria they use of "good looks" or "physical attractiveness" are really measures of age and health – smooth skin, lustrous hair, sprightly gait, flashing teeth. The emphasis men put on the bust and hips in their perception of a woman's figure are clearly biological criteria; the emphasis on a "tiny waist" may be a clue derived from the male need to prove paternity, namely that the woman is not pregnant.

As older men tend to have more resources and younger women greater reproductive potential, biology would predict, and observation confirms, that men will marry women who are younger than they are and the age gap is likely to be wider at a second marriage than a first.

There are important differences in the criteria used by men and women when selecting marriage partners (Buss and Barnes 1986). Women look for ambition, industriousness, and financial prospects while men are strongly influenced by physical attractiveness. Langhorne and Secord (1955) in a sample of 5000 college students found consistent differences in male and female ideals for marriage partners and Buss (1989) has described findings in this field as "so consistent across studies that they qualify as amongst the most robust and consistently replicated psychological findings that have been documented across several generations". In one prospective study, female "attractiveness" was more closely correlated with the husband's occupational status than was IQ or class origin (Elder 1969). Udry and Eckland (1984) found a one-point difference in a quantitative scale used to score the attractiveness of female college students was associated with a mean of $3000 higher income amongst their husbands later in life. Amongst Ache hunter-gatherers in Paraguay, men with a proven record of success as hunters have more surviving children, even though the tribe shares all the meat caught, and amongst the Kipsigis in Kenya those men who herd the most cows tend to have the most children.

Men, from a biological perspective, can afford to be less discriminating than women; a one-night-stand with a less desirable partner may still lead to pregnancy: to the man's wife, who has so much more reason to be cautious about reproduction, such behaviour is often particularly puzzling. Prostitution is an extreme example of the male agenda in mate selection. Although there are men who have sex with women for money, the overwhelming majority of prostitutes are women and nearly all provide sex for money (or drugs).

The female equivalent of male pornography may well be pulp romantic stories and as with male pornography, the woman's agenda is expressed without depth or realism. The best-selling authors tell the same story of a handsome prince meeting the young girl at the threshold of her search for a mate – and they end with a kiss and the promise of life-long protection and provisioning.

Sex Preference

The fact that a mammal, if successful in competition with other males, can father many children whereas a female is limited to a smaller number of offspring (because of the time it takes to carry, breast-feed and rear them) raises some interesting behavioural strategies amongst parents. Clutton-Brock (1984) and Clutton-Brock et al. (1985) have shown that female red deer will breast-feed male fawns longer than females. The likely explanation is that a doe, when she matures, is likely to mate and bear young whatever happens. But a buck will only compete with his fellows if he is strong enough: then the winner takes all. Therefore, the adult doe is more likely to see her genes in her grandchildren if she feeds a male fawn longer and gives him the best possible start in life. But the males do not have it all their own way. By being more competitive and aggressive, they are also injured and killed more frequently by their own species than are females.

A fascinating parallel exists between animal behaviour and human behaviour in the history of the aristocracy of Portugal. Between 1380 and 1580 A.D. the Portuguese aristocracy kept careful genealogical records and the *Peditura Lusitana* meticulously recorded the births, deaths and aristocratic title (a measure of wealth) of all the leading families. The behaviour of the Portuguese fits the prediction of biologists who have studied other mammals and birds: parents will make a differential investment in sons or daughters according to which sex is most likely to leave the greatest number of descendants (Boone 1988). Wealth is the stronger determinant of male reproductive performance than the female. Sons tend to inherit the social economic status of their parents, daughters if they are lucky can move up the social ladder. As the opportunities for geographical expansion in Portugal's empire were used up between the fourteenth and sixteenth centuries, reproduction in elite groups fell by 40% and the number of sons dying in warfare increased from less than 10% to almost 30% (Fig. 9.2).

The lower nobility favoured their daughters because, like all females, they would at least have a few children.

The younger sons of the higher Portuguese nobility were pushed out of society as bands of bachelor youths, who literally roamed the world as soldiers, fighting first against the Moslems in the south of Iberia, in the Crusades in the

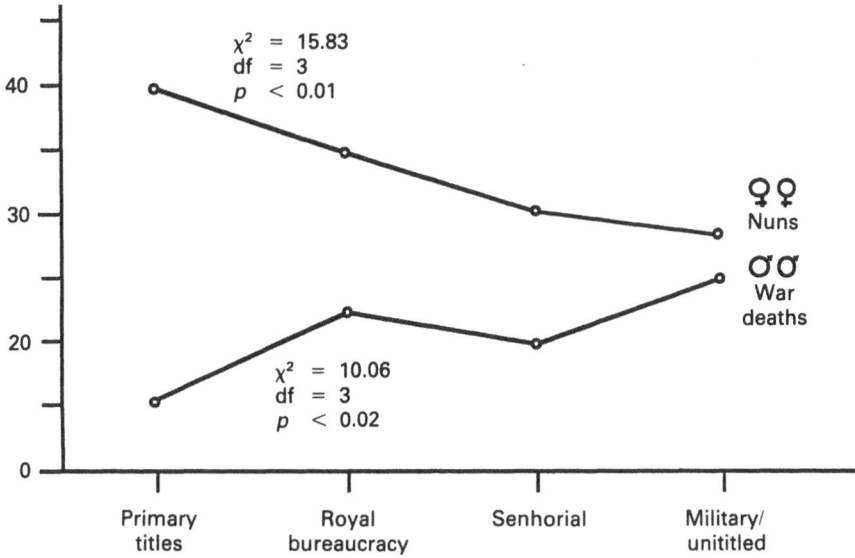

$\chi^2 = 15.83$
df $= 3$
$p < 0.01$

♀♀ Nuns

♂♂ War deaths

$\chi^2 = 10.06$
df $= 3$
$p < 0.02$

Primary titles · Royal bureaucracy · Senhorial · Military/ unititled

Figure 9.2. Proportion of sons dying in warfare and daughters entering nunneries by social status in the Portuguese aristocracy 1380–1580. (Redrawn from Boone 1988.)

Middle East and finally in India and the Far East. In a remarkable documentation of the subtleties of reproductive pressures, the more brothers a man had, the more likely he was to end up being killed in some far corner of the world.

The high nobility favoured their sons, as they had the greatest opportunities to stay at home and mate successfully. The upper classes, however, could not afford to divide their estates amongst their daughters and more and more of these entered nunneries (up to 40% by the sixteenth century). The daughter's dowry was paid into the convent and the virgin woman was "married" to the church. The family lost resources but did not risk any further division amongst numerous grandchildren. The same effect was achieved more brutally in some oriental cultures by simply killing females at birth.

In a complementary piece of historical research, this time a Protestant, agricultural society of the Netherlands in the seventeenth to nineteenth centuries, Voland (1988) compared the survival of children born to widows. When a woman lost her husband, she was likely to be poor and her sons would take her social rank with little chance of advancement; while her daughters were more likely to marry. The sons of widows were more likely to die than their daughters while amongst widowers there was no such differential in child loss. The data also demonstrate that widows whose first-born child died had 17% more chance of remarriage than women whose first-born survived and the first-born children of widows did indeed die more commonly than the first-born children of widowers (although the first-born of widowers died more frequently if the man remarried and a step-mother entered the family).

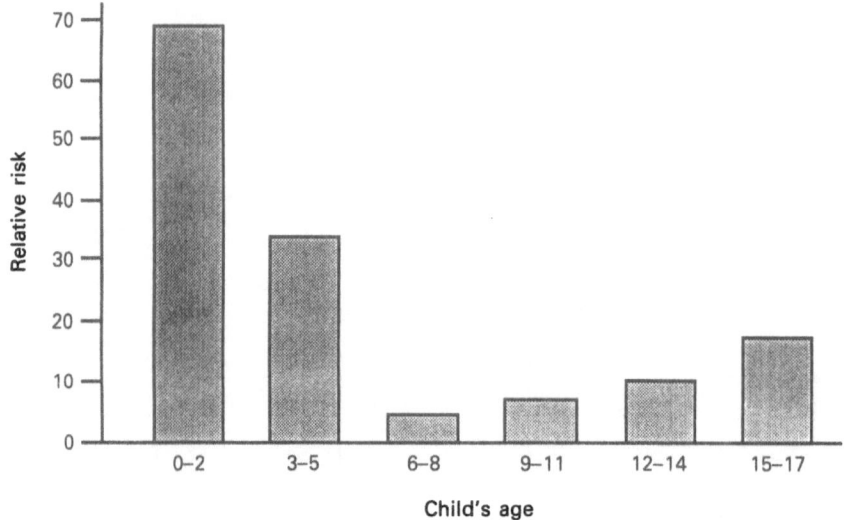

Figure 9.3. Relative risk of death due to murder by a step-parent or a person *in loco parentis* compared with that of a natural parent of offspring age 0–17 years of age. (Canadian homicide data 1976–83: redrawn from Daly and Wilson 1988.)

Infanticide

Reproduction in the higher primates is a slow process. Pregnancy in chimpanzees, gorillas and human beings lasts from seven to nine months and lactation for 18 months to four years. For most of the interval of lactation, the female will not ovulate. If the infant is stillborn and dies prematurely, then the stimuli to the nipple will cease and ovulation will return. In a polygynous species such as the gorilla, if a new male drives out a weaker one and takes over a harem, then he is likely to find that he has just risked his life to gain access to a group of females who are either pregnant or breast-feeding.

In a number of polygynous animals, a male who takes over a harem will systematically attempt to kill all suckling infants. This has been observed in lions, langurs and gorillas (Hrdy 1977). Data on human infanticide shows that step-parents, particularly men, are five to 70 times more likely to murder children than natural parents (Fig. 9.3). Poignantly, those *in loco* parents tend to murder teenagers just as they become aggressive and independent, while natural parents become increasingly tolerant of the offspring in whom they have made so much biological investment. Patterns of child abuse parallel those of infanticide and murder.

When women commit infanticide, it is for a different reason although, once again, the huge investment the female primate makes in reproduction is the key to the behaviour. If a young woman has an abnormal child, or if the relationship with the father breaks down, then it may be in her biological interest to kill the baby or, what in practice is often the same, not strive so hard to keep it alive. In this way, she brings forward the next possible pregnancy with a new

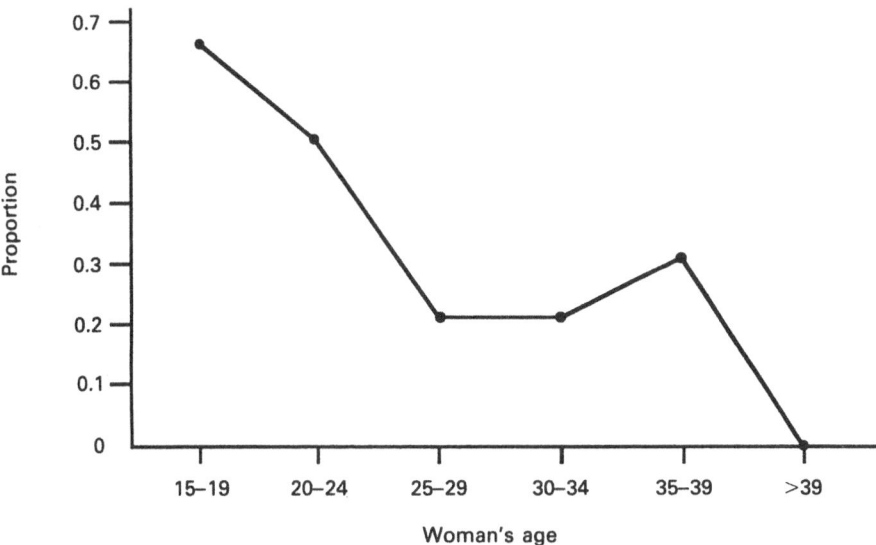

Figure 9.4. Proportion of birth ($n = 141$) ending in infanticide ($n = 54$) as a function of maternal age. (Redrawn from Bugos and McCarthy 1984.)

choice both for a healthy, sound infant or for a new and hopefully better relationship with a male.

The older the woman becomes, the less this strategy makes sense (Fig. 9.4). Again, homicide statistics show that human beings, like other mammals, can behave with a reproductive ruthlessness. A woman aged 20 has a good chance of mating and conceiving a child very quickly, whereas for a woman of 38 it may be her last chance to have a child. Amongst the preliterate Ayreo Indians of South America, young people choose their sexual partners by what in the West would be called romantic standards (Bugos and McCarthy 1986). If, however, a relationship breaks up during pregnancy, then it is in the "interest" of a young woman to kill her infant rather than bring up a child alone *and* have to wait for two or three years while she breast-feeds her child before becoming eligible to try and establish a new partnership.

Infanticide is rarely as open as amongst the Ayreo and is commonly occult, in the sense that the mother may not understand, and if asked, deny she was attempting to kill her child. Yet, by allotting resources in a particular way, she may decrease a child's chances of survival. In other words, human beings, like other animals, will manipulate the investment they make in their offspring to maximize their total reproductive potential over a lifetime. Once again, biology can explain behaviours. While our ethical and legal systems are predicated in largely non-biological values, it is interesting, and probably sensible, that society often finds extenuating circumstances when a woman kills her infant and passes a lenient ·sentence.

Abortion

Stallions that take over a new harem have been observed to kick the mares to the point of inducing an abortion. This behaviour, if valid, would be biologically comparable to examples of mammalian infanticide noted above. Human induced abortion seems to follow the same broad pattern of maternal age, poverty and marital status as infanticide.

Abortion in women, however, is unlike the other behaviours discussed above in that it depends on technology and often involves the participation of a second party. Indeed, it is interesting to speculate whether abortion would ever have become the basis of controlling legislation if some common herb, such as lettuce, for example, had the property to induce an abortion safely whenever it was ingested.

Biology is relevant to any ethical analysis of abortion, but in a very different way from the other behaviours discussed, because the drives that encourage or discourage abortion are less important in the abortion debate than are considerations about the status of the embryo and fetus: is abortion the moral equivalent of murder?

This question is all-too-often misunderstood: it is assumed it can be answered by biological observation, when it is really a question of religious belief.

Since scientific observation cannot determine "when life begins" then that judgement, however important, must be accepted as an assertion of religious belief, not as a statement of scientific fact. If that is the case, then it should be no more surprising that there are different interpretations of life before birth than there are different religious teachings about life after death. It should be no more surprising to find an abortion clinic in a city where many individuals sincerely believe abortion to be murder than it is to find a mosque, a synagogue and a church on the same road, even though they all make profoundly different assertions about the spiritual interpretation of the physical world.

There is, however, one area where embryology can provide a useful perspective on abortion. A high proportion of sperm (and possibly also of ova) are abnormal and incapable of fertilization. Amongst those eggs that are fertilized, up to half fail to develop normally and many are lost before the woman knows she is even pregnant. Chromosomal and other abnormalities lead to spontaneous abortion. Within the growing embryo itself, cell death is an essential part of development, shaping many organs, in particular the complex central nervous system. Spontaneous abortion, then, is a natural, healing process evolved to deal with the many errors that occur in the process of creating a new human being.

Contraception and Breast-feeding

In the ninth century, Ibn Al-Jawzi an Islamic jurist from Baghdad, perspicaciously suggested that man was distinguished from other animals by his use of contraception – "a donkey does not discharge into the she-ass because he seeks progeny, nor does he avoid offspring by practising withdrawal as men do".

In the midst of the contemporary population explosion, it is interesting to remember that human beings are probably the slowest breeding animal in existence, have a later puberty than any other animal, they alone have a universal discrete menopause and pregnancies are naturally spaced by long intervals of breast-feeding. The fertility of preliterate societies (Campbell and Wood 1988) is considerably lower than that of many contemporary agricultural societies, such as Kenya, where patterns of breast-feeding are beginning to change. Contraception restores the natural balance between population and the environment that has characterized most of human evolution. From a biological perspective, artificial feeding is an even more profound interruption of natural practices than artificial contraception. It increases fertility by eroding the natural suppression of ovulation which is an essential part of lactation and it endangers both the baby and the mother. Even in the Western world where parents use milk formula well, artificially fed babies have a higher morbidity than breast-fed ones. In the Third World (where milk formula is badly used with dirty water), there is a markedly increased risk of death amongst bottle-fed babies. Finally, there is increasing data that bottle-feeding instead of breast-feeding significantly increases the risk of breast cancer in the mother. Yet, theologians have rarely, if ever, commented upon the ethics of artificial milk formula.

The Judeao-Christian religion has made a number of critical assertions about the licitness of contraception practices (Noonan 1965). These begin with the somewhat difficult-to-interpret story of Onan (Genesis c 38) and reached a particularly hysterical condemnation of contraception and exposition of anti-feminist theology in St Augustine. In the contemporary world, the papal condemnation of contraception in *Humanae vitae* (1968) appears to have little direct effect on contraceptive practice amongst Catholics (Murphy 1981), but has a profound effect on public policy, the availability of contraception and even on medical research. Condemnation of contraception is not limited to the Catholic church and Anglicans took a similar stance: the 1908 Lambeth Conference regarded "with alarm, the growing practice of artificial restriction of a family".

The conflict about the ethics of contraception stems in part from the interpretations of Early Fathers of the Church regarding natural phenomena. They looked around them and saw domestic and farm animals only copulated in order to procreate, but as every modern reproductive phsyiologist knows, the choice of experimental animal is important when interpreting mammalian reproduction. It was not the fault of early theologians that their observations were flawed, but now that we have a better understanding of biology we should use it. The church's emphasis on the virtues of celibacy, the choice of the wrong animal and the cryptic story of Onan all combine to increase the Christian misinterpretation of human sexuality and condemnation of contraception.

St Augustine, logically, also condemned what today is known as "natural family planning", but in recent times, the use of periodic abstinence has been justified as a licit form of birth control. As we saw earlier, the concealment of ovulation in the human female is a unique human attribute, the basis of adult love and the biological foundation on which the human family, from a biological perspective, is built. From a biological perspective, contrived efforts to discover when a woman does or does not ovulate seem like an effort to turn a woman back into a monkey! If evolution (or a divine creator) had thought it useful to know when women ovulate, then women would not have lost the behavioural changes and physical vulval swellings that characterize ovulation in other related primates.

Conclusions

PERM II, the conference on which this volume is based, sought "the widest possible multi-disciplinary exchange" and a biological perspective illuminates many aspects of reproductive ethics. It is remarkable, for example, that underlying the records of births and deaths in mediaeval Portuguese noble families or homicides in Canada are a series of human behaviours which it has been observed make evolutionary sense for deer, lions, baboons and prairie dogs. Of course, the people involved do not know what they were doing, any more than the baboons understand why they follow certain reproductive strategies. What is convincing is the data across a range of human behaviours, from the probability of a young woman entering a nunnery to the possibility that her brother will die fighting to expand his country's possessions in India, do indeed fit a pattern which can be predicted on the grounds of evolutionary biology.

Biology cannot tell us how to behave in the modern world. It can often explain why we do certain things. Baroness Warnock states "My argument will be that, though the philosopher will not produce proof or certainty, yet analysis itself may be, in a modest way, useful. It may lead, though slowly, both to better decisions and to the possibility of explaining a decision once it is made" (page 21). The word biologist could just as easily be substituted for philosopher.

Byrne, who approaches sexual behaviour from a traditional perspective comes to many conclusions that overlap with these a biologist might propose (Chap. 10).

In the case of incest, biology, ethics and the law all pull in the same direction. In the case of marriage and mate selection, biology tells us that we are unstably balanced on a knife edge between monogamy and polygamy, encouraging society to treat various expressions of human sexuality and mating with some degree of tolerance. Overall, in technically complex societies, where women enjoy some degree of autonomy, cultural pressures are continuing where biological evolution left off and encouraging monogamy and the female reproductive agenda.

In the case of infanticide and the preference of the parents for a child of a particular sex, biology can help explain behaviours, but most people would accept that biological insights deserve to be over-ridden by our contemporary emphasis on the quality of all individuals. Nevertheless, in the long slow process of civilizing sex, our ethics and our laws, while we may condemn infanticide, we usually treat a woman who kills her baby more leniently than an adult who murders another adult.

It is also interesting to focus on areas where disciplines do not overlap in their assertions about sexual ethics. For example, in the case of contraception, biological perspectives are in direct contradiction to a major element in traditional Christian sexual ethics. It is to be hoped that biology can contribute in a valuable way to the ongoing debate on contraception, the outcome of which will influence the lives, health and happiness of hundreds of millions of women and their families – possibly even the future of life on earth.

In the case of abortion, biology cannot settle a debate which has deeply divided modern society. If the status of the embryo is indeed a religious assertion, then beliefs about abortion must surely be accommodated within a philosophy of religious tolerance. It is particularly sad that the USA, with its 200 years' history of religious tolerance, is the country most deeply divided over the abortion issue.

References

Aronson T (1988) The King in love: Edward VII's mistresses. Harper and Row, New York

Atiya N (1982) Khul-Khaal, five Egyptian women tell their stories. Syracuse University Press, New York

Bellis M, Baker R (1990) Animal Behaviour 40:998

Betzig L (1988) Mating and parenting in Darwinian perspective. In: Betzig L, Borgerhoff Mulder M, Turke P (eds) Human reproductive behaviour: a Darwinian perspective. Cambridge University Press, Cambridge

Boone JL (1988) Parental investment, social subordination and population processes amongst 15th and 10th century Portuguese nobility. In: Betzig L, Borgerhoff Molder M, Turke P (eds) Human reproductive behaviour. Cambridge University Press, Cambridge

Bugos PE, McCarthy LM (1984) Ayoreo infanticide: a case study. In: Hausfater G, Hrdy SB (eds) Infanticide: comparative and evolutionary perspectives. Aldine de Gruyter, New York

Buss DM (1989) Sex differences in human mate selection criteria: an evolutionary perspective. In: Crawford C, Smith M, Krebs D (eds) Sociobiology and psychology: ideas, issues and applications. Lawrence Erlbaum, Hillsdale, New Jersey, pp 335–351

Buss DM, Barnes MF (1986) Preferences in human mate selection. J Pers Soc Psychol 50:559–570

Campbell KL, Wood JW (1988) Fertility in traditional societies. In: Human fertility: social and biological determinants. Macmillan, London

Clutton-Brock TH (1984) Reproductive effect and terminal investment in iteroparous animals. Am Naturalist 123:212–29

Clutton-Brock TH, Albon SD, Guineo FE (1985) Parental investment and sex differences in juvenile mortality in birds and mammals. Nature 313:131–3

Daly M, Wilson M (1988) Homicide. Aldine de Gruyter, New York

de Waal F (1982) Chimpanzee politics: power and sex among apes. Harper and Row, New York

Elder GM (1969) Appearance and education in social nobility. Soc Rev 34:519–533

Evans-Pritchard EE (1971) The Azonde: history and political institutions. Clarendon Press, Oxford

Fedigan LM (1982) Primate paradigms: sex roles and social bonds. Eden Press, Montreal

Fisher RA (1930) The genetical theory of natural selection. Clarendon Press, Oxford

Fortes M (1969) The web of kinship amongst the Tallensi. Oxford University Press, Oxford

Freud S (1950) Totem and taboo. Norton, New York (first published 1913)

Hamilton WD (1964) The genetical evolution of social behaviour. J Theor Biol 7:1–52

Hrdy SB (1977) The langurs of Abu: female and male strategies of reproduction. Harvard University Press, Cambridge, Massachusetts

Jolly A (1985) The evolution of primate behaviour. Macmillan, London

Langhorne MC, Secord PF (1955) Variations in marital needs with age, sex, marital status and regional location. J Soc Psychol 41:19–37

Masie-Taylor CGN, Boyce AJ (eds) (1988) Human mating patterns. Cambridge University Press, Cambridge

McGinn TAJ (1989) The taxation of Roman prostitutes. Helios 16:79–110

McGinnis PR (1977) Sexual behaviour in free living chimpanzees: current relationships. In: Hamburg DA, McCown ER (eds) The Great Apes. Benjamin/Cummings, Menlo Park, California, pp 429–439

Murphy F (1981) Catholic Perspectives on Population Issues II. Population Bulletin, Population Reference Bureau, Inc. 35(6)

Noonan JT (1965) Tokos and atokion: an examination of natural law reasoning against usury and against contraception. Natural Law Forum 10:215–235

Pomeroy SB (1975) Goddesses, whores, wives and slaves: women in classical antiquity. Schocken Books, New York

Quaife GR (1979) Wanton wenches and wayward wives: peasants and illicit sex in early seventeenth century England. Croom Helm, London

Rasa AE, Vogel C, Voland E (eds) (1989) The sociobiology of sexual and reproductive strategies. Chapman and Hall, New York

Ranke-Heinemann U (1990) Eunuchs for heaven. Andre Deutsch, London

Shepher J (1971) Mate selection among second generation kibbutz adolescents and adults. Arch Sex Behav 1:293–307

Short RV (1985) Species differences in reproductive mechanisms. In: Reproduction in mammals: 4. Reproductive fitness. Cambridge University Press, Cambridge, p. 24

Shields WM, Shields LM (1987) Forceable rape: an evolutionary perspective. Ethol Sociobol 4:115–136

Shostak M (1981) Nisa: the life and words of a !Kung woman. Harvard University Press, Cambridge, Massachusetts

Symonds D (1979) The evolution of human sexuality. Oxford University Press, Oxford

Thornhill R, Thornhill NW (1979) Human rape: the strengths of the evolutionary perspective. In: Crawford C, Smith M, Krebs D (eds) Sociobiology and psychology: ideas, issues and applications. Lawrence Erlbaum, Hillsdale, New Jersey

Trivers RL (1972) Parental investment and sexual selection. In: Campbell B (ed) Sexual selection and the descent of man: 1871–1971. Aldine, Chicago

Trivers R (1985) Social evolution. Benjamin/Cummings Publishing, Menlo Park, California

Udry JR, Eckland BK (1984) Benefits of being attractive: differential payoffs for men and women. Psychol Rep 54:47–56

van den Berghe PL (1987) Incest taboos and avoidance: some Africa applications. In: Crawford C, Smith M, Krebs D (eds) Sociobiology and psychology: ideas, issues and applications. Lawrence Erlbaum, Hillsdale, New Jersey

Voland E (1988) Differential infant and child mortality in evolutionary perspective: data from late 17th to 19th century. Ostriesland (Germany) In: Betzig L, Borgerhoff-Mulder M, Turke P (eds). Human reproductive behaviour: a Darwinian perspective. Cambridge University Press

CHAPTER 10

The Ethics of Sexual Restraint

Peter Byrne

This paper is based on the unargued premise that the spread of serious sexually transmitted diseases such as AIDS is promoted by promiscuous and casual sexual behaviour. The question it addresses is what ethical significance attaches to this alleged fact. The assumption is that the threat of sexually transmitted disease places a premium on having few sexual partners rather than many and on knowing enough about those sexual partners to be assured that they too are not promiscuous or casual in their sexual behaviour. But what kind of premium is this?

These questions are interesting to a moralist because of their connections with recent debates about whether there is any ethical significance in sexual behaviour at all. Many contemporary philosophical writers on ethics have contended that sexual behaviour generates of itself no moral norms or virtues. There are no such things as sexual vice and virtue. Some ordinary vices (such as cruelty) and virtues (such as promise-keeping) can be exemplified in sexual conduct. But their role is limited and little is to be learnt about them from their application in the sexual sphere. Sex is, by and large, a private matter concerned with the pursuit of pleasures. Morality has little to say about it, except in so far as sex gives occasion to apply some general rules of an unproblematic kind governing interaction between people. Rules forbidding cruelty to others, governing exchange of contracts and proscribing trespass on the person in the absence of consent all apply. But it is only because sexual encounters are interactions between persons that they occasion the application of such principles. There is nothing in the nature of sexual activity itself that generates a distinction between good and bad sex, and such general moral rules as apply to sexual behaviour allow little room for an ethics of sex, while sex, for its part, sheds little, if any, light on these rules. Their source and value is located elsewhere.

This view of the moral triviality of sex contradicts an age-old perception in the Western moral tradition that a large part of personal virtue and of the human good arises out of, or is displayed in, the direction and exercise of sexuality. This is why the recent dismissal of the moral significance of sex is interesting. Sexually transmitted disease (particularly the AIDS pandemic) has been used by supporters of the moral tradition to attempt to rebut the contemporary liberalisation and trivialisation of sexual ethics (compare Byrne 1989).

We have in the debates and disagreements described so far material for the moral discussion of sexuality and sexually transmitted disease. But it must be said at the outset that those responsible for the treatment and prevention of sexually transmitted disease may have grounds for thinking such philosophical issues unimportant for their work. One thing is sure, it may be said: effective treatment and education for the prevention of sexually transmitted disease has to be guided by a morally neutral attitude toward the varied behaviours which express human sexuality. If there is a moral message associated with education in the health aspects of sexual conduct this is bound to mean that such education loses its impact. If there is a "tone" of moralism or moral condemnation within the ethos of STD clinics this is likely to deprive them of clients. In practice, even if the moralism toward sex of the tradition can be vindicated, the health educator or clinician concerned with sexually transmitted disease has to adopt, for practical purposes, the liberalising, trivialising attitude toward sex of much recent moral philosophy.

No one could deny the force of the above point. Direct moralising about sex is likely to be counter-productive in the fight against sexually transmitted disease. But this does not mean that the debate about the possibility of a substantial sexual ethic is merely of academic interest. For if we took the view that such an ethic could be vindicated, it would be open to use to argue that *indirect* means of propagating its values were available and that these could have important implications in the cultivation of attitudes which resulted in less promiscuous and casual sexual behaviour. For example, a traditional sexual ethic gives grounds for the condemnation and censorship of pornographic and obscene publications. Acting on those grounds might in turn be connected with discouraging the attitudes to the human body and to sexual gratification encountered in a culture where promiscuous and casual sex finds support.

The liberalising and trivialising view of sex which opposes the idea that there are any valid norms proscribing casual and promiscuous sex rests upon the key notion that there can be no wrong in behaviour which does not cause tangible harm to others. Unless and until the defender of traditional sexual ethics can show that there are ideals for personal conduct which should bind all, regardless of whether conduct which runs counter to them threatens others, then casual and promiscuous sex remains a valid expression of a personal lifestyle. (This mode of arguing about sexual promiscuity should be distinguished from that which holds that promiscuity is ethically or aesthetically liberating. I shall not discuss the provision of a serious rationale for promiscuity provided by prophets of sexual liberation, who link it to some ideal of the good life or good community.)

Many defenders of the liberalising view I shall consider take as their inspiration the arguments of John Stewart Mill's *On Liberty*. In particular they would fasten on two statements: first that the only reason society has to restrict the conduct of an individual is that it causes tangible harm to others; second that each man is the best judge of what is in his own interest (Mill 1964: 72–3 and 133). It can be doubted whether Mill's statements are, in fact, the rejection of the idea that there is a best way of life for individuals that many take them for (see Cowling 1963: 25–6, 33). Yet out of Mill has grown a picture of the nature of morality which altogether excludes the possibility of their being a right way of ordering personal life, and with it, sexual relations and behaviour.

The common philosophical view which rules out any norms for the ordering of personal life can be summed up as follows:

    i. Individuals possess interests which are prior to their encounter and relationships with others

   ii. The pursuit of interests by individuals is always liable to generate conflict

  iii. The point of moral principles and social norms is to provide means of ordering, resolving and limiting these conflicts

  iv. The general point of morality is to establish persons as beings each with their own unique sets of interests and to maximise the ability of each to realise his set of interests, granted that the pursuit of individual sets of interests is always likely to cause conflict. (Adapted from Harrison 1989: 304).

This perspective has a number of important philosophical consequences. Morality turns out to have a role only in the region where the interests of two or more individuals touch. Morality is about conflict avoidance and co-operation for the sake of pursuing interest-satisfaction. The paradigm source of moral obligation becomes the bargain or contract. Self-respect (and allied notions, such as respect for persons) becomes a matter of respecting individuals as bargaining agents. Its conditions are those necessary for making bargains free, unforced, honest and the like. No sense can be made of the pursuit of individual interest being "wrong" if that pursuit in no way interferes with others' pursuit of their interests. No sense can be made of there being a human good: an ideally best form of life for any human being as such. The human good comprises only those basic goods which human beings require to function as interest-pursuing, bargain-making agents. It is vital in all this that "interests" be understood as meaning no more than "preferences". To admit the thought that some things might genuinely be in a person's best interests as a moral being, even though he has no desire for these things, is to unravel all the threads of this perspective. Then there would be more to morality than bargaining and conflict-avoidance to facilitate the pursuit of individual life-styles; then we would have a standpoint from which some freely made contracts could be judged nonetheless to be morally unacceptable; then the notion of respect for persons might include more than respect for those conditions which enabled human beings to exist as bargaining agents; then we would have an objective human good against which to measure the pursuits of any individual.

Consider what this ethic of preference-pursuit has to say about sexual restraint and sexually transmitted disease. It becomes imperative on this view to make facts about the transmission of sexual diseases widely available, for such knowledge bears on how some people want to pursue their sexual preferences. Such facts *may* act as an important constraint on some life-styles. But they will only do so if those concerned do not wish to accept the health risks involved. If they have no distaste for illness then any links between promiscuity and sexually transmitted disease lose their normative force. It is in this spirit, perhaps, that contemporary libertarians protest about public health measures to discourage smoking, excessive drinking and the like that go beyond the mere provision of information. Facts about the transmission of sexual disease affect the morality of sexual encounters mainly in so far as sexual partners are not honest with one another about their life-styles. Concealment of sexual practices such as promiscuity materially affects the freedom of the agreement two casual sexual partners make to exchange sexual favours and the use of their respective bodies.

But if they are open and honest with one another, then morality has nothing to say about whatever they agree upon.

Overall the liberalising, trivialising view of sex this moral perspective engenders leads to calls for what has been described as a "sexual democracy" (Weeks 1986: 120–1). It is important to note, again, that a particular notion of democracy is used here. It is not democracy understood as the means of achieving some objective good, as if, following eighteenth century democratic theorists, we believe human virtue can be realised by the many and not just the few and that the means to attaining this realisation is through the greatest possible spread of full citizenship and civil liberty. Democracy, on many a contemporary view, has no end in view apart from the maximising of preferences. It is because there is no objective personal good to be achieved that democracy becomes necessary: it is a device for maximising choice, mandated because there is no objective good to be attained through the exercise of choice. Adherents of older conceptions of democracy of course find this totally unacceptable, on the grounds that it makes the machinery of democracy an end in itself and not the means whereby good can be successfully attained and shared (compare Kristol, in Holbrook 1973: 192).

If we have the modern liberal's opinion of the nature and desirability of sexual and political democracy, then even the possibility of a sexually transmitted pandemic such as AIDS becomes of limited moral importance. For a liberal of this type can have no quarrel with a society freely choosing to lower the quality of its collective health (though even he may have some qualms about the implications for future generations in such a choice).

I have said that there are other understandings of social and political democracy than the contemporary liberal's. With those alternatives will go alternative understandings of respect for persons and allied notions. The nature of these alternatives can be explored through considering the issues of liberty and slavery. Thence we may return to the examination of objective sexual and personal ideals.

Mill considered the objection to his libertarian social philosophy that it could raise no objections to someone voluntarily selling himself into bondage (Mill 1964: 57–8). His cursory dismissal of this objection makes sense if we follow that interpretation of his liberalism which sees it as strongly committed to a positive norm of the best life for society and the individual, while contending that social and political liberty is the best means for this ideal to be promoted. A conception of liberty and morality as rooted in preference-satisfaction and the absence of any objective ideals for a good human life cannot, surely, object to someone freely bargaining himself into bondage, provided that this adversely affects no one else's interests. There can be no objection to the voluntary relinquishment of autonomy while the value of autonomy is seen as merely instrumental (it being the means whereby one is enabled to pursue one's preferences), and if a preference-set favours its abandonment. What is wrong in human slavery is that it is customarily the result of brute force or of bargains that are materially unfree. If we value respect for persons and the self-respect of each, we must respect the right of each to abandon his autonomy in a free bargain. For respect for persons here means nothing other than respect for each as a free bargaining agent.

The paradox in the above conclusion is that it is precisely the notion of respect for persons that old-fashioned liberals will appeal to as showing the inherent wrongness of human bondage. This shows their commitment to respect for persons is to a presumed objective human ideal. Slavery is a violation of what we owe to ourselves and others as creatures with a certain endowment which we must honour regardless of choice. *This* liberal must, then, do what defenders of objective sexual norms are challenged to do by their critics: find a wrongness in the conduct they condemn which is not that of harming others, coercing or deceiving them or otherwise breaking obligations freely entered into (compare Harris 1985: 190–1).

We can argue that what is violated in the relationship between master and slave is a form of respect for persons that is at the heart of moral relationship and which cannot be accounted for in terms of the libertarian philosophy of choice outlined above.

What is wrong with the relation between master and slave, regardless of whether it is entered into freely or not, is that after it is constituted the parties to it do not exist for each other as persons. The slave as mere chattel finds his wishes and interests of no intrinsic importance to the master. His actuality as a being with certain beliefs, desires and feelings is not regarded. Indeed, should his master begin to pay attention to it, then the relationship would be transformed from one of pure bondage. The master suffers a corresponding loss of personal actuality. That his slave pays attention to his beliefs, wishes and feelings is not a consequence of the slave having any interest in these for themselves, but simply arises out of the slave being forced by sheer power to have fear of them. So the master does not find his sense of his own interior life and needs confirmed in the recognition that the slave apparently gives these through his attention and obedience. The slave's recognition is simply that due to a force whose moods and behaviour must be reckoned with if pain is to be avoided. It is not qualitatively different in this respect from that which may be due to a powerful and threatening non-human object.

Neither master nor slave, then, find their reality as persons confirmed in their relationship. Such confirmation arises in normal relationships out of the mutual recognition of feelings, attention to and respect for the other's beliefs and desires. This is how human beings exist for each other as persons in relationship.

What is the harm in the voluntary slave's condition? It is not necessarily the tangible harm of libertarian philosophy. The master may keep the slave happy and in good condition for economic reasons. The slave may not be distressed. He may relish the fact that he no longer needs to display the mental and moral effort necessary to engage with others as one person among many. But we would judge that someone who was happy without the desire for self-respect has a moral psychology which can only be repudiated. Contentment with *this* lot is in itself a sign of moral corruption. The contented slave may be said no longer to exist as a person in the eyes of others, and therefore for himself (compare Dent 1988: 50). To live like this is to suffer great harm, because, we might say, we need to exist as persons for each other; but the harm and need in question can only be fully understood if we are allowed to bring in a notion of moral harm, one that is judged relative to a picture of the good life for a human being and the flourishing of the distinctive traits of the human. Those who would endorse my judgement would of course estimate that the general loss of this mode of self-respect will lead to forms of experienced unhappiness in the long run. But if we found someone who *could* endure being a person

who did not exist as such for others (having in the slave's case no more actuality
than that of a useful animal), that would for us be sign of a mind and
consciousness depraved, corrupted and pitiable.

My brief discussion of slavery is meant to introduce a defence of a traditional
ethic of sexual restraint in a number of ways. It indicates problems in a modern
conception of freedom. It introduces a notion of self-respect and right relation
with others that may be re-used in describing what is wrong with casual and
promiscuous sex. It fastens on the *psychology* of those who flout traditional
understandings of respect for self and person: this psychology being the object
of moral judgement and censure. It endeavours to establish the legitimacy of a
non-libertarian notion of harm.

On the view outlined here the harm that the traditionalist may see in
promiscuous sex is a function of a number of factors. Primarily it will consist
in a violation of a normatively valid mode of being-for-others and -for-self that
should inform any morally respectworthy relation between human beings. The
mode of relationship between casual sexual partners and the moral psychology
that supports that relationship is the primary object of judgement (compare
Green 1989: 530). In addition the traditionalist will want to point to tangible
harmful consequences that result from these modes of relationship and
attitudes. Sexually transmitted disease could be one such consequence, unwanted
pregnancies another. There is no reason why a range of distinctive factors should
not be part of a mutually supporting case for a common conclusion. One point
that I think difficult to resurrect in the traditionalist's case is the morality of
rules which once gave a detailed proscription of narrowly defined types of sexual
act. This type of sexual ethic is probably only viable given belief in a certain
form of natural law ethic which finds few champions even among moral
theologians today. Given a primary stress on the modes of relationship and
attitudes to self and others in a worthwhile defence of a non-libertarian sexual
ethic, the emphasis will be on a morality of virtues, rather than rules. This
approach is compatible, then, with an older fashioned liberal's distrust of a
detailed and socially enforced set of rules about precise categories of forbidden
sexual acts.

What is wrong with casual and promiscuous sex is that it is sex without love
and in the absence of any mutual regard and affection between partners. The
two fifths of homosexual males reported to have had 500 sexual partners in a
survey of the late 1970s (Armytage 1980: 167) must have attitudes so structured
as not to feel any attachment to their partners once the pleasures of sex were
over. Love and affection is an encumbrance to promiscuous modes of sexuality
because they beckon toward involvement in the life and feelings of the beloved
and thus against abandonment of him or her and against the move onto the
next partner. Sexual excitement in such relationships cannot be the outcome of
resonance with the feelings of the beloved. As has been pointed out by many
authors, the pleasures gained in normal, loving sexual encounters are in large
measure reciprocal and reflexive. One gains pleasure through the experience of
giving it. Pleasure exists through imagining and feeling how the other responds
to one's acts. Such pleasures can only exist for those able to conceive of their
partners as persons whose feelings and perceptions are worth attending and
responding to. Pleasure of this sort is destroyed by the thought on either side

that responses are faked or produced by rote. Despite its obviously sensual nature, we have here a genuinely inter-personal encounter that is morally structured (see Holbrook 1973: 9).

Sexual union in the non-casual relationship is a form of interaction between human beings in which the actuality of the partners as persons is affirmed. The closeness of the physical intimacy is matched by a uniquely intimate way in which one person exists for another as a being with feelings, beliefs and values. Sexual excitement in the casual, promiscuous union is not achieved through the sharing of personhood, but through mechanical contact, in which the other need not exist as person but only as flesh capable of providing friction for other flesh; or the excitement might be obtained through images of the other as a "conquest" whose capture feeds a sense of power and of one's own attractiveness. Either way the traditionalist in sexual morality will argue that such sex does not represent merely a lower kind, short of full inter-personal union, but still having a value as sex which some find satisfying. He will regard it as a perversion of sex, in the sense of something which reverses its proper nature, turning what is good into something which is harmful. In the same way, we might contend that freely contracted bondage is a perversion of autonomy, reversing the value of what is otherwise good. Perversion and reversal of value might be evident in two aspects of the moral psychology of the casual sexual agent.

First the recognition and confirmation of self and personhood is reversed. The casual sexual agent must not think that his partner's involvement with him betrays any interest or resonance with him as a person. The partners must actually *exclude* regard for the other from the terms of the relationship. The casual sexual agent must meet and tolerate others in the most intimate physical closeness with no thought that these others are respectworthy as full persons and with no thought that their involvement with *him* shows any interest they might have in him as a person. Thus the behaviour exemplifies a psychology in which others cannot be encountered as persons and which sets no store by oneself being confirmed as a person. In this connection it is interesting to note the physical and mental devices prostitutes habitually employ to separate the physical unions with their clients from any thoughts about their personal worth or private existence. They must build defences against the idea that their professional sexual activity devalues them as persons in the minds of themselves and others (Green 1989: 530).

Second the union of mind and body in loving sex is reversed. Far from the sexual excitement being a deeply felt set of bodily sensations resulting from encountering another as a full person and in whom one's own full self is engaged, excitement results from bodily contact in which one's full self must be disengaged and the full range of the other's existence as a self ignored. Such a mode of sex can be accused of involving a Cartesian dualism of the person put into action and the reverse therefore of a proper attitude towards one's own body and the bodies of others.

Central to the traditionalist's condemnation of casual and promiscuous sex is the thought that it reverses and cripples the capacity to love. Love's centrality in a morally healthy society can be supported by reference to the human need for self-confirmation and to the importance of the family and of parental love. "Moral health" is here judged by what is supposed necessary for society to maintain respect for persons and for its members as beings who can respect themselves.

I am paramountly confirmed as a person in the eyes of others when I become an object of someone else's love. Then my thoughts, feelings and projects are recognised and given value because I am the object of an intimacy which is exclusive (to some degree) and cherishing (Dent 1988: 115). Then I become of unconditional interest and worth to another, for it is characteristic of love that the beloved does not matter simply as another with whom one must co-operate to gain one's own ends. In love one takes the other's good as an end for oneself. One's range of interests becomes expanded to include those dictated by concern for the other. Self-confirmation is established as a basic human need because it is the foundation of that self-respect necessary to function as an autonomous being (this points to an anti-individualist foundation for freedom). Parental and family love is normally the means whereby this self-confirmation is given to us as children and without it, or some substitute for it, no one would be able to enter the adult world as a being with self-respect. It is through being an object of love as a child that I am initially established as a being of worth and capable of self-esteem. The giving of love to children and their reception of self-confirmation through it is particularly difficult, when viewed from the outside. For the younger a human being the more demands he makes upon others for care and attention and the less he is able to respond by returning reciprocal aid and esteem. The demand that love be unconditional and promote the other's well-being and self-esteem regardless of reciprocal benefit strikes deep in the case of the care of children (Green 1989: 529). Why should anyone wish to offer such love? In the loving family this question gets a straightforward answer. Since the child is the outcome and embodiment of the couple's love for one another it is established from the outset as an object of love. Loving the child is a natural extension of loving one another. If they love one another and regard each other as having unconditional worth they need no further motive to love their child. But this mutual love between parents is strongly based on and perfected by sexual desire. Therefore it is necessary for any society that wishes to see children brought up as objects of unconditional love to maintain the link between sexual desire and love. Attitudes and modes of behaviour which embody or promote a severance between sex and mutually regarding love are inimical to the conditions necessary for the establishment of people as beings needing and deserving of confirmation as persons. (Karen Green has summed up another version of this argument, with an acknowledged debt to Freud, in Green 1989: 529–30.)

The moral case against casual and promiscuous sexual behaviour, then, concentrates in the first instance on the attitudes and sentiments shown in it. Such behaviour embodies in itself attitudes toward others and toward one's own body which fall short, in significant ways, of respect for persons and of self-respect. Furthermore it will tend to weaken the connection between sex and love which society has an interest in maintaining in so far as it desires the proper establishment of children as moral beings. If, in addition, casual and promiscuous sex has deleterious consequences of a more tangible kind (such as in the spreading of serious sexually transmitted disease) this would be further reason for regarding it as wrong. There could be many layers in our adverse judgement on it. One obvious danger to be avoided, however, is drawing the conclusion that AIDS, or anything similar, triumphantly *proves* the moral case put forward on other grounds, as if it were established as "Nature's judgement" on the promiscuous

– a non-human confirmation of what moralists down the centuries had been urging. Only the crudest personification of the processes of disease could make sense of such reasoning. It should be resisted easily even by those of theistic persuasion. The god who is so closely involved in such "judgements of Nature" is theologically incredible.

Adverse judgement on casual and promiscuous sex will take us near to the terms of a traditional sexual ethic. It may well not be so heavily act- or rule-centred as in the past (for the reasons outlined above). However, it does not follow that if we wish to alter the behaviour of those most at risk from such conduct, we should plaster them with moral condemnations. Moralising, now and in the past, is and has been a poor modifier of behaviour. Lesser targets must be aimed at. Though it must be pointed out that one message underlying propaganda about condoms, safe sex and the like is of more general moral significance: this is the thought that sex has consequences.

If it is morally important to maintain a conviction of the importance of the connection between sex and love, there are things that society is mandated to do, in my opinion. The traditional family emerges as something of moral value. As such, there are things that society can do to foster and support it. (This need not be at the cost of condemning other forms of stable, loving relationship.) Pornography emerges as an evil out of the same arguments which establish loving sex as a good. The way in which the pornographic object is displayed typically embodies attitudes towards it which depersonalise it and are contrary to regarding it as a thing of esteem or worth. Feminists are right to regard pornography centred on females as degrading women. Here there may be grounds for social action. To maintain that society has an interest in fostering the connection between sex and love is in general to establish a *prima facie*, defeasible social concern with what is published on sex.

If we reason in favour of the promotion of one set of attitudes toward sexuality and are prepared to at least countenance socially enforced restrictions on material embodying contrary attitudes, then we will be forced to reject the contemporary liberal's conception of the proper sphere of moral and social norms. We shall be countenancing restrictions on the liberty of some to pursue their preferences in private and in free association with others where such pursuit does not tangibly interfere with the liberty of others to pursue their preferences. Contemporary liberals find this unintelligible because it is obviously contrary to the essence of morality as they define it.

It is no use entering into detailed debates about sexual ethics unless we are prepared to point to the general differences about the nature of morality that so frequently underlie them. The restrictive attitudes I have tried to articulate here make sense if one allows two thoughts. The first is that the good of being allowed to pursue a given preference may relate to the value of the object of that preference. There are some goods and evils independent of preference. The freedom to pursue certain evils may not be of sufficient value to be worth protecting. The second is the thought that what establishes the worth of an individual's liberty to pursue his preferences relates to things that can only be socially created and maintained. These include him being a creature possessed of self-worth and -esteem, one whose preferences and projects matter to him. Such factors make the exercise of autonomy worthwhile. But to ground the establishment of worthwhile autonomy objective restraints will have to be placed on pursuit of preferences through the promotion of some forms of human relationship over others. It will require a society committed to some non-procedural goods.

We return to the contemporary philosophical consensus on the nature of moral and social norms I summarised from Harrison (see above). At the heart of that consensus is the thought that what is substantively good is created by human preferences alone. Moral and social norms are concerned with procedural rules for maximising the choice of individually established goods, given conditions which make conflicts of goods inevitable. There is no way in which human sexuality can be seen as an important area of ethical reflection if this conception of morality is correct. Contrariwise, if we do consider sexuality to be of profound moral significance, we have every reason to question this philosophical consensus on the nature of morality. Questioning will lead to different, older conceptions of the basis and value of liberty.

References

Armytage W (1980) Changing incidence and patterns of sexually transmitted disease. In: Armytage W, Chester R, Peel J (eds) Changing patterns in sexual behaviour. Academic Press, London, pp. 159–170

Byrne P (1989) AIDS: the moral, social and legal issues. In: Byrne P (ed) Health, rights and resources. King's Fund/Oxford University Press, London, pp 11–34

Cowling M (1963) Mill and liberalism. Cambridge University Press, Cambridge

Dent NJH (1988) Rousseau. Blackwell, Oxford

Green K (1989) Prostitution, exploitation and taboo. *Philosophy* 64: no 250, 525–534

Harris J (1985) The value of life. Routledge, London

Harrison B (1989) Morality and interest. *Philosophy* 64: no 249, 303–322

Holbrook D (1973) The case against pornography. Library Press, La Salle, Illinois

Kristol I (1973) Is this what we wanted. In: Holbrook D (ed) *The case against pornography*. Library Press, La Salle, Illinois, pp. 187–194

Mill JS (1964) On liberty. Dent, London

Weeks J (1986) Sexuality. Horwood/Tavistock, London

CHAPTER 11

Clinical Research and the Consumer

Leonie Somorjay

In the introduction to a paper prepared for the February 1988 meeting of the WHO European Advisory committee for Health Research, the sociologist Margaret Stacey wrote:

> All areas associated with reproduction are of profound importance for individuals and for society at large; they are not, and cannot be, conceived as merely clinical matters. Reproductive techniques affect the health of individuals beyond the immediate event of birth and also influence, as well as reflect, the basic values of societies. Reproduction is about the future of the society; the way it is handled will inevitably affect that future biologically and socially.

Her paper was timely; it raised a number of vital issues at a time when legislation about embryo research was under discussion, and in the UK the Department of Health was beginning to consider the ethics of gene therapy. She was observing a society in which technical "progress" in almost everything to do with pregnancy and childbirth had far outstripped the necessary ethical debate, other than in certain rarified quarters (like research ethics committees), and certainly as far as the general public was concerned. Additionally, society is grappling with changes in the whole context for childbirth, which have been brought about by contraception, AIDS, rising divorce rates, the decline of religious belief and the proliferation of "alternative" family structures. Finally, a life event which throughout history has been regarded as women's domain, and inappropriate for men, has over the last 40 years become dominated by them (Stacey 1988).

In the last few years there has been some recognition of the need to consult with "consumers", those who are affected by the decisions reached by medical researchers, lawyers, philosphers, theologians and ethicists; contributions from some of them make up most of this volume. There is now more, and better, patient information and ethics committees have more authority and include more lay representatives.

The National Childbirth Trust (NCT) has little to do directly with infertility, assisted conception or genetic research, but its antenatal teachers have in their classes, from time to time, women or couples whose pregnancies have triggered off unresolved problems associated with a previous abortion, or who have had assisted conceptions. It is important, then, for the teachers to have sufficient understanding of the particular stresses associated with fertility problems and their treatment to be able to offer appropriate support.

In recent years, the NCT has had a research involvement with three major studies – the randomised controlled trial comparing chorion villus sampling (CVS) and amniocentesis, the CLASP (or aspirin) trials and the MAIN trial, which is a study comparing different treatments for inverted or non-protractile nipples. The Trust has helped to write patient information material for the first two, and is directly involved in the MAIN trial, one of the two arms of which is organised through the NCT network. In addition, the Trust has conducted its own in-house studies on a variety of topics: although these have not been scientific trials, they have their own validity, serve as consciousness raisers and goad others into action.

It is important to identify the issues which are important to the National Childbirth Trust as consumers of clinical research. Three questions must be addressed:

1. General issues: What are the important issues for consumers of clinical research?
2. Specific issues: What are the specific issues for infertility patients?
3. Wider issues: What are the issues for society as a whole?

General Issues

The general issues for consumers of clinical research are:
1. Costs and benefits – safety, efficiency, resources, alternatives
2. Information, counselling, follow-up
3. Informed consent
4. Methodology
5. Accountability – how is the research regulated, is it supported by a research ethics committee, how is it funded, how are the results disseminated?

Specific Issues

The general issues can be discussed specifically in relation to the infertile patient and his or her partner and family.

In a society where the norm is to have children, infertility is always painful, usually traumatic and often accompanied by feelings of guilt and worthlessness. The infertile are very vulnerable, the unwilling victims of confused ideas and inconsistent practice. Jalna Hanmer (1991) suggests that some, at least, of this confusion arises from an anomaly inherent in any consideration of the new reproductive technologies, that is, that such technologies, if successful, claim to restore their "natural" rights to the infertile while being themselves "unnatural". Additionally, such technologies require the intervention of third parties, constituting an invasion of privacy which to some is extremely distressing. The process of reproduction is necessarily separated from the act of intercourse and it should not seem surprising that this is profoundly disturbing to some sections of the population. People do not normally feel neutral on this subject – they are either firmly in favour of or against research into problems of infertility and equally firmly for or against treatment for themselves.

Costs and Benefits

There are issues of safety and efficacy which are relevant to the physical and mental health of infertility patients and, importantly, their partners and families. However, any assessment of costs and benefits must include other considerations – premature referral, status and self-image, loss of autonomy, costs, treatment approach and options.

Some couples are being referred to infertility clinics far too early – after as little as six months of trying to conceive.

As infertility services become increasingly available, infertility is no longer regarded inevitably as "just one of those things" or, worse, a sort of Divine punishment. Increasingly, infertility is regarded as treatable, with a reasonable expectation of a satisfactory outcome. There is plenty of evidence that couples experiencing difficulty in conceiving feel under pressure to "do something about it", and may go on a fertility programme to avoid coming to terms with their infertility or to silence inquisitive families and friends. Jalna Hanmer (1991) considers that in some cases "going on the programme" confers a status which, while not a substitute for the status of parenthood, is preferable to that assigned to the infertile. She and others, including some of the infertile themselves, question whether treatment is always the right option. *Issue*, the journal of the National Association for the Childless, recently (summer 1990) featured two accounts of alternative coping strategies; undoubtedly, some people find happiness and fulfilment in life without children.

The loss of control over their own bodies experienced by women who conceive after fertility treatment can be very disconcerting to them. While there are good reasons for closely monitoring their pregnancies and deliveries, the threat to their own autonomy is an issue for them, as it is for all childbearing women and those involved in childbirth education.

Those who are able to conceive without help are not screened for their suitability as parents, but clients for a fertility programme are. It must be devastating to be told that one is "unsuitable" medically or socially, particularly when all around are more "unsuitable" natural parents. The language used is also emotive – "poor sperm", "hostile mucus". Although counselling services are improving, more are needed to help those who may suffer shattered self-images, see themselves as unacceptable, undesirable, even unloveable.

Figures for numbers of babies born as a result of assisted conception are available, but they are "broad brush" figures. They conceal two findings: apparently some centres have never had a live birth and up to 50% of the babies are born with temporary or permanent health problems – which may well be partly a function of the number of twin or higher order births (Botting et al. 1990), although there are other factors. At the very least, there is a large commitment in terms of hospital resources (caesarian operations, intensive care cots and so on) compared to those required for the population as a whole.

The costs of infertility programmes must be borne in mind, for the drugs for one stimulated treatment cycle cost about £500. Commercial and academic research interests are involved, and some companies which assist IVF in some parts of the world are promoting birth control in others, often with the same products.

Much of the work associated with infertility is being done by innovative techniques at the frontiers of technology, but the same effort should be applied to the prevention of infertility. Comparatively few resources are devoted to applying existing knowledge about pre-conception care, preventing and treating low-grade infections, and ameliorating environmental factors, all of which are known to be causes of some infertility.

Infertile couples are to a large extent at the mercy of fashion and finance, as indeed are childbearing couples. Treatment options vary from centre to centre at present, though all patients should in the future receive information about the full range of alternatives, if the guidelines in the HFEA's draft Code of Practice (1991) are adopted.

Information, Counselling and Follow-up

Richard Lilford (1990) has said that "good ethics starts with good factual information". Although some people might put values as the starting point, all would agree that good information is important, even vital, in this complex and sensitive area. The draft Code of Practice is encouraging in this regard, detailing the kind of information which ought to be given to all patients.

The need for "proper counselling" was acknowledged in the UK Human Fertility and Embryology Act (1990), and the draft Code of Practice identifies three types of counselling: implications counselling, support counselling and therapeutic counselling. The National Childbirth Trust welcomes the extent to which the recommendations of the King's Fund Centre Counselling Committee have been adopted and supports the proposed establishment of independent, non-directive counselling services, by suitably qualified persons in an unhurried manner in conditions of comfort and privacy. The NCT further suggests that there should be two counsellors available, one a woman.

Informed Consent

Everyone has the right to give or withhold consent. Consent to research should always be obtained, and the draft Code of Practice states that no licensed treatment should be given without written consent, other than in exceptional circumstances where treatment is life-saving and an unconscious patient cannot indicate her wishes. Normally, consent should follow the provision of written information and the opportunity for discussion and counselling, with time for reflection ideally away from the clinical environment. In practice, however, many factors make truly informed consent difficult to achieve: a patient may not be offered a full range of options, there may be restraints on resources, there may not be enough time, doctors may judge a patient or her family to be unable to understand or cope with certain information, patients may feel pressured by fear or guilt into making decisions they would not otherwise have made. Research indicates that "the majority of people are not able to make highly rational decisions" but Lilford still concludes, rightly, that "these frequently irrational individual decisions are much better than the often equally irrational decisions which may be made on behalf of individuals". Gorowitz (1990) goes further: "Informed consent is valuable morally and therapeutically, is legally necessary, is challenging and difficult to achieve and it can never, in any situation of any complexity, be satisfactorily achieved in a perfunctory or bureaucratic manner".

Methodology

Consumers must be sure that studies are well designed and the protocols governing them take some account of their views. Only in this way will research generate sound evidence on which to base practice, whilst also inspiring the confidence and cooperation of participants and patients alike. Guidelines for good practice in this area include those recently prepared by the Standing Joint Committee of the British Paediatric Association and the Royal College of Obstetricians and Gynaecologists (1991).

Accountability

There are a number of important issues in connection with accountability, three of which are of particular concern to the consumer: independence, representation on research ethics committees and the implementation of the results of research.

Consumers would like to be sure that researchers are able to operate independently of their funders. The general public is not reassured by discovering, for instance, that research designed to test whether or not there is an association between giving vitamin supplements to children and their IQs is funded by the suppliers of the supplements.

Consumers would like better representation on ethics committees. The guidelines on the structure and function of ethics committees in the 1990 report of the Interim Licensing Authority (ILA) in the UK go some way to ensure this, but two lay members are too few, especially if one is there primarily to contribute legal expertise. It is, perhaps, surprising that the guidelines discourage the inclusion of a representative of a "special interest group": it may be thought very valuable to have a representative of an infertility organisation or support group.

Consumers are interested in the results of research and how these results are put into practice. They also need to be sure that research which, however inconveniently, has yielded the "wrong" results is also published. In the UK, Iain Chalmers and the National Perinatal Epidemiological Unit have highlighted the importance of identifying this particularly insidious form of bias (Chalmers 1989).

Wider Issues

Both the development of new reproductive technologies and the prospect, however remote, of gene therapy raise a number of moral questions which have many dimensions – spiritual, social, economic, environmental, political and others. Whether advances in reproductive technology are contemplated with ease or unease depends on the individual's moral, and maybe spiritual, perspective. It also depends on whether the person's horizons extend beyond the boundaries of the developed world: a Sudanese farmer or a Kurdish refugee would have a vastly different set of priorities from an urban Briton, for instance.

It is particularly important to consider:

1. The structure and nature of populations, and the concept of normality
2. Changes in emphasis in medicine and their implications for research allocation
3. The lack of public debate about these issues

Infertility treatment, and to a much greater extent genetic manipulation, have the potential to alter the structure and nature of populations in profound ways. If surrogacy, in its modern form with the necessary involvement of third parties, or "virgin birth" became widely practised new kinship norms would be established.

Social values change rapidly in response to medical innovations. Abortion was illegal in the UK 20 years ago: now it is widely viewed as an acceptable, even sometimes morally desirable, option. Parents are under increasing pressure to agree to screening for fetal abnormality and to an abortion if the fetus is found to be defective. Compassion and care for the weaker, disabled members of society is giving way to the expectation that all babies should be born perfect, and less tolerance of deviations from the norm. If genetic manipulation becomes acceptable, one wonders how long it will be before the option to do nothing, to let nature take its course, is lost.

Technology seems to be altering morality. At the first PERM conference, Pamela Sims (Sims and Cameron 1989) perceived a shift in emphasis in medicine, from the Hippocratic injunctions to "heal" and "do no harm" to a fundamentally humanist ideal based on quality of life and the relief of suffering. The former emphasises the sanctity of life, the latter "respect for life". Now, the draft Code of Practice takes as its starting point "respect for", not "sanctity of" life; indeed, it could do no other.

Technology and rarified research may bring only tiny benefits, at great expense, to very small numbers of people. They divert attention from unglamorous low technology and social measures aimed at prevention, simple cures, "coming-to-terms-with" strategies and support. The National Childbirth Trust is neither "pro-life" nor the opposite. It has a wide agenda and ethical issues are a prime interest of only some members; through them and concerned members of other similar organisations, the lay public can and should play a part in the debate to determine who decides who is an "acceptable" human being, and on what basis. It is essential to widen discussion of the issues surrounding ethics in reproductive medicine from its present narrow confines into the public arena.

References

Botting B, Macfarlane A, Price F (1990) Three, four and more: a study of triplet and higher order births. HMSO, London

Chalmers I (1989) Evaluating the effects of care during pregnancy and childbirth. In: Chalmers I, Enkin M, Keirse MJNC (eds) Effective care in pregnancy and childbirth. Oxford University Press, Oxford, pp 3–38

Gorowitz S (1990) Informed consent. In: Bromham D, Dalton M, Jackson J (eds) Philosophical ethics in reproductive medicine. Manchester University Press, Manchester and New York, pp 228–235

Hanmer J (1991) The wider implications of new reproductive technologies. Royal Society of Medicine Forum on Maternity and the Newborn, February 1991

Human Fertilization and Embryology Authority (1991) Code of practice: consultation document. Human Fertilization and Embryology Authority, London

Interim Licensing Authority for Human In Vitro Fertilization and Embryology (1990) Fifth report. ILA, London

Lilford R (1990) What is informed consent? In: Bromham D, Dalton M, Jackson J (eds) Philosophical ethics in reproductive medicine. Manchester University Press, Manchester and New York

Sims P, Cameron N (1989) New medicine for old – the demise of the Hippocratic tradition. In: Bromham D, Forsythe E, Dalton M (eds) Ethical problems in reproductive medicine. National Association of Family Planning Doctors, London, pp 34–35

Stacey M (1988) The manipulation of the birth process: research implications. Meeting of the WHO European Advisory Committee for Health Research, February 1988

Standing Joint Committee of the British Paediatric Association and the Royal College of Obstetricians and Gynaecologists (1991) A checklist of questions to ask when evaluating proposed research during pregnancy and following birth.

CHAPTER 12

Is It Ethical To Be Efficient?

J. Hutton and A.K. Maynard

It has frequently been contended that economic considerations have no place in decisions about the medical treatment of patients. If doctors are to recommend the most appropriate course of action for the patient being treated the relative cost of different therapeutic regimens should not influence the choice. For those holding this view any attempt by the doctor to consider the efficiency of treatment would contravene the ethics which should govern the doctor–patient relationship. Some of those adhering to this principle of clinical freedom are prepared to allow some place for the consideration of efficiency in the use of health care resources, but see this as the responsibility of managers not doctors. This separates resource allocation decisions from clinical decisions in a very artificial way, given that one of the major resources used by the health care system is the time of clinicians.

The difficulty in justifying clinical freedom from constraint, when all health care systems do not have access to unlimited resources, has led to a reformulation of the relationship between ethics and efficiency by health economists, for example Williams (1988, 1990). The revised version goes so far as to suggest that it may be unethical not to be efficient, and its supporters can be found amongst clinicians as well as economists (Hoffenberg 1987). Where resources are limited, what is given to one patient affects what can be given to others, and a social dimension must be introduced to consideration of ethics.

More recent attempts to set out ethical principles for the practice of medicine have included the traditional elements such as "to do no harm", "to preserve life", and "to alleviate suffering" (however contradictory these may prove in some circumstances). They have also attempted to deal with the question of the interdependence of decisions about different patients. For example, Ruark et al. (1988) include "to deal justly with patients" as an additional ethical requirement. If this is added to the doctor's responsibilities he or she will be unable to devote unlimited resources to the treatment of one patient, regardless of the ultimate clinical effectiveness, without considering how much benefit other patients might have gained from the resources.

An understanding of the issue depends on clear definition of the terms and a recognition that efficiency is also a value-laden concept. Consequently the next section will set out what the authors understand by the term efficiency. The following sections develop the concept of efficiency most appropriate to a publicly funded health care system such as the UK National Health Service

(NHS) and illustrate some of the techniques used by economists to measure efficiency in health service provision. The final section reviews the economic issues which arise in reproductive medicine and the ethical problems likely to be encountered in attempting to measure efficiency in such services.

Efficiency in Health Care

The term efficiency, implying lack of waste in general usage, has a more specific meaning in economics, built up from a multi-faceted analysis of optimum resource utilisation. For the optimum (or socially efficient) use of resources to occur, three conditions must hold:

1. In whatever use they are put, maximum output must be achieved from physical inputs to a productive process
2. The goods and services which are produced must be produced using the least cost combination of resources
3. The goods and services produced must be those most desired by society and must be produced in the desired quantities.

The fulfilment of those three conditions of technical efficiency, cost-effectiveness and overall social efficiency is discussed in more detail in the health context in Culyer (1989). Micro-economics has a well-developed theoretical framework which demonstrates the ability of a competitive economic system to achieve overall social efficiency. If conditions of perfect competition do not exist then the optimal position for society may differ from that which the competitive model would predict. For example, if the production of goods and services exhibits economies of scale from co-ordination, then competition may not achieve the least cost level of production. Similarly, if the production and consumption of goods and services have influences beyond the immediate parties in a transaction, so-called external effects, then satisfactory private transactions may be unsatisfactory from a social standpoint. These arguments are set out in all intermediate micro-economics texts, see for example Ng (1979).

The fact that health care is likely to exhibit the above characteristics was recognised early in the development of health economics as a separate sub-discipline (Culyer 1971). There is a further difficulty in the use of the competitive model in health care which involves ethics as well as efficiency. Demand and the ability to pay for goods and services is dependent on the distribution of income. Only if the current distribution of income is considered socially optimal can the allocation of health care on the basis of ability-to-pay be acceptable. It has been the desire to achieve equal access for all patients with a given need for care, regardless of financial or social circumstances, as much as any perception of increased efficiency from co-ordinated services, which has led to the development of state-funded and social-insurance-based systems of health care provision.

A final problem in basing analysis of health care on conventional welfare economics is the ability of individuals to make informed and rational decisions, when they are usually reliant on the expert advice of health professionals as to the best course of action. The implications of this are explored by Williams

(1990) and the importance of defining the concept of efficiency being used is emphasised by Brazier et al. (1990). If it is accepted that individuals trying to act in their own self-interest may not have the knowledge to demand appropriate health care, then willingness-to-pay in a market context will not be a correct indicator of the benefits of health care. If, on the other hand it is accepted that for each patient there are potential gains from treatment which can be directly measured (independently of costs and charges), then the achievement of maximum health benefits from given resources can be used as an indicator of efficiency. The key features of the two approaches are summarised in Table 12.1.

Efficiency in the NHS

In a system of publicly-funded health care provision, with virtually no charges at the point of use of services, an objective indicator of benefit is necessary to compare the relative merits of treating different illnesses and patient groups. In the face of politically imposed budget constraints it is impossible to provide treatment for all those who might obtain some positive benefit. Priorities are determined by a mixture of professional judgement by those providing care, and explicit political decisions implemented through the health service management structure. For various reasons this may fail to produce a socially desirable outcome (see Table 12.2).

In an attempt to correct for some of these problems, the current changes being introduced by the UK government are an amalgam of the last three items of column one in Table 12.1, and the first two items of column two (Secretaries of State 1989). It is not proposed to debate the merits of these changes here; a detailed review can be found in Culyer et al. (1990). As far as this discussion is concerned the changes do not alter the basis on which the efficiency of NHS services should be judged i.e. the quantity of health benefits produced per unit of resources used.

Table 12.1. Ideology and efficiency in health care

	Competitive System	Planned System
Individual choice	Individuals are the best judges of their own interests	Individuals often have insufficient knowledge to judge their own best interests
Social priorities	Willingness-to-pay should determine which services are provided to whom	Priorities should be determined by social judgements about need
Supplier motivation	Financial gain should motivate suppliers of services	Suppliers should be motivated by professional ethics and dedication to public service
Cost control	Competition will regulate prices	Central review will control costs
Quality control	Consumer demand will regulate quality of services	Professional standards will ensure quality of services

Table 12.2. Efficiency problems in a planned health care system

---

Freedom from direct financial contribution may lead patients to seek inappropriate treatment

Priorities may be determined by professional satisfaction rather than social need

Providers may not see cost-effectiveness as a priority

Managers may lack the necessary information to identify cost-effective uses of resources

Attention is focused on more easily measured aspects of health status, e.g., mortality rates

---

If an index of health benefits can be derived, which is sufficiently general to allow comparison of the outcomes of a whole range of treatments, then it can be used at three different levels in assessing efficiency. For any method of treatment it could be used to determine whether patients were getting maximum benefit from the use of committed resources, e.g. doctors' time, medical equipment and drugs, or whether some re-organisation of the use of those resources could increase benefit. The index could also be used to decide which of a range of possible treatments for a particular patient group would produce maximum benefit. Ultimately, such an index could be used to determine whether the maximum benefit was being obtained from the overall health care budget, or whether changes in the patient groups or illnesses treated would lead to increased total benefit.

Many different indices of health benefit have been used in economic evaluations, see for example Torrance (1986), but in seeking a general index of benefit with the widest possible use there is general agreement on the appropriateness of the concept of the quality-adjusted-life-year (QALY). The traditional measure of outcome most used in clinical trials has been the survival rate. Whilst prolongation of life is an important element of benefit from health care it is not the only element which patients take into account. Many medical interventions do not have any impact on length of life, but may have a major impact on quality of life through, for example, relief of pain or increase in mobility. A general indicator must be able to compare the benefits of treatments offering different combinations of improvement to both the length and health-related quality of life. The "health-related" qualification is important for, just as length of life is influenced by many factors other than health care, so overall quality of life depends on many things, of which health might be considered amongst the more important. In effect, using a scale from zero (dead) to one (good health) all health states are given a relative weight which is used to compare the value of survival with different degrees of physical or social disability.

Measurement of Health-Related Quality of Life

The construction of an index of health-related quality of life, with which to convert survival rates into measures of quality-adjusted-life-years gained, involves several stages of observation and analysis as shown in Table 12.3. Stages 1 and 2 are dependent on the purpose of the study and the generality required in interpreting the results. The dimensions and categories can be very specific to a particular illness or much broader for use with all types of patient. Stage 3 can be carried out by an observer, but it is preferable for the patient's own opinion to dominate the categorisation. Self-assessment questionnaires completed by patients are a common method of achieving this. An algorithm can be used to link patient response to specific questions to the dimensions of the index. Obtaining the relative weights for health states is a crucial part of the process and several methods have been used. Magnitude estimation, time-trade-off and standard gamble approaches all have their drawbacks (Torrance 1986). For decisions in a social context a fundamental issue is whose value judgements should influence the weighting? Interested groups include patients and their relatives, doctors, health service managers, politicians, the general public as potential patients, and the general public as taxpayers.

Much of the work at the University of York in developing QALY measures in the UK context has been based on a set of health-related quality of life dimensions and categories (reflecting the impact of ill-health on social functioning) first put forward by Rosser and Watts (1972) (see Table 12.4). Using the magnitude estimation approach, a set of relative weights was later derived from a sample of 70 patients, health care workers and members of the general public (Kind et al. 1982). The stages of the calculation of this index are described in more detail in Gudex and Kind (1988). The relative weights, shown in Table 12.5, although based on a relatively small, selected sample of respondents, were for many years the only available source for the derivation of quality-adjusted life years in the UK. Other measures existed, but were either disease-specific rather than general, or had a profile format which did not allow the calculation

Table 12.3. Construction of an index of health-related quality of life and its use in economic analysis

---

1. Define the important *dimensions* of health-related quality of life

2. Define methods of measuring or *categorising* each of the dimensions

3. Design a method of *classifying* patients within these categories

4. Devise a set of relative *weights* for the categories to allow the calculation of a quantitative measure of the benefit of moving from one category to another
   Having obtained the relative weights for the health states, defined on combinations of categories from each dimension, it is possible to proceed to calculation of QALYs gained or lost

5. Calculate the *expected survival period* for patients *with and without* the health care intervention under analysis

6. Estimate the *health-related quality of life* associated with *each year* of survival

7. Apply the appropriate quality *weights to each year* of survival

8. *Subtract* the total QALYs for a typical patient without treatment from the total QALYs for a patient with treatment

9. Estimate the *costs* of the different forms of treatment being compared (including "do-nothing option")

10. Discount to produce a *net present value of costs*

11. Discount benefits to produce a *net present value of QALYs* gained

12. Calculate *cost per QALY gained* for each treatment

Table 12.4. Rosser's classification of illness states

Disability		Distress	
I	No disability	A.	No distress
II	Slight social disability	B.	Mild
III	Severe social disability and/or slight impairment of performance at work Able to do all housework except very heavy tasks	C.	Moderate
		D.	Severe
IV	Choice of work or performance at work very severely limited Housewives and old people able to do light housework only but able to go out shopping		
V	Unable to undertake any paid employment Unable to continue any education Old people confined to home except for escorted outings and short walks and unable to do shopping Housewives able only to perform a few simple tasks		
VI	Confined to chair or to wheelchair or able to move around in the house only with support from an assistant		
VII	Confined to bed		
VIII	Unconscious		

Source: Rosser and Watts (1972).

Table 12.5. Transformed valuations for 29 health states

Disability	A	B	C	D
I	1.000	0.995	0.990	0.967
II	0.990	0.986	0.973	0.932
III	0.980	0.972	0.956	0.912
IV	0.964	0.956	0.942	0.870
V	0.946	0.935	0.900	0.700
VI	0.875	0.845	0.680	0.000
VII	0.677	0.564	0.000	−1.486
VIII	−1.028	–	–	–

Fixed points: healthy = 1; dead = 0

See: Kind et al. (1982).

of a single index. Recent research has attempted to re-estimate the weights for the Rosser health state using different population samples, and collaborative work with other European centres has produced a new approach (The Euroqol Team 1990) which is being tested in several countries.

The completion of the QALY calculation using the weights (Table 12.3, Stages 5–8) requires information on the prognosis of patients, with and without treatment, and on the initial health state. Evidence from clinical trials is required for the calculation of expected survival periods. Quality of life measured directly from samples of patients is desirable but often this is not possible and expert clinical opinion has to be used (Williams 1985). To use QALYs in economic evaluations requires their combination with cost data to produce cost-effectiveness measures of the cost per QALY form. For detailed discussion of this part of the process (Table 12.3, Stages 9–12) see Williams (1985) and Gudex and Kind (1988). Discounting is used, as in all applications of economic appraisal, to allow for social preferences for benefits sooner rather than later and for costs to be postponed as long as possible. Some examples of the results of this process are shown in Table 12.6. Although the cost per QALY for the obstetric intervention is higher than the others this does not mean that it is not worthwhile (in fact much higher figures have been calculated for other treatments). Even after the calculation of the relative cost of achieving benefits by different means, there is still need for social judgement on how much it is worth spending to gain a QALY; or whether there are other important elements in the decision not included in the QALY calculation; and particularly on issues of equity between patient groups.

Economic Issues in Reproductive Medicine

The range of interventions possible in the field of reproductive medicine raises many problems in the application of economics, and it is not surprising that those studies carried out have concentrated on cost rather than benefit measurement. Several attempts have been made to estimate the resource savings which might result from prenatal screening for foetal abnormalities, for example, Henderson (1982). In the remainder of this paper the issues will be discussed in the context of in vitro fertilisation (IVF), which has not previously been given detailed attention by economists.

Page (1989) has produced estimates of the cost of providing an IVF service and used these to calculate various cost-effectiveness ratios. Defining success as the achievement of a maternity (i.e., a surviving baby) the cost per success was found to be £11 000. While this figure could be used in comparison with similar estimates for other methods of treating infertility, it is only a beginning in comparing the benefits of IVF with other clinical services. The estimation of comparing utility-based benefit measures, such as QALYs is never easy, but IVF poses particular problems in this area, which have implications not just in IVF but for the whole process of benefit measurement in health care.

Table 12.6. Costs and benefits of selected procedures: cost per QALY gained (£1983)

Pacemaker implantation	700
Hip replacement	750
Heart transplantation	5000
Hospital haemodialysis	14000
Neo-natal intensive care (500–999 g)	21000

Sources: Williams (1985); Boyle et al. (1983).

It is customary in benefit measurement to concentrate on the "patient", although it is often recognised that significant benefits may also accrue to others, such as the patient's family, as a result of successful treatment. In IVF the concept of "patient" is less easily applied as infertility is a problem for a couple, neither of whom may be ill in the conventionally accepted sense. The loss of quality of life resulting from infertility is most likely to lie in the distress dimension of Table 12.4, and is likely to apply to both partners, although the impact on personal relationships may affect social functioning in other ways. In terms of length of life no benefit is expected, in fact by attempting a pregnancy the woman is accepting a risk of reduced length of life.

The process of measurement of health-related quality of life would again raise the question of whether general measures are sufficiently sensitive to detect real improvements, or whether generality of comparison should be sacrificed in order to obtain some detailed measures of specific benefits. The immediate objective of any study should determine this, but if the ultimate aim is to demonstrate the benefit of IVF in relation to general NHS service provision in other clinical fields then comparison at the general level is necessary. The timing of assessment of quality of life is of great importance. In the case of IVF key points would be before IVF was recommended; after each IVF cycle; during pregnancy; and after the birth. It should be borne in mind that, during pregnancy and after the birth, short-term deteriorations in quality of life might be observed from the impact of parenthood on a couple's whole lifestyle, if current measurement techniques are used. This might give an inappropriate indication that quality of life for previously infertile couples was reduced by IVF. Equivalent measurements of quality of life for those undergoing IVF unsuccessfully would also be required at similar time intervals from the commencement of the treatment. These could be used as controls to assess the marginal impact of success, but would also be of interest in showing whether any benefits, in terms of reduced distress, resulted from the increased understanding of their situation gained by couples undergoing IVF unsuccessfully.

The problem of identifying the fundamental benefit of IVF using currently available methods requires further research and testing of the various indices in the context of clinical trials. One possible method of controlling for the short-term impact of parenthood could be to measure quality of life in a sample of couples, without particular clinical problems, who conceived without the need for IVF. Using data from this group, before and after the birth, together with data from the successful and unsuccessful IVF groups might be more informative.

Another issue frequently raised in the context of reproductive medicine is whether the utility to the child should enter into the calculation. The conventional economic view is that it is the utility of those making a decision which should be considered, and also the effect of that decision on anyone else who is a member of society at the time the decision is made. The impact of the decision on future generations is only taken on board indirectly, through any altruistic feelings of the current generation which might lead them to sacrifice current benefits for the general good of society in the future. Self-assessment of one's own utility is at the core of economic theory, and ex ante prediction of the impact of decisions on the as yet unborn does not fit easily into this framework. There is, however, an ethical requirement to consider the circumstances in which a child might be brought up, when offering treatment for infertility to particular couples. This cannot be incorporated in the efficiency calculations which relate more to the question of whether a service should be provided in the aggregate.

Conclusions

In outlining the principles of economic evaluation in health care an attempt has been made to show that they can be applied in reproductive medicine. The particular problems which arise are related as much to the difficulties of measurement in this clinical area, as to any extra ethical problems. However, in the UK context the overall ethical question of public or private provision of services must be addressed. If we regard ability-to-pay as the appropriate indicator of the real value of health care, then those who feel sufficiently strongly that they wish to have IVF will find the money to use private services. If we regard infertility treatment as a socially worthwhile service, access to which should be equal, regardless of income, then a case for provision in the NHS must be made. To assess the relative priority to be given to such services when allocating constrained NHS resources, economic evaluation is being used increasingly by NHS managers. Research to demonstrate more clearly the extent of the benefits of services such as IVF, in relation to their costs, would assist the pursuit of efficiency and ethical consistency in the NHS.

References

Brazier J, Hutton J, Jeavons R (1990) Evaluating the reform of the NHS. In: Culyer AJ, Maynard AK, Posnett J (eds) Competition in health care: reforming the NHS. Macmillan, Basingstoke

Boyle MH, Torrance GW, Sinclair JC, Horwood SP (1983) Economic evaluation of neonatal intensive care of very-low-birth-weight infants. N Engl J Med 308:1330–1337

Culyer AJ (1971) The nature of the commodity health care and its efficient allocation. Oxford Economic Papers 23:189–211

Culyer AJ (1989) The normative economics of health care finance and provision. Oxford Review of Economic Policy 5:34–58

Culyer AJ, Maynard AK, Posnett J (eds) (1990) Competition in health care: reforming the NHS. Macmillan, Basingstoke

Euroqol Group (1990) Euroqol – a new facility for the measurement of health related quality of life. Health Policy 16:199–208

Gudex C, Kind P (1988) The QALY toolkit. Discussion Paper no. 38, Centre for Health Economics, University of York

Henderson J (1982) An economic appraisal of the benefits of screening for open spina bifida. Soc Sci Med 16:545–560

Hoffenberg R (1987) Clinical freedom. Nuffield Provincial Hospitals Trust, London

Kind P, Rosser R, Williams AH (1982) Valuation of quality of life. In: Jones-Lee MW (ed) The value of life and safety. Elsevier North-Holland, Amsterdam

Ng YK (1979) Welfare economics. Macmillan, Basingstoke

Page H (1989) Economic appraisal of in vitro fertilisation: discussion paper. J R Soc Med 82:99–102

Rosser RM, Watts VC (1972) The measurement of hospital output. Int J Epidemiol 1:361–367

Ruark JE, Raffin TA, Stanford University Medical Centre Committee on Ethics (1988) Initiating and withdrawing life support: principles and practice in adult medicine. N Eng J Med 318:25–30

Secretaries of State for Health, Wales, N. Ireland, Scotland (1989) Working for patients. HMSO, London

Torrance GW (1986) Measurement of health state utilities for economic appraisal: a review. J Health
    Economics 5:1–30
Williams AH (1985) Economics of coronary artery by-pass grafting. Br Med J 291:326–329
Williams AH (1988) Health economics, the end of clinical freedom? Br Med J 297:1183–1186
Williams AH (1990) Ethics, clinical freedom and the doctors' role. In: Culyer AJ, Maynard AK,
    Posnett J (eds). Competition in health care: reforming the NHS. Macmillan, Basingstoke,
    pp 178–191

CHAPTER 13

Screening and Discriminating: Resource Implications of the New Technology

W.R. Sheaff

Suppose it is 2011. The Humane Genome Project (HGP) finished 5 years ago, making new forms of genetic screening of very young embryos and foetuses possible. Older types of screening can now be carried out earlier and more reliably (e.g., to screen for the sex of the foetus and for ethnically-related conditions such as sickle cell anaemia). Young foetuses can now also be screened for predisposition to other conditions. Imagine these include so-called "deviances" such as homosexuality, alcoholism, criminality and manic depression (Tyler 1991); inherited dispositions to disease such as Parkinsonism or certain cancers and to mental illness; physical defects ranging from short-sightedness to quadriplegia; mild mental handicap; and personality traits ranging from general "intelligence" to athleticism.

Also suppose that the HGP makes many new forms of gene and embryo therapy possible. The new screening would enable foetuses displaying any of the above conditions to be aborted early. If intra-uteral embryo surgery and the genetic medical treatment of humans developed apace it would become possible to engineer away the genetic causes of these putatively undesirable dispositions. Yet it would also become possible to retrieve ever more marginally viable premature babies (at least those who pass the screening for genetic desirability), many of whom would survive to a life of handicap, pain and hospitalisation. Together these techniques would enable clinicians, and whoever influences them, to select characteristics of children which as recently as 1991 had been the result of genetic accident. Such techniques can be labelled the "new genetic engineering".

Such prognoses easily attract cliches about "brave new worlds". Yet twentieth-century history is not very reassuring that they can be dismissed as alarmist. In the 1930s financial crises and economic recession in an advanced industrial society brought to power a notoriously eugenicist regime and it is unlikely that the industrialised world has seen its last recession or financial crisis. Among British moral philosophers a Darwinist and eugenicist tendency was active until the early 1940s (e.g., Stephen 1882; Huxley 1947). Overtly racist political parties reappeared in parts of Europe from the 1970s. Yet it is arguable that genetic screening would be only slightly less discriminatory in more familiar circumstances. Clinicians already have a considerable degree of clinical autonomy to practise in the (eugenic) interests of "society" or "science". A libertarian government could advance economic and moral arguments for letting "parents" and firms buy and use genetic screening and engineering with minimal regulation, and any government can make a politically attractive case for resourcing genetic research that promises new cures (Tyler 1991). Commercialised NHS health-care providers would find genetic screening an attractive "income generator" and a marketing "leader" for sales of genetic engineering procedures. Private health insurers might readily buy procedures to prevent births of potentially expensive patients or avoid insuring people with high genetic risks. Eugenicist pressure groups could give the slogan "every child a wanted child" a new meaning.

One journalist has therefore suggested that genetic screening would generate a dangerous repertoire of techniques for

> . . . eugenically minded embryo surgeons and social reformers: employers who would want individual genetic profiles of prospective employees to see where their defects lay; insurance companies who would seek to "tax" those defects with higher premiums; the defence establishment which could fashion new, more terrible race-specific biological weapons; an insatiable commercial sector, bereft of any sense of moral direction, and the masses themselves, driven as they are by fear of failure, sickness and death, and for whom such a scheme promises the final solution.
>
> (Tyler 1991)

Meanwhile more effective health services – for example, health promotion and *bona fide* preventive programmes – would lose resources to genetic screening and engineering. Andrew Tyler adds that genetic screening and engineering will wreak large, long-term, unpredictable and uncontrollable harm. They will prime a genetic time-bomb of new diseases and mutations and stimulate new genetic, pharmaceutical and surgical activities, mostly unnecessary and iatrogenic. What was intended to be discrimination in favour of the recipients of genetic screening may well turn out to be discrimination against them. On these views genetic screening is discriminatory and a waste of health service resources.

Tyler's warning is not necessarily the most historically plausible prediction that could be made about the onset of genetic screening of foetuses nor the most ethically coherent objection to it. However it does illustrate anxieties felt by a wider public than clinicians, scientists and moral philosophers (which is why a journalistic rather than a scientific text has been cited). We could call this scenario the "eugenic nightmare". It is unattractive enough to raise ethical worries about whether genetic screening is inherently discriminatory in a morally objectionable sense and about what policy health services and government should follow towards resourcing it.

To assess whether genetic screening is discriminatory one must define "genetic screening", determine what moral criteria of discrimination the anti-eugenicists are appealing to, then see whether genetic screening satisfies these criteria (or is likely to). The smallest risk of ethical question-begging comes with a minimal definition of "screening". "Genetic screening" can then be defined as "the technologies used to investigate the genetic characteristics of a human or human foetus".

What makes the eugenic nightmare discriminatory is less simple to define. Accounts such as Tyler's usually concentrate on predictions, either regarding the moral conclusions as self-evident or smuggling them in under cover of rhetoric (e.g., "the final solution"), persuasive definitions (e.g., "tax those defects") or tendentious descriptions (e.g., "bereft of any sense of moral direction"). The point of calling genetic screening "discriminatory" is to liken screening to paradigms of discrimination which are generally taken to be morally objectionable – above all racial and sexual discrimination. Three types of ethical objection are commonly brought against these types of discrimination.

Formal objections to racial or sexual discrimination see it as a mistake in moral logic, an inconsistency. Exactly what type the putative inconsistency is, varies from ethical theory to ethical theory. Some argue that the racist or sexist is flouting requirements for moral judgements to be universalisable or reciprocally acceptable of moral judgements, and these requirements may be understood as requirements of moral logic or rules of moral language (Hare 1952; Gewirth 1986). An appeal to game theory might argue that the racist or sexist fails to follow the procedures making for rational choice (cf., Gauthier 1987). The objection may be that the racist or sexist applies incompatible criteria of moral judgement to cases which are essentially similar or applies extraneous, logically irrelevant (racial or sexual) criteria in making his moral judgements (Daniels 1985).

Substantive moral misjudgement is the second category of mistake attributed to the racist or sexist. The suggestion here is that the racist or sexist fails not so much in logic as in moral perception or moral character. Again ethical theories differ in how they characterise this mistake. Some would regard it as a failure to appreciate or participate in the moral "form of life"; others as a failure to apprehend or intuit moral truths (Beehler 1978). More concretely, the racist or sexist is accused of failing to perceive that the notion of personhood applies to non-whites and to women in exactly the same way, and confers the same moral rights, duties and status, as it does to adult males. What applies to notions of personhood applies also to various teleological accounts of the human essence and its moral implications (MacIntyre 1981). According to autonomist theories, the discriminator has exercised moral choice in an incomplete, perverse or unintelligible way (e.g., Hare's famous "fanatic"; Hare 1952). Neo-Aristotelean theories might present racism or sexism as a failure in exercising the virtue of justice or a defect of moral character (Murdoch 1970; MacIntyre 1981).

A third ethical mistake which racial or sexual discriminators allegedly make is in their predictive knowledge. The locus of dispute does not lie primarily in what the morally desirable ends of social life are (individual liberty, health, opportunity for creative and stimulating work, rich and varied social relations etc.) although different ethical objections to discrimination have variously characterised these purposes as the maximisation of happiness, as a classless society, as a higher evolutionary state, and in other ways (Marx and Engels 1969; Mill 1969; Stephen 1882). Writers in this vein criticise the racist or sexist for failing to see that racial or sexual discrimination would practically prevent construction of the morally desirable society, in the sense that discrimination causally prevents the realisation of maximal levels of happiness, possibilities for self-realisation or whatever else characterises that goal. There will be less happiness (for racists too) in a racist society; even for men sexism is a political obstacle to a society which maximises human self-realisation; and so on. Moral assumptions stand behind these claims but the central objection to discrimination is on instrumental grounds.

To show by analogy that genetic screening is discriminatory would require showing that its advocates make at least one of these mistakes. Its opponents implicitly suggest that all three mistakes are made. In the nightmare scenario, screening enables foetuses to be aborted when they are not of the sex the parents prefer, or are genetically predisposed to handicaps, deviancy or disease, or would cost too much to care for. Yet these are not criteria which excuse the killing of adults so it is inconsistent to apply such criteria in killing humans at the foetal stage. The only widely accepted moral excuses for killing adults are in self defence, to punish murder (and this is contested) or in a just war (and then only combatants or unavoidable "collateral" civilian victims). Then, however, the victim has to be an actual, not a potential, member of one of these categories. If mere potential for deviancy, disease or handicap were grounds to kill adults none of us would be safe. Assume that medical treatment of children, and *a fortiori* medical experimentation upon them, is morally permissible only if the intervention is in the child's interest (Helsinki Declaration A5, A11, C4, reprinted in Wall 1989). Consistently applying these criteria to foetuses would preclude most (not all) of the genetic screening and engineering envisaged in the eugenic nightmare.

Choosing the sex of one's children could easily become self-defeating. If, in the child's interest, parents decided that boys would lead more worthwile lives than girls in a sexist world and used screening for the "selective reduction" of female foetuses, the resulting sex imbalance in the population would (for other reasons) defeat the intention of serving the child's interests. If genetic inequality and disorders are inevitable, it might be argued, allocating the results by lottery – the unmanaged, natural genetic lottery – is procedurally the fairest allocation that can be devised (cf., Harris 1986). Any alternative is bound to be less fair, hence discriminatory.

In accusing the genetic screeners of a failure of moral judgement the anti-screener could argue that anyone capable of moral perception can perceive that attributes such as non-athleticism, unintelligence or homosexuality are morally neutral and that it is simply morally wrong – discriminatory – to suppress them by genetic engineering, screening or any other means. Supposing it were morally legitimate to prevent or punish genuinely "deviant" behaviour (e.g., habitual minor criminality), deprivation of life seems hardly a proportionate or just response. Race-specific weapons are presumably objectionable both as weapons and as racist. Those who judge abortion in general to be wrong will also object to genetic engineering or screening if they think it assists or involves abortion. Some who oppose abortion, contraception and other developments in reproductive medicine come close to arguing – although rarely explicitly – against these technologies for weakening the natural sanctions supporting a non-permissive code of sexual conduct (Gillick 1985). Genetic screening and engineering also weaken these sanctions. Added to a claim that permissive sexual moralities are discriminatory against women (Gillick 1985), this yields a conclusion that genetic engineering and screening are indirectly discriminatory. That race and sex are irrelevant to moral status and moral decisions is also a substantive moral judgement.

Predictions about employers' or insurers' screening presume the effects would be discriminatory restrictions of economic or social "life chances". Anxieties about genetic time-bombs and iatrogenic over-activity by health services and their suppliers rest upon predictions about the effects of commercialisation in sacrificing people's health to commercial imperatives (and assume that this is morally unacceptable). Opponents of genetic screening could add that implicitly labelling such groups as alcoholics or the handicapped as people who ought never have been born is more likely to reinforce social discrimination against these groups than the opposite. The cuts which the cost of genetic screening and engineering will impose on services for other groups are bound to be discriminatory against these losers, and perhaps indirectly discriminatory against other groups (e.g., largely female informal carers). If health-care providers promote genetic screening and engineering to generate income, the rich will benefit from having healthy children with characteristics to their parents' choice and the poor will not. A new social discrimination will replace the natural genetic lottery and supplement the other ways in which inequalities in health status arise from class differences. We have already noted the alleged uses of screening as a medium for implementing overtly discriminatory social policies.

The three types of argument make unequal contributions to the "eugenic nightmare" objection to genetic screening. The charge of inconsistency tacitly involves substantive judgements about what is morally relevant and what is morally legitimate to consider in practical judgements, and about what characteristics of actions have to satisfy the requirements for universalisability of reciprocal acceptability. Where the genetic engineering is carried out upon foetuses it presupposes that foetuses are persons having at least the rights that, say, neonates do. The argument from potential is one way to maintain this. Another, Darwinist or eugenicist, way might be to say that the moral significance of humans lies partly in their genetic uniqueness but the advocate of genetic screening and engineering forgets that this also applies to foetuses. Any attempt to show that a given procedure – here, the natural genetic lottery – is procedurally fair relies on a substantive moral judgement on what outcomes from that procedure are fair or unfair (Daniels 1985). The objection to grounding moral claims on a foetus' potential appeals to moral practice, in other domains, that grounds a moral decision (e.g., to punish someone or keep a promise) on the other person's actual moral status, not a counterfactual potential. At root these appeals to consistency are not purely formal but tacitly also rest upon substantive moral assumptions.

A few of the substantive moral objections to the eugenic nightmare are narrow and contentious enough to be unlikely to persuade those who do not already accept that, say, abortion or liberal sexual attitudes are wrong. "Potentially human" is notoriously difficult to define in ways that proscribe destroying foetuses but not other potentially human entities (e.g., by prohibiting celibacy). If objections to the eugenicist nightmare appealed to Darwinian or eugenicist ethical theory, they would depend on another dubious support. Most of the substantive moral assumptions, however, are at the opposite pole. They include the judgements that killing is wrong (except in rare cases outside the geneticists' domain), that deviancy should be tolerated if possible and any response to it should be in proportion to whatever harm it does, an appeal for beneficence and against unnecessary social discrimination, and demands for moral consistency. These are consensual enough to give opponents of screening and genetic engineering common moral ground on which to appeal to supporters of the new genetic technologies. But because these moral judgements are so general, the opponent of the eugenic nightmare confronts the problem of showing that genetic screening and the new genetic engineering do actually fall under these moral judgements.

This is why most of the persuasive work of making the eugenic nightmare, and hence genetic screening and engineering, seem unattractive is done by arguments of the third sort. They predict effects of genetic engineering and screening which look morally unacceptable given the broader moral positions that supporters and opponents of screening and genetic engineering share. On examining it we find that the predictions are of a specific kind, having less than first appears to do with the technology of screening itself.

This is because the intrinsic ethical significance of screening techniques themselves is slight. Screening is a morally neutral technology. To define terms: a "technology" can be defined as a set of physical means of production and the technical knowledge embodied in their construction and use. A technology could be defined as morally neutral or non-neutral according to the moral character of the direct physical effects of its main application – the application for which it was designed. (The adjective "main" is used to pre-empt detours into deviant or secondary uses, as for instance when bricks are used as weapons or museum exhibits or works of art.) On this definition some technologies – for instance weapons technologies or the so-called "technologies of repression" (British Society for Social Responsibility in Science 1976) – are evidently not morally neutral because their main application is to inflict harm on populations. Others are morally non-neutral in the opposite way – for instance technologies of anaesthesia. Others again are morally ambivalent, for instance nuclear physics technologies.

Taken as a diagnostic method, genetic screening is not like this. Its main application is simply to produce biological knowledge about particular people or foetuses. Genetic screening is discriminatory only in the sense of discriminating whether, as a point of fact, specific genetic conditions apply to a particular foetus. This information indicates what further clinical intervention (if any) is necessary to achieve whatever further purposes are served by the treatment plan or by the clinician's or patient's practical decision. This necessity too is a purely factual matter. The moral significance of genetic screening *per se* is, therefore, at most as a means to these further ends; that is, as a means to meet an instrumental need (Sheaff 1988). It does not intrinsically meet or frustrate "needs" in any more strongly moral sense of the term, "needs" as one form of moral end ("that which a person ought to have", cf., Doyal and Gough 1984). Whatever ethical colour it has, is only derived from the further ends it serves (the same holds of most diagnostic methods). Despite his equivocation about the fallibility and pseudo-scientificity of genetics, Tyler for one does not deny that rectifying congenital disorders is a no less possible source of this moral colour than the development of race-specific biological weapons.

Only the most specialised or unimaginative researcher would see screening as an end in itself. In practice screening is embedded in a treatment plan (Jennet 1983) and used to direct and monitor it. The direction which the treatment plan takes, the effects it has and the purposes it serves are determined by many factors. They include the clinician's own preferences (including his or her ethical standpoint), what techniques are known for acting upon the information yielded by genetic screening, the patient's consent, and what health workers and physical resources are immediately available. A treatment plan is devised and implemented through a health system which itself stands within wider social structures. They influence in turn which types of treatment receive investment for research and development, the effects and purposes of the health-care organisation within which the treatment plan occurs, how practical alternative treatment plans are, and how effective clinical care is likely to be (McKeown 1976; Black 1980). All this influences the effects and purposes of the treatment plan, and hence the moral colour of its screening component.

Ambiguity afflicts the term "screening" because different amounts of these practical contexts can get defined into the term along with its core meaning of a diagnostic technology. "Screening" can be defined either narrowly and technically (as above) or as a health-care programme combining the technology itself with a health-system context, even as a social or political programme (with the diagnostic technology as one means among many). Prognoses of eugenic nightmares caused by "screening" (including the one cited above) trade on this ambiguity, arguing from an opposition to employers' and insurers' "screening" to opposition to the "screening" technology, the human genome project and the diagnostic applications of its findings. To make the prognosis possible, let alone plausible, contextual infilling must be added to the bare technical possibilities of genetic screening and the HGP. An incomplete summary of what is added now follows.

"The masses", including intending parents, are assumed not to want girls or "deviant" children; nor (with better moral excuse) handicapped children. Any moral qualms they might have about abortion or genetic engineering to remove undesirable characteristics would soon evaporate. They would prefer to select the characteristics of their child which were previously determined by genetic accident, and to alter their own characteristics if that would postpone "failure, sickness and death". They command the health-care resources to do all this, whether purchasing power in a conventional market, or the means of making "customer-friendly" internal markets respond to their wishes. Yet they are ignorant, compliant or desperate enough to submit to eugenic experimentation.

To postulate the eugenic nightmare one has also to assume that doctors have the clinical autonomy to develop genetic technologies as described above, and to apply them. They control sufficient research and development resources, investment and working capital, or can get them by selling applications of genetic screening. Either they are oblivious to the moral results and politically compliant, interested only in developing genetic screening and engineering for its own sake or to gain academic or professional status; or the very opposite. The opposite assumption – purely for the sake of argument! – is of a conservative medical profession adopting a radical libertarian economic view that any legal way of earning income is morally acceptable, and susceptible to eugenicist doctrines. They (or similarly motivated managers) can reinvest the profits in developing the marketable aspects of genetic screening. Patients have so little real control over health-care resources – including their own bodies – as to become material for eugenic experiments. It is further assumed that doctors would respond to financial or professional incentives by retrieving yet more babies of marginal viability (they can call off resources to do this too) but regard patients as fair game for eugenic experiments. "Vain of their skills", these doctors will promise new cures to secure funding and endorse a potentially profitable pseudo-science, applying it prematurely with small knowledge of the biological consequences, secure in the knowledge that no deterrent means exist to make them accountable for reimbursing the misused resources, for compensating the victims or for contributing to other external costs of their decisions.

One has also to assume that the health system can provide – "can" both technically and financially – a repertoire of techniques based partly upon genetic screening: genetic interventions, *in utero* surgery besides the successful identification of putative genes corresponding to predisposition to alcoholism, criminality, manic depression and other "deviances". The health system as a whole is assumed to remain underfunded relative to needs – presumably because of an ageing population, the relative price effect, the comparative economic backwardness of the UK and cash-limited NHS budgets. High technology developments such as genetic medicine exacerbate the problem. The commercialis-ation of health care at least allows and resources insurers and providers to research, develop and implement screening and a connected repertoire of techniques (including abortion); and at most creates an economic incentive to do so as an income generator or cost saver (respectively).

Health system managers and governments are assumed to tolerate, resource, advocate or exploit these developments. They let "parents" buy and use genetic screening and engineering. They tolerate abortion and let "eugenically minded embryo surgeons and social reformers" pursue these interests. Government resources and uses health care partly as a means of preventing or controlling the genetically-influenced behaviours it classifies as morally "deviant". Govern-ment also resources and supports the defence establishment's development of race-specific biological weapons. Business is seen as capable of resourcing the use of genetic methods to maintain a profitable and compliant work-force, and to have economic incentives to do so. Insurance companies use genetic screening results to justify raising premiums or reducing cover (but seldom the reverse). Prospects of profit outweigh the claims of business ethics (against exploiting public credulity) or health-care ethics (against iatrogenic technologies). Lastly a certain economic and social background is assumed: economic stagnation and a libertarian government with rather authoritarian views towards deviancy.

How realistic these assumptions are, under what conditions they might become true, and whether they are consistent, are questions I leave open. My point is simply *that* such assumptions are necessary to get the eugenicist scenario started at all. A crude form of the implication is this: what makes the eugenicist scenario discriminatory are the choices made by parents, doctors, health service managers, firms and governments; not the screening technology as such. More realistically, what makes the scenario discriminatory is the complex interplay of individual choices, professional and economic incentives, patterns of resource flow, a policy setting and an economic climate in health care: in short, the structure of the health system itself. "Structure", because the organisational framework for health care and the incentives it offers determine how screening is used, partly by determining what individual decisions appear to be prudent – or moral – in the circumstances, partly through the interplay of innumerable individual decisions. This structure brings results that derive from the conscious decision of every participant in the health system and (especially in the case of markets) were intended by none of them. The infilling assumptions were listed at such length partly to substantiate the claim about their number and complexity, partly to illustrate a further point.

A major determinant of these effects is resource allocation within the health system. In social and organisational theory it is controversial how far the non-economic characteristics of a health system (the forms of professionalisation that emerge, the moral climate within it, its managerial arrangements etc.) are determined by its economic characteristics. What is not controversial is the large part resource allocation plays in determining what health-care technologies are developed, and how innovations such as genetic screening are applied. Indeed the production of scientific knowledge itself is increasingly organised on bureaucratic lines and increasingly influenced by who allocates (research, development, educational and capital) resources, and how.

Four aspects (at least) of resource allocation are involved. Because of the way the NHS has been funded, the most obvious to British minds is the question of what resources government would have to provide for the health system to permit genetic screening and engineering to reach the innovation and dissemination stages of these products' life cycles (Stocking 1985). Questions of what the opportunity cost would be elsewhere in the health system, and whether the resulting reallocation of resources is defensible, arise in consequence. However the foregoing list of assumptions behind the eugenic nightmare prognosis shows that other resourcing issues are involved.

A second aspect of resource allocation is what sorts of clinical behaviour the system of resource allocation rewards at the individual level. The rewards in question are not simply cash payments. Health workers are no less motivated by non-financial aims such as the pursuit of knowledge and developing services for the good that can be done to patients; but even these motives require resources to realise. So a third aspect of health system resource allocation concerns whole health-care organisations, interacting with other parts of the health system: what sorts of health-care activity attract the resources necessary to expand themselves? The first aspect of health resource allocation is a special case of this general question, the form it takes in directly managed, publicly-funded health services where such matters are decided consciously, as a result of policy. Other methods of deciding such matters are possible. One procedural method, for instance, stipulates how "managed competition" will occur and accepts whatever resource allocations result from that process.

Fourthly, there is the aspect of who has rights (here *de facto* rights, whether or not morally defensible or legally articulated) to dispose of the resources that constitute a health service; money, property in buildings and equipment, the time and work of health workers, intellectual property and so on (clinical autonomy can in this sense be seen as a special sort of property right). In a directly-managed, publicly-owned health system, these property rights manifest themselves as a set of managerial practices and administrative regulation. In conventional or "internal" markets they take more overt and familiar form as property rights exercised in commercial transactions. In the relations between a health service and its consumers (i.e., patients and the healthy population) the corresponding issue is: what effect does consumer influence have on the use of health service resources, and through what mechanism? An analogous issue arises in relation to the buyer of the service, when this is not the consumer (as in internal markets).

Questions about resource implications of new technology such as genetic screening should therefore be reformulated in wider terms than the quantity of resources. Questions about whether genetic screening is discriminatory also require reformulating. Genetic screening technology is indeed required to realise the eugenic nightmare – but so are very many other technologies. What some opponents of screening assume is that screening, above all, makes the nightmare possible. This is true only in the limited sense that prohibiting the development of genetic screening would disarm eugenicists of one technical means for realising the nightmare. But even this claim is dubious. Lack of genetic screening techniques did not hinder the Nazis. The question which this begs is: why disarm them at *this* point, by removing an ethically neutral technology? One would not argue that the technical development of railways should be halted because railways were indispensable – much more necessary than genetic screening – for the concentration camps. What made the "final solution" a reality was not technologies so much as a profound economic and social crisis and the ensuing war.

The question of whether genetic screening is discriminatory is starting to look an odd – indeed a leading – question. It presupposes that of the whole concatenation of social systems and political events that make up the nightmare scenario, the main locale at which health-care ethicists face a practical, or a moral, question is in deciding whether to develop or apply a diagnostic technique. One can easily understand that this is how the issue spontaneously presents itself to a specialist in reproductive technologies; but in health policy terms it is a profoundly conservative leading question. An ambiguity in the term "screening" has allowed the moral effects of a whole health system to be attributed solely to its technology. The question it excludes (unless "screening" is defined to include a great deal of organisational context) is no less practically significant, and much more critical for determining whether in practice genetic screening is discriminatory. It is: what sort of health system, or what sort of social system, is likeliest to use a neutral technology to create a eugenic nightmare (or the opposite)?

Neither are the most ethically important resource implications of ethically neutral new technologies such as genetic screening found only by asking: "what effect on scarcity will genetic screening have?"; "what ethically defensible claim for resources for genetic screening can be formulated?"; or even "will genetic screening sharpen or palliate ethical dilemmas in the use of scarce resources?" Ethically important resource implications are more likely to be revealed by addressing more complex, but also less question-begging problems. Among them are: "what systems of health resource allocation and what property relations in health services are more likely, and which less likely, to make screening practically discriminatory?"; "does the development of new technology itself influence the development of health resource allocative systems, and hence indirectly affect ways in which health systems become discriminatory as a result?"; and "does genetic screening re-open moral dilemmas about the role of health workers (e.g., on the proper extent and uses of clinical autonomy)?" These are primarily theoretical questions, settled by appeal to factual evidence; although for their answers to be of practical, or policy, import still requires ethical judgements on when discrimination is objectionable, and why.

At present in Britain the different sets of answers to these questions can be summarised as a policy choice between the types of health structure available to a developed industrial society. Four "ideal types" are a conventional market, a (Bismarckian) system of social insurance, an internal market (both social insurance and internal markets are now being proposed in the USSR; Sheaff 1990; Ryan 1991) and a directly managed public system (John Roberts proposed an earlier form of this typology in personal discussions with the author). A comparative discussion of the implications of these resource-allocative systems for discrimination in genetic screening is beyond the scope of a short paper on philosophical ethics, except to indicate briefly the likeliest conclusions. On the face of it the probability of the eugenic nightmare (or something like it) coming true seems least remote with a conventional market system, less likely with an internal market and a social insurance system, and least likely under a publicly funded and directly managed system. In essence the reasons for suggesting this lie in the ways the four types of system differ in the degrees of freedom to market new products and the (converse) degree of public control; in the strength and ubiquity of commercial imperatives; in their ability to countervail pressures to prioritise high-technology, high value-added curative services; in the scope and incentives for managing consumer reactions through marketing methods; and (when it comes to scarcity) in their comparative efficiency in terms of meeting needs for health care (the well-known problems of market failure in health care).

Whether genetic screening is discriminatory in practice depends as much upon social and political assumptions as upon ethical arguments. However the price that geneticists and others pay for maintaining that genetic screening is a morally neutral technology is one of refocusing ethical debates about discrimination onto the health policy arena. Health policy and health service management might be none the worse for that.

References

Beehler R (1978) Moral life. Blackwell, Oxford

Black D (1980) Inequalities in health. Department of Health and Social Security, London. [The Black Report]

British Society for Social Responsibility in Science (1976) The new technology of repression BSSRS, London

Daniels N (1985) Just health care. Cambridge University Press, Cambridge

Doyal L, Gough I (1984) A theory of human needs. Critical social policy 10: 6–36

Gauthier D (1987) Morals by agreement. Oxford University Press, Oxford

Gewirth A (1986) Why rights are indispensable. Mind 95: 329–344

Gillick V (1985) Contraception for children; whose choice? Whose responsibility? Ethical Issues in Caring Conference, Manchester, 7 September 1985

Hare RM (1952) The language of morals. Clarendon Press, Oxford

Harris J (1986) The Survival Lottery. In: Singer P (ed) Applied ethics. Oxford University Press, Oxford

Huxley J (1947) Evolutionary ethics. Pilot Press, London

Jennet B (1983) High technology medicine. Nuffield Provincial Hospitals Trust, London

MacIntyre A (1981) After virtue. Duckworth, London

Marx K, Engels F (1969) Manifesto of the Communist Party. Progress, Moscow

McDowell J (1979) Virtue and reason. The Monist 1xii: 331–350

McKeown T (1976) The role of medicine. Nuffield Provincial Hospitals Trust, London

Mill JS (1969) Utilitarianism. Fontana, London

Murdoch I (1970) The sovereignty of good. Routledge Kegan Paul, London

Ryan M (1991) USSR letter: Health Insurance in the Soviet Union. Br Med J 302 (6769) 170 (19th January 1991).

Sheaff WR (1988) Needs and justice in health resource allocation. In: Fairbairn G, Fairbairn S (eds) Ethical issues in caring. Avebury, Aldershot

Sheaff WR (1990) An international comparison; the Leningrad experiment. In: Cook H (ed) The NHS – private sector interface. Longman, Harlow

Stephen L (1882) The science of ethics. Smith and Elder, London

Stocking B (1985) Initiative and inertia. Case studies in the NHS. Nuffield Provincial Hospitals
    Trust, London
Tyler A (1991) The Frankenstein Factor. Guardian 16–17 March 1991 pp 8–9, 27
Wall A (1989) Ethics and the health service manager. Kings Fund, London

CHAPTER 14

Epidemiology of Induced Abortion

S.L. Barron

Some unkind things have been said and written about the ability of statistics to mislead. There is always more than one way to present the facts and the choice of information and its presentation inevitably reflects the bias of the author. My purpose is to provide some information about induced abortion as a prelude to the discussions about the ethics of termination of pregnancy. Debates about abortion tend to become emotional, and I hope it will be helpful to start with an examination of the large amount of information now available, much of it from governmental sources.

Reliable information about spontaneous abortion is very hard to find since the condition is often unrecognised and there is no system, such as compulsory notification, for collecting the data. On the other hand, the liberalisation of the laws on abortion in Europe and the USA has greatly increased the amount of available information about legally induced abortion. In England, Wales and Scotland the Abortion Act (1967), which became effective in April 1968, included a provision for compulsory notification and as a result there is now an extensive collection of reliable data which is published as Abortion Statistics (Scottish Health Service 1990; OPCS 1991). Similar arrangements operate in other European countries whilst in the USA the data are collected on a voluntary basis by the Centers for Disease Control (CDC) (Koonin et al. 1990). An excellent summary of world data can be found in publications from the Guttmacher Institute (Tietze and Henshaw 1986; Henshaw and Morrow 1990).

When the figures for England and Wales were first published there was surprise and concern at the high number of notifications. The numbers were, in fact, inflated by an influx into SE England of women from the European Continent and from Ireland. As European countries changed their laws, the number of abortions in foreign women, shown as the gap between all notifications and those to resident women, declined (Fig. 14.1). It is interesting that the number of abortions notified for British residents was not far off the 100 000 abortions per year which were thought to have been performed illegally prior to the 1967 Abortion Act (Leete 1976).

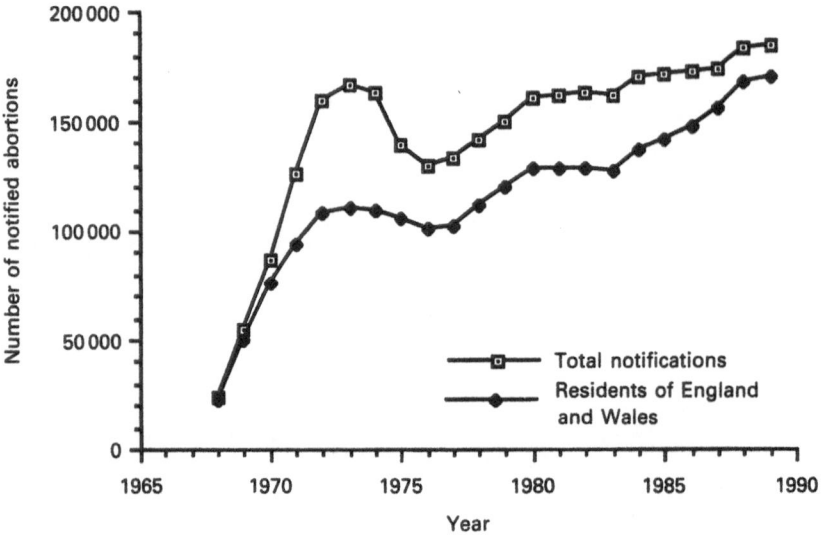

Figure 14.1. Notified abortions in England and Wales1968–1989. Source: OPCS Abortion Statistics.

Abortion Rates and Ratios

The recorded number of abortions in a given population depends on the age structure, age-specific fertility and the effective use made of contraception. Within the population, abortion rates will also vary according to marital status and parity. In looking at published statistics, it is important to note whether or not the data include women who have come from abroad and the tables published by OPCS distinguish those which apply to residents of England and Wales. It can be misleading to look only at absolute numbers, if they do not take into account the nature and structure of the fertile population.

Geographical Variation in Britain

There is wide variation in the abortion rate among the 14 English Regional Health Authorities, with the Thames Regions having the highest rates, followed by the West Midlands and Mersey (Table 14.1). Fewer than half of all abortions are carried out in the NHS and this figure also varies very much from 85% in the Northern Region to only 17% in the West Midlands Region. It is interesting to note that those Regions with the poorest NHS provision also tend to have the highest abortion rates (Barron 1984).

The Effect of Age and Marital Status

Since fertility is highest in women aged from 20 to 30, abortion rates in this age group have a disproportionate effect on overall rates. The demographic

Table 14.1. Abortion rates per 1000 women aged 15–44, in different regions of England

Regional Health Authority	rate/1000
NE Thames	25.6
NW Thames	22.2
SE Thames	20.8
SW Thames	17.8
West Midlands	16.2
North Western	14.0
Mersey	13.9
Oxford	13.7
Wessex	12.5
Yorkshire	12.4
Trent	12.1
East Anglia	11.2
South Western	10.6
Northern	10.4

structure of the population, which reflects changes in the birth rate over the years, determines the number of those women who are at risk of pregnancy. Although the number of abortions has steadily increased, the abortion rate (which is measured per 1000 women aged 15 to 44) hardly changed between 1974 and 1983 so that the increased numbers reflected population change rather than an increased use of abortion. More recently, however, the abortion rate has shown an upward trend (Fig. 14.2). The point is further illustrated in Fig. 14.3 which shows the increase in the percentage of conceptions which ended in abortion.

There is a very marked difference in behaviour between the single and married. Fertility is high in women under 30 but the abortion rate in young married women is very low when compared with single women of the same age. Only

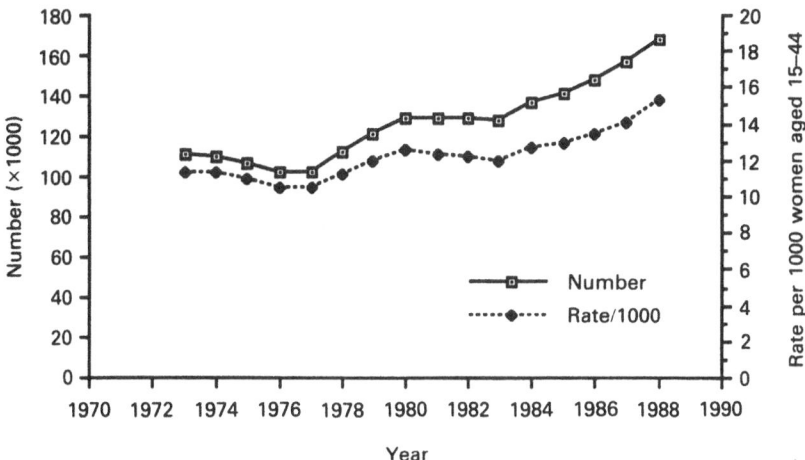

Figure 14.2. Notified abortions in residents of England and Wales, with rates per 1000 women aged 15 to 44 years. Source: OPCS Abortion Statistics.

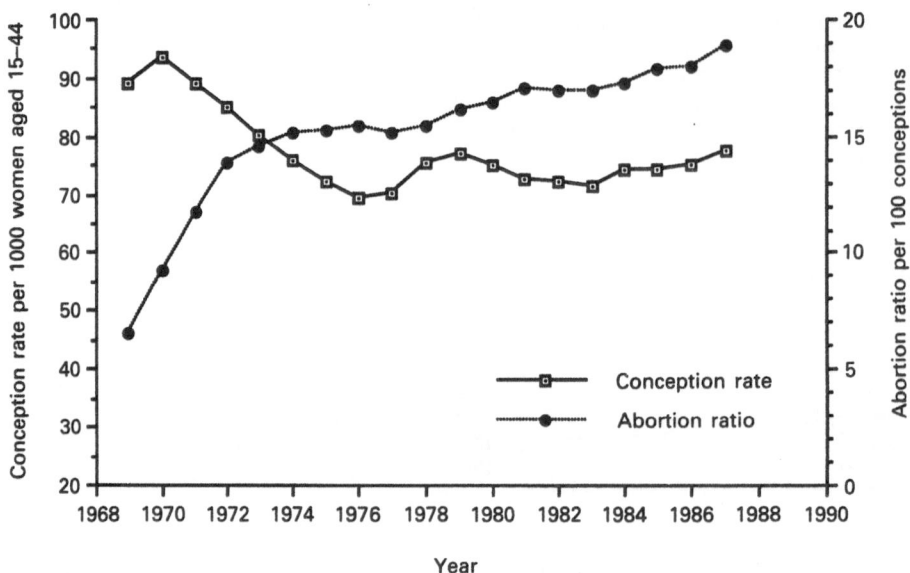

Figure 14.3. Outcome of known conceptions in women aged 15 to 44 years, for England and Wales.

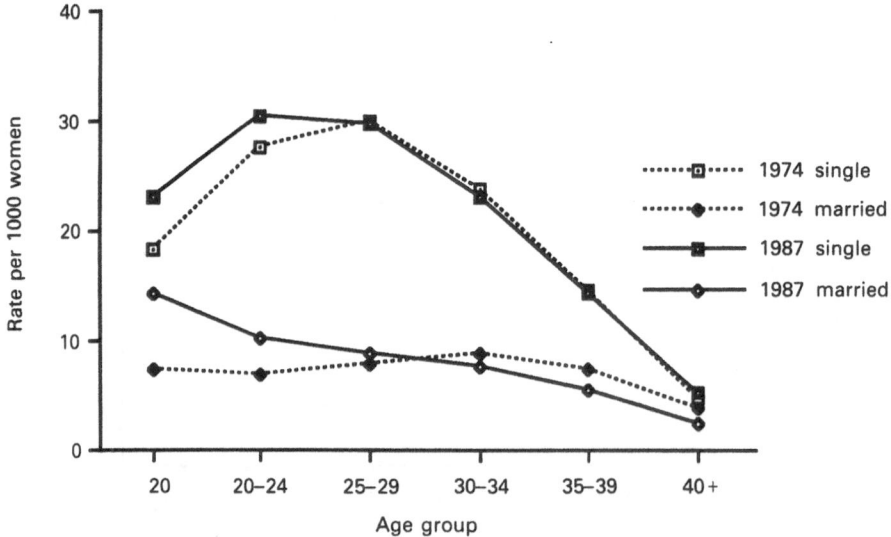

Figure 14.4. Abortion rates in 1974 and 1987 in single and married residents of different ages in England and Wales.

in the over-40s do the rates of single and married come close together. The pattern has not changed over the years between 1974 and 1987 (Fig. 14.4).

In Britain there has been particular concern about girls under 16, following the Court ruling in the Gillick Case (Barron 1986). It was feared that the need to obtain parental consent before a girl under 16 could be prescribed contraception might lead to an increase in unwanted pregnancy and abortion. So far that fear is unfounded. The age-specific rates for the very young are shown in Fig. 14.5. Although the number of notifications has declined, the age-specific abortion rate has hardly changed, a further illustration of the importance of looking at rates rather than absolute numbers.

The abortion ratio is the number of abortions per 100 live births. It is, therefore, independent of age-specific fertility but gives a measure of the use of abortion and reflects the effectiveness of contraception, assuming that the abortions were all unplanned pregnancies (which is not always the case). The marked differences with age and marital status, described above, are seen even more clearly (Fig. 14.6). The pattern has not changed between 1974 and 1984, although the ratios and rates have both increased over time.

The age-specific trend is not the same in all groups. In Fig. 14.7, which is based on known conceptions (i.e., legal abortions, still and live births), the abortion ratio has increased steadily in the under-twenties, very little in women aged under 25, and has shown a slow decline in the use of abortion by women aged 40 or more.

The demographic effect of the use of abortion by women outside marriage is shown in Fig. 14.8, which covers a time span of 19 years. After the rise which followed the introduction of the Abortion Act, the abortion rate has hardly changed, but what is striking is how pre-marital conceptions (births legitimised by later marriage) have declined. Single parenthood or abortion seems to be

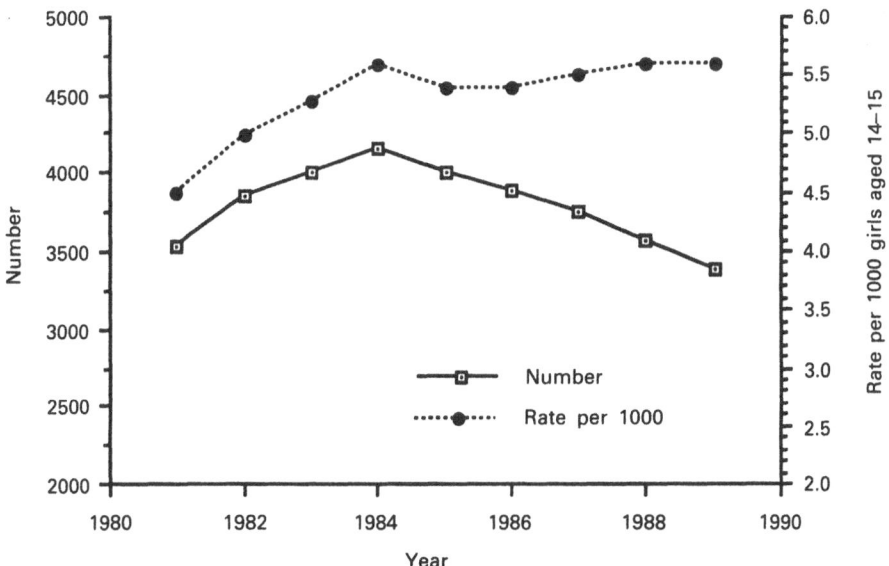

Figure 14.5. Abortion rates in under-16 year olds, in England and Wales from 1980 to 1989.

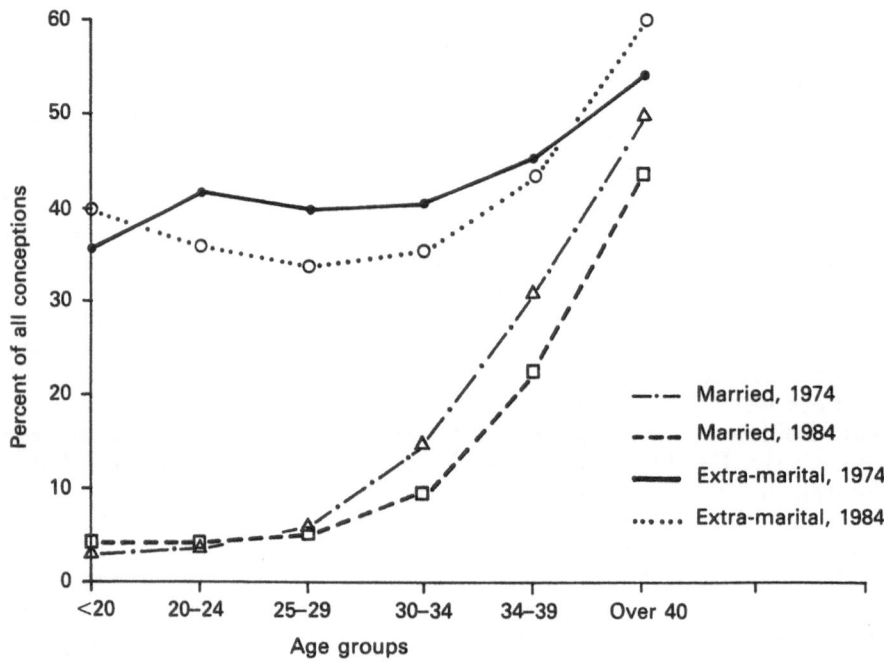

Figure 14.6. Conceptions ending in abortion in England and Wales. Source: OPCS Abortion Report.

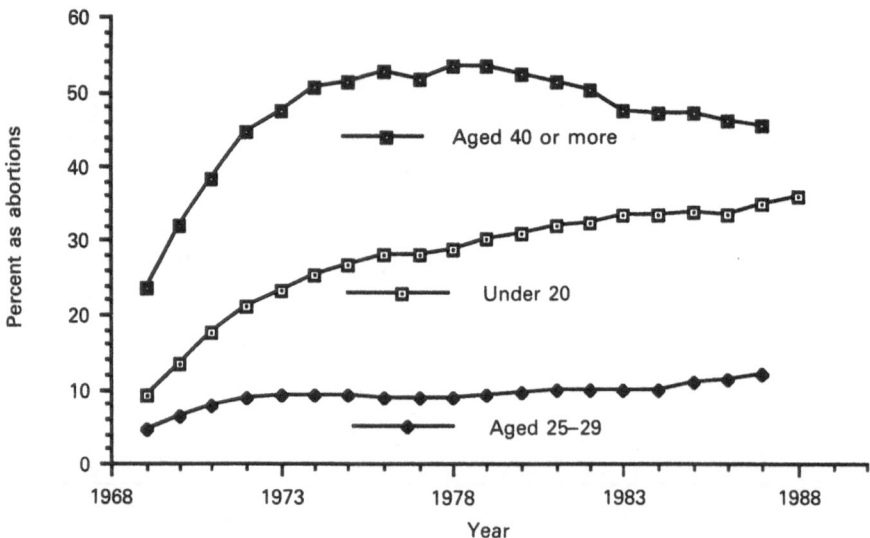

Figure 14.7. Abortion rates in women of different ages in England and Wales, 1969–1988.

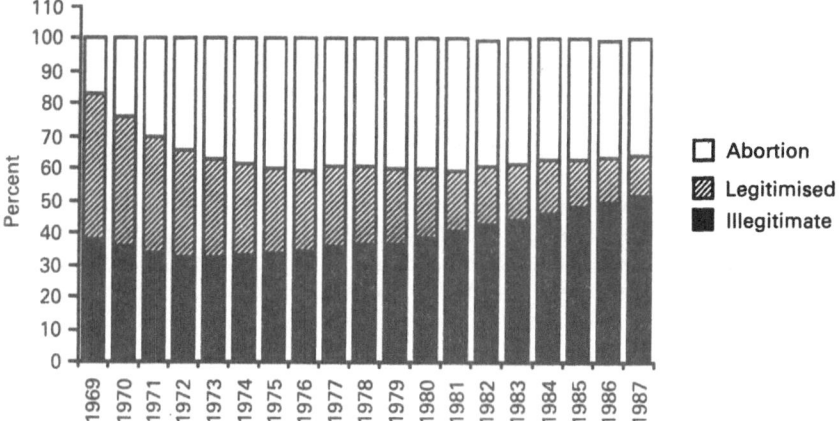

Figure 14.8. Outcome of pregnancy outside marriage, for residents of England and Wales, 1969–1987.

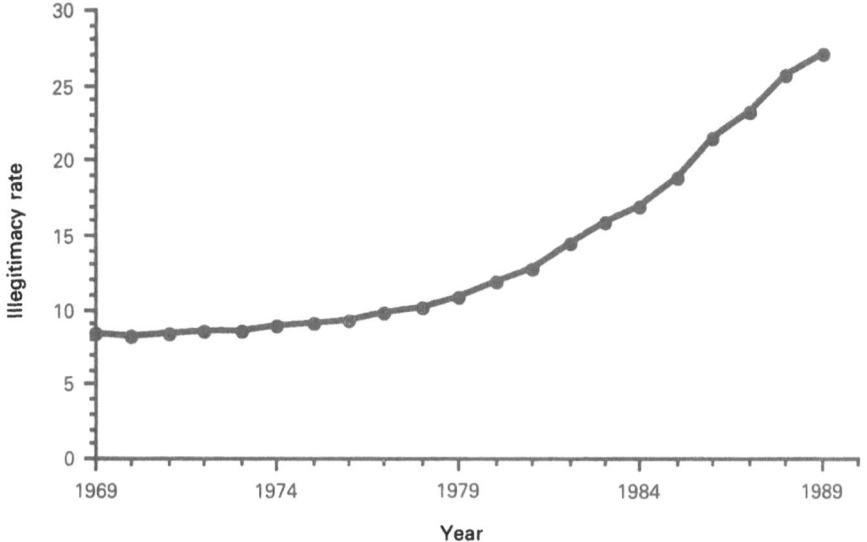

Figure 14.9. Illegitimacy rates in England and Wales per 100 live births, 1969–1989.

preferred to "shot-gun marriage". The net result has been a rapid and continuous increase in the illegitimacy rate, which now exceeds 30% (Fig. 14.9).

Morbidity and Mortality of Induced Abortion

Deaths from abortion in England and Wales can be followed from 1952 in the Reports of Confidential Enquiries into Maternal Deaths (Department of Health and Social Security 1957–1989 and Departments of Health 1991) which are published every three years. In the first of these triennial reports to be published after the introduction of the Abortion Act, the number of recorded deaths from induced abortion rose because of the greatly increased number being performed by relatively inexperienced operators. There was, however, a corresponding fall in deaths from illegal abortions (Fig. 14.10). Successive reports demonstrated that mortality from induced abortion, both legal and illegal, declined out of proportion to the general fall in maternal mortality. In 1970–2 abortion mortality was 25.3 per million pregnancies and accounted for 21% of all maternal deaths; in 1985–7 abortion mortality had fallen to 2.3 and accounted for only 4% of deaths (Table 14.2). Mortality figures from the USA show a similar fall (Fig. 14.11), but mortality was lower in the USA than in England and Wales in the early seventies. The two reasons thought to be responsible were the use in Britain of hysterotomy, especially when combined with sterilisation, and the tendency in Britain to perform the operation relatively late in pregnancy. There is still a tendency to perform the operation later in Britain than in the USA, because of the organisational problems of the NHS (Barron 1984), but there has been some improvement over the years 1972–1987 in the proportion of abortions carried out before 13 weeks (Fig. 14.12).

What is equally interesting is the way in which deaths from "spontaneous" abortion also fell. This fall coincided with a fall in the admission of septic abortions to NHS hospitals (Barron 1981) and adds credence to the assertion that many so-called spontaneous abortions were in fact illegally induced.

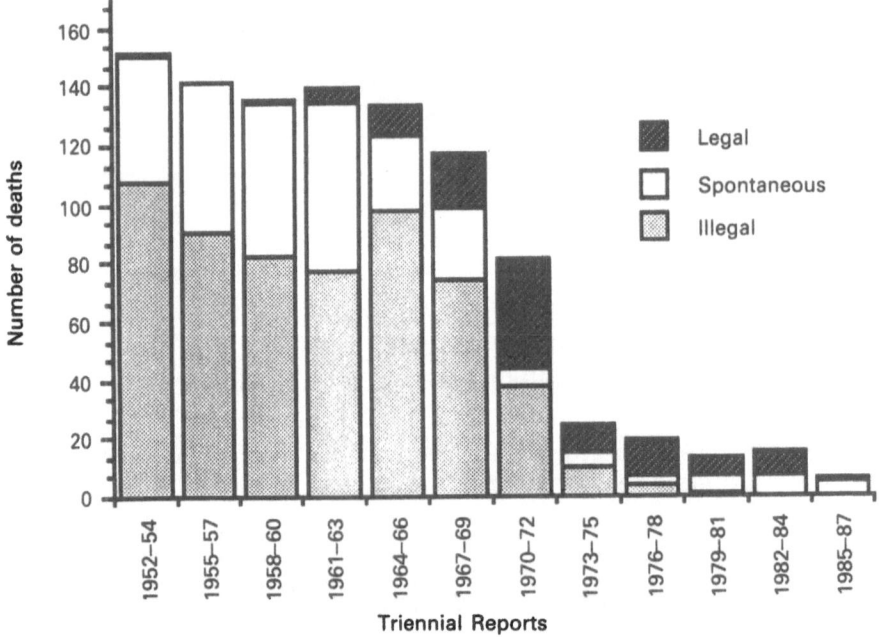

Figure 14.10. Deaths from abortion in England and Wales, 1952–1987. Source: Report of confidential enquiries into maternal deaths in the United Kingdom, 1985–1987.

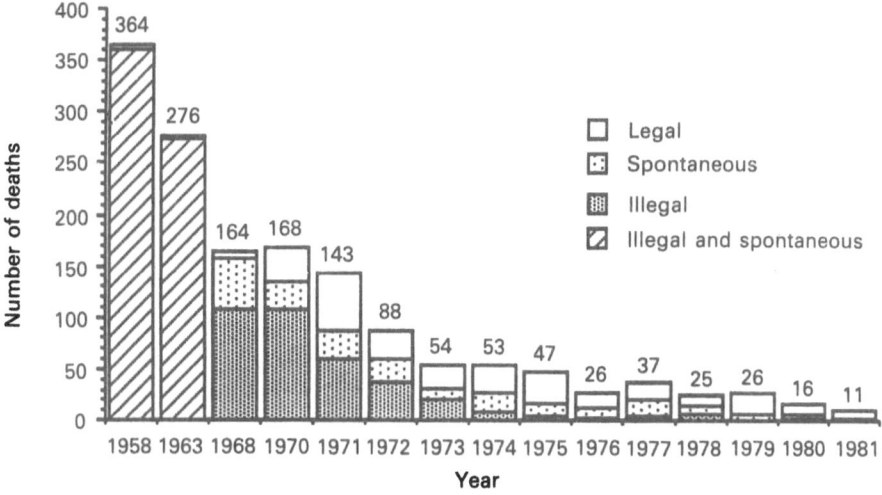

Figure 14.11. Deaths from abortion in the USA, 1958–1981.

Table 14.2. Mortality from abortion in England and Wales, 1970–1987

Triennium	Maternal mortality	Abortion mortality	% allmortality
1970–1972	118.7	25.3	21.0
1973–1975	88.0	10.5	19.0
1976–1978	93.4	6.0	6.4
1979–1981	70.0	5.5	7.9
1982–1984	55.0	4.4	8.0
1985–1987	45.6	1.9	4.0

Rates are per million estimated pregnancies.
Source: Report of Confidential Enquiries into Maternal Deaths in the United Kingdom, 1985–87.
HMSO, London, 1991.

Method of Abortion

The choice of method, and the related morbidity, is closely related to gestation.

First Trimester

Prior to 12 weeks gestation, vacuum aspiration (or suction curettage) is the method of choice and was used in 91% of cases in England and Wales in 1987. The new anti-progestin drug RU486, which is about to be licensed for use in Britain, promises to reduce the need for an operation, but its use will be heavily constrained by law and it will be some time before its effect on management becomes clear.

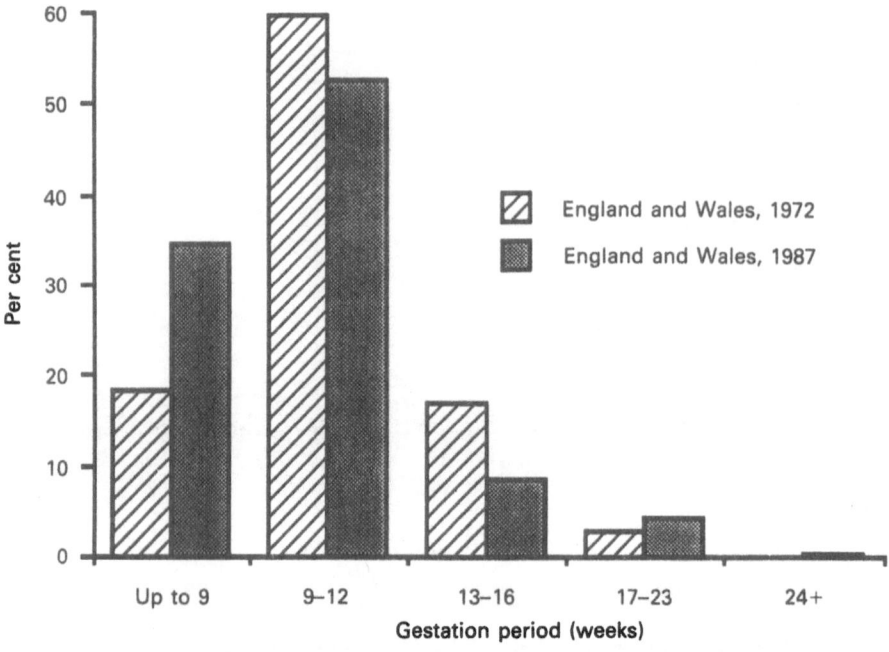

Figure 14.12. Comparison of periods of gestation at abortion in England and Wales in 1972 and 1987.

Second Trimester

Beyond 12 weeks, in order to evacuate the contents of the uterus through the cervix by curettage, it may be necessary to dilate the cervix over 14 mm, which increases the risk of splitting the cervix or of rupturing the uterus. A number of other methods are more commonly used:

Hysterotomy, which is a miniature Caesarean section, requires an abdominal operation and several days stay in hospital

Intra-uterine injection of pharmacological agents, such as hypertonic saline, prostaglandins or urea, which stimulate the uterus to abort the conceptus

Dilatation and evacuation (D & E) is a development of suction curettage (Fink 1973) and is more popular in the USA than in Britain. It may be carried out in one or two stages.

In Britain the most popular method for second trimester abortion is the injection into the uterus of a prostaglandin which induces uterine contractions and subsequent dilatation of the cervix over several hours. The fetus is eventually aborted in the bed and this may cause distress to the woman and to the nurses who care for her. Newer analogues of prostaglandins, such as gemeprost, are administered as a vaginal pessary and avoid the need for an injection but this is only a marginal improvement. D & E, on the other hand, is performed entirely under anaesthesia and takes minutes rather than hours. In expert hands the method is safer than prostaglandins (Fig. 14.13 and Table 14.3) (Cates and Grimes 1981; Grimes and Schultz 1985; Atrash et al. 1987) but the operation

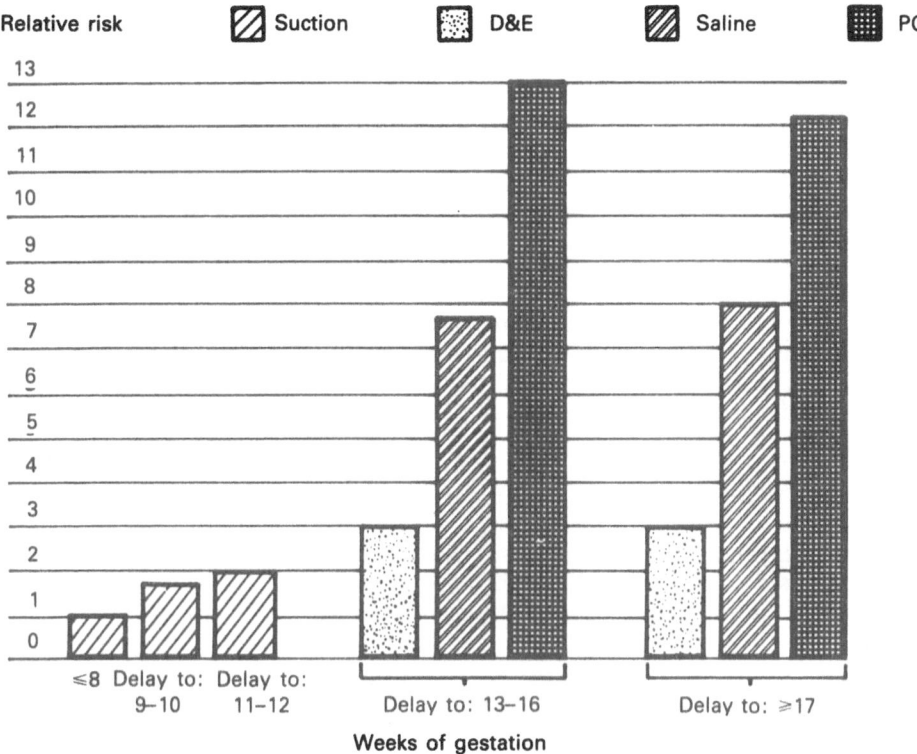

Figure 14.13. Relative mortality risk of different methods of abortion.

requires a lot of skill and is very distasteful to the surgeon and theatre staff. In England and Wales the procedure is carried out mainly by a few specialist gynaecologists in the private sector (Stanwell-Smith 1984).

Table 14.3. Abortion mortality by gestation and method in the USA, 1972–1982 (Atrash et al. 1987)

Method	< 13 weeks	13–15 weeks	16–20 weeks	21 weeks+	Total	Relative risk
Curettage	0.8 (82)[1]				0.8 (82)	1
D & E		3.6 (14)	9.5 (12)	10.4 (2)	5.1 (28)	6.2[2]
Instillation		5.0 (5)	10.9 (41)	11.7 (10)	10.1 (56)	12.3[2]
Hysterotomy/ hysterectomy	41.9 (3)	62.8 (3)	80.9 (4)	115 (1)	44.8 (11)	54.4[2]
All methods	0.86 (85)	4.3 (22)	11.1 (22)	11.8 (13)	1.6 (177)	
N=	9 996 356	555 730	529 698	118 876	11 200 660	

[1] Number of deaths in parentheses.
[2] Significant at $p < 0.5$.

Short-term Complications

The official notifications of abortion in Britain include a record of any complication that occurred before the patient left hospital. The most common complications are sepsis, haemorrhage and surgical trauma to the uterus and the incidence, calculated from data for England and Wales from 1985–1989, is summarised in Table 14.4. These rates are under estimates because they do not include later complications that require re-admission. For that we are dependent on special studies such as the Joint Program for the Study of Abortion (JPSA) in the USA (Tietze and Lewit 1972) or the Joint Study of the Royal Colleges (Joint Study 1985). The immediate morbidity in the first 21 days was observed by follow-up and the results are shown in Table 14.4 alongside the official statistics. Overall morbidity was 8.9% which included psychiatric morbidity some of it from pre-existing psychosis.

Long-term Sequelae Following Abortion

In Eastern Europe, where abortion was freely available long before 1967, concern was expressed in a paper from Hungary (Czeizel et al. 1970) at the apparent increase in the prevalence of premature birth. Other fears were expressed that abortion might lead to infertility or psychiatric illness. A number of attempts have been made to determine the long term sequelae, the largest being a multinational study by WHO (WHO Task Force 1979). The difficulty with all such studies is to agree on the nature of the control group, since any pregnancy will carry some kind of sequel. In the WHO study, pregnancies following an induced abortion were compared with those following spontaneous abortion, live birth and with first-ever pregnancies. It became obvious that the women in each of these groups differed markedly from one another, and particularly from those who had a previous induced abortion. Once allowance had been made for factors like cigarette smoking and contraceptive failure, most of the observed differences between the groups disappeared. There was no good evidence of an increase in the incidence of premature birth, low birth weight or cervical incompetence which could be ascribed to early induced abortion.

Another factor which bedevils studies of this kind is what is called "differential

Table 14.4. Immediate morbidity following abortion

Complication	OPCS		RCGP/RCOG Study	
	Number	rate(%)	Number	rate(%)
Infection	305	0.03	218	3.6
Haemorrhage	1746	0.2	122	2.0
Trauma	1062	0.12	37	0.6
Thrombo-embolism	–	–	29	0.5
Psychiatric	–	–	140	2.4
Total	4166	0.47	546	8.9
No. of operations	886 207		6105	

Sources: OPCS Abortion Statistics AB 12–16: Joint Study of RCGP & RCOG (1985).

recall" in which there is the tendency for women who have a problem such as infertility to recall an induced abortion as a cause for subsequent failure, whilst those who do not suffer ignore, or even deny, the history of a previous induced abortion. The only solution to the problem is to undertake a prospective follow-up, which is notoriously difficult because of the reluctance of such women to agree to be identified or followed up. The unique British system of general practice within the National Health Service has enabled the Royal Colleges of General Practitioners and Obstetricians and Gynaecologists to mount a successful joint follow-up study (Kay and Frank 1981; Joint Study 1985; Frank et al. 1985). Patients with an unplanned pregnancy were followed up over a period of 10 years even through changes of name and residence and it was possible to compare the outcome of those who underwent abortion with control groups who continued with their pregnancy. The results were similar to those of the WHO study, with no significant differences in birth weight or gestation. A Congressional Report from the USA also came to the conclusion that there was no evidence of any serious somatic or psychiatric sequelae following abortion (Koop 1989).

Experience in Other Countries

In Eastern Europe, particularly USSR, Hungary and Yugoslavia, abortion was preferred to contraception as a method of controlling fertility, and although such attitudes are changing (Kapor-Stanulovic and Beric 1975), abortion rates are very high compared with the rest of Europe and USA (Table 14.5). Put into perspective, abortion rates in England and Wales are in the middle range for Western Europe and much lower than in the USA. Even in Ireland, which has no abortion law, there is still a legal abortion rate of at least 4.8 per 1000 recorded from women who came to Britain.

Table 14.5. International comparison of abortion rates and ratios

Country	rate/1000 women	ratio/100 births
USSR (best estimate)	111.9	54.9
Bulgaria	64.7	50.7
Cuba	58.0	45.3
USA	28.0	29.7
Sweden	19.8	24.9
Italy	15.3	25.7
England and Wales	*11.7*	*18.0*
Ireland (notifications in England and Wales)	4.8	5.9
German Fed Rep (best estimate)	7.0	12.8

Romania

The experience of Romania is of particular interest because their very liberal abortion laws were replaced by Ceausescu in 1966, for political reasons, by strong pro-natalist policies which prohibited abortion. What followed was a temporary fall in the birth rate and an increase in abortion mortality which has been described by Tietze (Tietze and Henshaw 1986). I am very grateful to Dr. Nana from Bucharest for more recent figures which demonstrate that suppression of legal abortion merely leads to illegal operations and a rise in maternal mortality (Figs 14.14, 14.15). In the light of the Romanian experience, the proposal to reverse the law on abortion in Poland makes me apprehensive.

Conclusion

Much as we should like to avoid it, induced abortion seems to be part of human reproductive behaviour. Although contraception can go a long way towards reducing the need for abortion, many pregnancies are perceived to be unwanted only after they are conceived and it seems unlikely that unwanted pregnancies can be entirely prevented. If abortions are to be done, it is best that they are done openly, safely and above all, quickly. Experience suggests that attempting to reduce abortion by suppressing it is counter-productive.

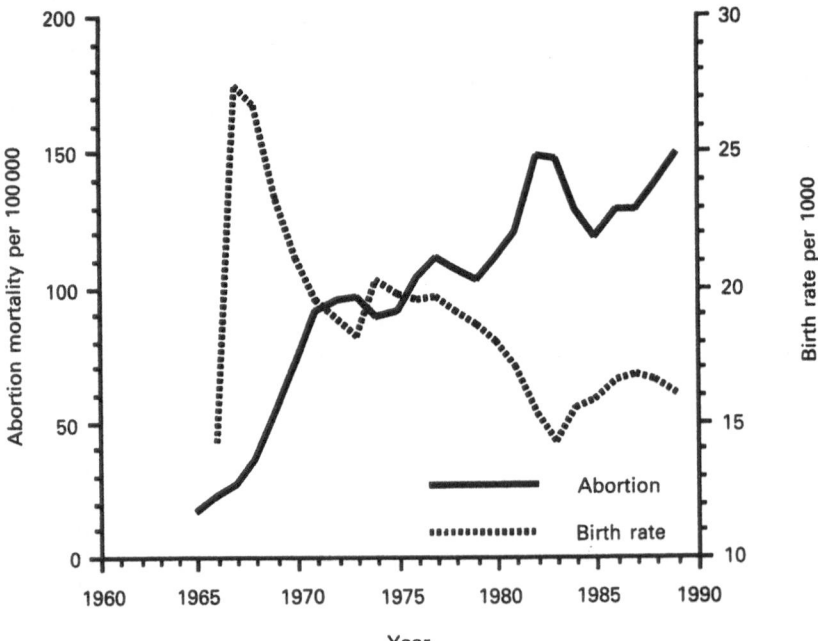

Figure 14.14. Birth rate and abortion mortality in Romania from the restrictive decree of 1966 to 1989. Source: Nana (personal communication).

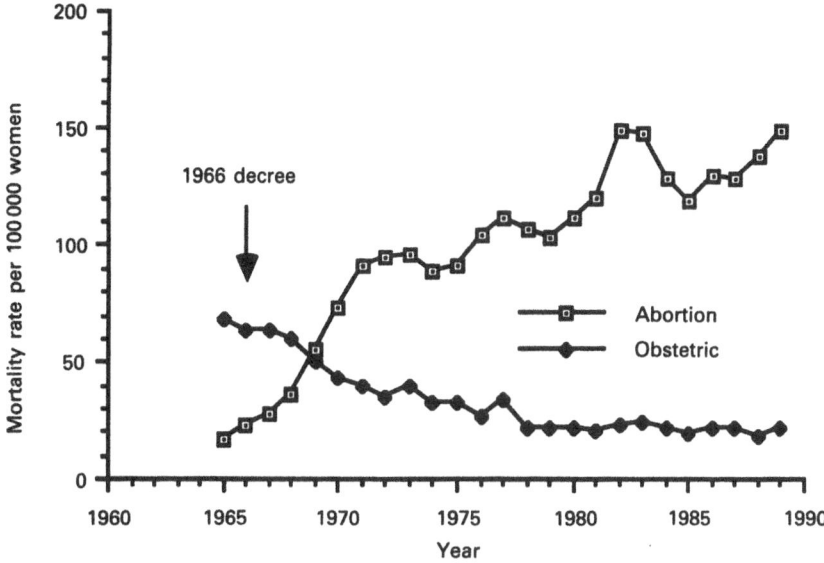

Figure 14.15. The Romanian experience of abortion. Source: Nana (personal communication).

References

Atrash HK, MacKay HT, Binkin NJ, Hogue CJ (1987) Legal abortion mortality in the United States: 1972 to 1982. Am J Obstet Gynecol 156:605–612

Barron SL (1981) Abortion and health. In: Hodgson JE (ed) Abortion and sterilization. Academic Press, London, pp 121–137

Barron SL (1984) Service aspects of abortion. In: Alberman E, Dennis KJ (eds) Late Abortions in England and Wales. RCOG, London, pp 83–102

Barron SL (1986) Sexual activity in girls under sixteen years of age. Br J Obstet Gynaecol 93:787–793

Cates W, Grimes DA (1981) Morbidity and mortality of abortion in the United States. In: Hodgson JE (ed) Abortion and sterilization. Academic Press, London, pp 154–180

Czeizel A, Bognar Z, Tusnady G, Revez P (1970) Changes in mean birth-weight and proportion of low-weight births in Hungary, Br J Prev Soc Med 24:146–153

Department of Health and Social Security (1957–1989) Reports on Confidential Enquiries into Maternal Deaths in England and Wales. Eleven triennial reports from 1952–1954 to 1982–1984, inclusive. Her Majesty's Stationery Office, London

Departments of Health (1991) Report on Confidential Enquiries into Maternal Deaths in the United Kingdom, 1985–87. Her Majesty's Stationery Office, London

Fink AI (1973) Midtrimester abortion. Lancet i:263–264

Frank PI, Kay CR, Lewis TLT, Parish S (1985) Outcome of pregnancy following induced abortion. Br J Obstet Gynaecol 92:308–316

Grimes DJ, Schultz KF (1985) The comparative safety of second-trimester abortion methods. In: Abortion: medical progress and social implications. Pitman, London, pp 83–101 (Ciba foundation symposium 115)

Henshaw SK, Morrow E (1990) Induced abortion: a world review, 1990 Supplement. Alan Guttmacher Institute, New York

Joint Study of Royal College of General Practitioners and the Royal College of Obstetricians and Gynaecologists (1985) Induced abortion operations and their early sequelae. J R Coll Gen Pract 35:175–180

Kapor-Stanulovic N, Beric B (1975) Family planning in Yugoslavia with special reference to the Province of Vojvodina. J Biosoc Sci 5:179–185

Kay CR, Frank PI (1981) Characteristics of women recruited to a long-term study of the sequelae of induced abortion. J R Coll Gen Pract 31:473–477

Koonin LK, Atrash HK, Smith JC, Ramick M (1990) Abortion surveillance, 1986–1987. In: CDC Surveillance Summaries, June 1990. MMWR 1990 (No SS-2) 23–60

Koop CE (1989) Surgeon General's Report on Abortion. Congressional record, 21 March 1989. US Government Printing Office, Washington, DC

Leete R (1976) Some comments on the demographic and social effects of the 1967 Abortion Act. J Biosoc Sci 8:229–251

OPCS (1987) Birth statistics, series FM1 no. 13. HMSO, London

OPCS (1991) Abortion Statistics 1989. Series AB no. 16. HMSO, London

OPCS Monitor (1987) Trends in conceptions to women resident in England and Wales: 1975–85. Series FM1 87/2. OPCS, London

Scottish Health Service (1990) Scottish Health Statistics 1990 and earlier volumes. Common Services Agency, Edinburgh

Stanwell-Smith R (1984) Procedures used for legal abortion. In: Alberman E, Dennis KJ (eds) Late Abortions in England and Wales: report of confidential enquiry by Royal College of Obstetricians and Gynaecologists. RCOG, London, pp 45–66

Tietze C, Lewit S (1972) Joint Program for the Study of Abortion (JPSA). Stud Fam Plann 4:97–122

Tietze C (1983) Induced Abortion. In: Barron SL, Thomson AM (eds) Obstetrical epidemiology. Academic Press, London, pp 319–346

Tietze C, Henshaw SK (1986) Induced abortion: a world review, 6th edn. Alan Guttmacher Institute, New York

WHO Task Force (1979) Gestation, birth-weight and spontaneous abortion in pregnancy after induced abortion. Lancet i:142–145

CHAPTER 15

The Complex Problem of Abortion

Peter Millican

The problem of the morality of abortion is one of the most complex and controversial in the entire field of applied ethics. It may therefore appear rather surprising that the most popular proposed "solutions" to it are extremely simple and straightforward, based on clear-cut universal rules which typically either condemn abortion severely in virtually every case or else deem it to be morally quite unproblematic, and hence permissible whenever the mother wishes. This polarised situation in the theoretical debate, however, is in clear contrast with the abortion law in many countries (including Britain), where abortions are treated very differently according to the stage of pregnancy at which they are carried out, so that early abortions are permitted relatively easily, whereas very late abortions are sanctioned only in exceptional cases. It seems likely, moreover, that in thus taking account of the time of an abortion, the law genuinely reflects the weight of public opinion – there may be no overall consensus on the underlying moral issues, but it does appear to be part of "commonsense" morality to accept that, whatever the ultimate rights and wrongs of abortion in general may be, at any rate abortion early in pregnancy is morally greatly preferable to late abortion. Let us call this "the developmental view", since it holds that the moral gravity of abortion increases with the degree of development of the fetus.[1]

It is, as I have said, surprising that the theoretical debate on such a complex issue should be so polarised. But what is far more surprising, and even paradoxical, is that the various polarised positions, which are so at odds with each other, should all present themselves as the logical working out of the commonsense moral framework which is itself far more moderate than any of them.[2] This I dub the "polarisation paradox", and one of the primary aims of this paper is to investigate what lies behind it, and how it might be resolved. My diagnosis will be that the abortion debate has been polarised precisely because it has been grossly oversimplified, in that the various protagonists have tended to look for a single general rule to solve the entire problem, when a relatively subtle and sensitive approach would be far more appropriate to the complexity of the issue. Once the search for a simple solution is abandoned, we shall see that it is relatively easy to provide some justification for the commonsense developmental view, and in doing so, to undermine the appeal of the extreme positions which have hitherto held the field. I shall here be able to offer no more than a sketch of how such a justification might go, but I hope that this sketch will be enough to suggest that progress can be made.

All this, however, may seem somewhat academic to those of a strong religious persuasion, whose part in the abortion debate has been too significant to ignore, but who are likely to be quite unimpressed by appeals to "commonsense" morality when they believe themselves to have at hand a far more authoritative and reliable moral guide. It is important to face up to this issue, for (at least in the West) the Christian religion has been the inspiration for most of those who have, over the years, advocated an extreme "conservative" position. Before turning to the main business of the paper, therefore, it is appropriate to ask whether, for the believer, religion can legitimately cut through the complexities of the moral debate, and establish independently the sort of extreme position which I am here opposing. I shall argue that it cannot, and that therefore even the religious believer, if he wishes to achieve a rationally defensible view, cannot expect to ignore or bypass the twists and turns of this complex moral debate.[3] We shall also see, incidentally, that the most prominent conservative tradition, that of the Roman Catholic Church, provides a far less secure foundation than is generally supposed even for a purely religiously-based rejection of the commonsense developmental view.

Why Religion Provides No Simple Answer

Although it is very common for those on the conservative side of the abortion debate to appeal to religion to support their case, such an appeal is far more problematic than is usually appreciated. One very obvious point is that, at least in any pluralist society such as our own, all religious principles are themselves highly controversial, so that those who base their opposition to abortion on the authority of, say, the Roman Catholic Church, can expect to convince only those who already share similar religious commitments. Moreover even those Roman Catholics who are convinced by such an appeal to authority may be reluctant to impose their views on people outside the Church: it is perfectly consistent to believe that something is wrong without also believing that one has a right to prohibit others from doing it.[4] Such an imposition of one's own moral views on others is likely to seem particularly questionable when those views are overtly based on religious doctrines which are themselves very hard to defend.[5]

It is, then, at least problematic to appeal to religious authority in order to establish any law which is to be binding on those of other faiths or of none. But perhaps surprisingly, there are also serious practical and theoretical difficulties even for the rational believer who wishes to base his personal moral opinions on such an authority. Two of the most serious of these difficulties derive from the doubtfulness of many religions' moral implications, and the relative certainty of some "commonsense" moral beliefs. The first difficulty can perhaps best be illustrated by giving a brief sketch of the history of the Roman Catholic attitude to abortion, by far the most significant religious influence on the abortion debate in the West.

Roman Catholic Teaching On Abortion

It seems to be almost universally assumed in public debate that the Roman Catholic position on abortion has always been clear, straightforward, and historically consistent. It is indeed true that the Roman Church has always condemned the vast majority of abortions, but this condemnation has over the years been made with greatly differing force, on the basis of a variety of reasons, and with a changing list of exceptions and qualifications. Catholic theologians have disputed at great length about the moral implications of Christianity, but many of their arguments, which have been highly influential in determining the development of the Church's official doctrine, would probably now seem very questionable to many of those who nevertheless ascribe great authority to the current official position. This position is that the fetus is to be treated as a human person from the "first instant" of conception, and that abortion is therefore tantamount to homicide, excusable only in cases where it is an indirect effect of medical intervention whose direct intention is to save the mother's life, as in the case of the removal of a Fallopian tube in an ectopic pregnancy, or the removal of a cancerous uterus. We shall see that it is far from clear whether modern Roman Catholics should feel themselves committed to endorsing such a doctrine.

Much of the historical Christian debate was centred around the interpretation of Exodus 21: 22–25, the only passage of obvious relevance in the Old Testament. In the Revised Standard Version this is translated as follows:

> [22]When men strive together, and hurt a woman with child, so that there is a miscarriage, and yet no harm follows, the one who hurt her shall be fined, according as the woman's husband shall lay upon him; and he shall pay as the judges determine. [23]If any harm follows, then you shall give life for life, [24]eye for eye, tooth for tooth, hand for hand, foot for foot, [25]burn for burn, wound for wound, stripe for stripe.

It is clear from the context that "harm" here means harm to the woman, but in the influential Greek Septuagint version, this passage was mistranslated to state that "you shall give life for life" not only where the mother dies, but also where a "formed" fetus dies (that is, a fetus sufficiently developed to have a recognisably human form). Over the centuries most prominent moral theologians (e.g., Jerome, Augustine, Gratian, Lombard, Aquinas, Sanchez, Liguori)[6] accordingly drew a distinction between the abortion of an early ("unformed") and of a late fetus, usually taking only the latter, at most, to be equivalent to homicide, on the grounds that only a "formed" fetus could be "ensouled". The Septuagint mistranslation may have been indirectly influenced by the Aristotelian theory of progressive ensoulment,[7] which was itself to have a significant independent impact on scholastic thought (principally through Aquinas) after Aristotle's major biological writings had been translated into Latin near the beginning of the thirteenth century. According to Aristotle the fetus is initially infused with a nutritive or vegetative soul, then a sensitive or animal soul, and finally manifests a rational or human soul at the (misleadingly named) stage of "animation", occurring after about 40 days of gestation in the case of males, and 80 to 90 days in the case of females. Like the Exodus passage from the Septuagint, this theory was understood to imply that early abortion is not homicide, since it does not involve the killing of a being with a human soul.

None of this should be taken to suggest that the Church condoned early abortion, except in a small number of very special cases. For early abortion was indeed condemned, sometimes as strongly as late abortion, but *not* on the grounds that it was tantamount to homicide. The usual complaint was instead that it was "contrary to nature",[8] so that early abortion would thus be on the same level as the supposedly fairly serious sin of contraception. Most took the two to be roughly equivalent, though Sanchez, for example, thought contraception to be the more unequivocally evil, because of its association with sexual pleasure, whereas early abortion he took to be sometimes permissible. It was not until after the Second Vatican Council in 1965 that the modern distinction was clearly drawn, with abortion at any stage, but not contraception, being declared a "horrible crime".

The distinction between early and late abortion seems to have lost favour for two principal reasons. First, medical advances began to suggest that the development of the fetus was gradual from conception onwards, with no sharp discontinuity to mark the supposed event of ensoulment. The *Medico-Legal Questions* (1621) of Paolo Zacchia was particularly influential in thus undermining the Aristotelian orthodoxy in medical circles (and, much later, amongst theologians), though Zacchia himself retained the idea that late abortion was significantly more serious than early abortion. The second, and theologically more crucial, objection to progressive ensoulment came in the nineteenth century from the increasingly popular cult of the Immaculate Conception of Mary: the doctrine (with no biblical foundation) that Jesus' mother was herself conceived without sin. The point here was that the feast of the Immaculate Conception had been finally settled in the previous century as 8 December, exactly nine months prior to the feast of her birth on 8 September. This looked quite illogical unless Mary's sinless rational soul had come into being at the time of her physical conception, and accordingly, when Pius IX in 1854 "infallibly" proclaimed the Immaculate Conception as a dogma of the church, he stated that Mary had been free from sin "in the first instant of her conception". Consistently, it was this same Pope who, in 1869, finally gave implicit official endorsement to the doctrine of immediate animation, by extending the ultimate punishment of excommunication to all abortions, with no distinction between early and late.

From all this it can be seen that the Roman Catholic position on abortion has developed over a long period subject to many influences, including the interpretation and (mis-) translation of biblical texts,[9] prominent philosophical theories,[10] the development of biological science, many moral judgements about related issues such as contraception and sexual behaviour, and, not least, consistency with theological doctrines.[11] A strict Roman Catholic may be confident that the seal of Papal Infallibility on the Immaculate Conception is sufficient to guarantee the doctrine of immediate animation,[12] and therefore to demonstrate that all abortion is homicide. But for any Christian who has no such confidence, and in particular, for one who denies the traditional belief in the wrongness of contraception and the associated negative attitude to sex, it is far from clear that the Church's historical debate on abortion provides any convincing evidence for the claim that Christian principles require opposition to abortion in virtually all cases, let alone for the extreme Roman Catholic view that all abortion is homicide. Indeed it seems a betrayal of the Church's distinguished history of ethical debate to presume that any such simplistic answer can be derived straightforwardly from the essential core of Christianity. Applied

Christian moral teaching has always been influenced by the science and philosophy of its time: it has never been an exercise in purely *a priori* deduction from religious first principles. Thus for example the interpretation of the central Christian command to "love one's neighbour" has always been determined, in the context of abortion, by contemporary views on the stage at which the fetus begins to count as one's "neighbour", that is, as a person. For most of the history of Christianity it has been accepted that this question is a factual one, not a question of fundamental religious doctrine but one subject to metaphysical and scientific investigation and discovery. Modern Roman Catholics, who appeal to the current orthodoxy as though any faithful Christian must immediately endorse it on religious grounds alone, are therefore contradicting the spirit of the very tradition to which they appeal.

The Moral Route to Knowledge of God's Will

Any reasonable religious believer who is aware of the multitude of faiths, of the equal commitment and conviction of many of those who follow them, and of the lack of independently compelling arguments to vindicate any one of them, must surely acknowledge that, from an objective point of view, his religious beliefs are somewhat less than certain. Also, as we have seen, the moral implications of any particular religion can themselves be very uncertain, and even where they are not, there can be serious doubt as to the legitimacy of imposing them on others. Furthermore, and very significantly, all of these three uncertainties will multiply together and thus amplify, indicating that any direct inference from religion to morality is likely to be highly problematic. But there is yet another important point, related to this, which becomes apparent when we focus on the inference in the reverse direction, from morality to religion.

The point is a simple one, probably best made with an extreme example. Suppose that I am a devoted Christian, with what I take to be strong grounds for my faith (based on personal religious experiences, perhaps), and that I also believe, on similar grounds, that Christianity commits me to accepting the entire Bible as the inspired word of God. Reading it one day, I come across the following passage:

> [16][When you make war against] the cities of these peoples that the Lord your God gives you for an inheritance, you shall save alive nothing that breathes, [17] but you shall utterly destroy them, the Hittites and the Amorites, the Canaanites and the Perizzites, the Hivites and the Jebusites, as the Lord your God has commanded.
> (Deuteronomy 20: 16–17 (RSV))

No doubt my initial reaction in such a case would be surprise that a good God should order the genocide of six whole nations, but the standard fundamentalist response is to provide God with excuses: "no doubt the Hittites, the Amorites and all the rest were appallingly corrupt, worshipping golden calves and performing other such evil deeds, so that they indeed deserved to die, and since God is not only good but also perfectly just, He had to give them what was coming to them", or something of that kind. But it is arguable that such a response itself manifests gross moral corruption; that if there is one thing here that I can be totally sure of, it is that multiple genocide and the slaughter of children is an abomination, and that to advocate such things is unequivocally evil. No matter how convinced I am of my religion, or of its fundamentalist implications, there is simply no way that I can justifiably be more sure of these things that I am of that simple moral truth. So even if my reasons for taking the Bible as the inspired word of a good God are compelling by any *normal* standards, nevertheless those reasons will be completely dwarfed by my certainty of the wrongness of genocide. I should conclude either that this passage in the Bible does not express God's will, or else that a good God does not exist (although of course a different Supreme Being might exist, such as an evil one, but then presumably we would be wrong to obey such a being).[13]

To put this more generally, in some cases our independent moral judgements may be more reliable than our religious speculations – indeed the history of theological dispute suggests that this will often be so. But then, if there is a God and He is good, it follows that our most reliable route to knowledge of His will may be through independent moral argument rather than through theology. The consequences of this are considerable. For example it is all too often taken for granted that any Christian must endorse similar moral views to those taken by other Christians down the centuries: views typically based on absolutist principles rather than on the weighing of consequences. But if our independent moral thinking leads us to conclude that utilitarianism, say, is correct, then this *need* not imply that we must choose between our belief in a good God and our confidence in that moral thinking – we might instead conclude that God is Himself a utilitarian, no doubt with His own excellent and thoroughly consequentialist reasons for having advocated (if indeed He did so) a straightforward absolutist morality in less sophisticated times!

To conclude, it is clear that all religious beliefs are uncertain, while the practical moral implications of the world's major religions are in many cases equally uncertain. On the other hand, sometimes our moral thinking can be compelling on its own terms, without any appeal to religious authority, and with a force sufficient to overrule any such authority if the two conflict. Putting all these points together, it follows that even for the committed believer, religion gives no easy escape from examining, on their own merits, the rights and wrongs of moral issues, and in particular, of abortion.

The Shape of the Abortion Debate

Before embarking on an examination of some of the arguments that have been most prominent within the abortion debate, it is worth first briefly considering the nature of applied moral argument in general. We can then see how the debate fits into a standard pattern, an insight which may provide the key to its eventual resolution.

The Need for a Moral Baseline

A fundamental point, first noticed by David Hume (Hume 1740 pp 469–70) and accordingly known as "Hume's Law", is that moral rules cannot be logically derived from purely non-moral facts: hence any argument that is validly to yield a moral conclusion must include at least one premise which is (explicitly or implicitly) morally loaded. Now if any such argument is to be not only valid but also convincing, the moral premise in question must obviously be accepted in advance by those who are to be persuaded of the conclusion: if they do not accept that crucial premise, then the argument will be powerless to persuade them of anything.[14] It therefore follows that effective moral argument can never take place in a moral vacuum, but has to begin from some baseline which is (at least in the context) taken for granted.

The moral baseline from which the abortion debate starts is constituted by various judgements about the morality of killing and reproduction which are, within our culture, almost universally accepted (albeit with some controversial exceptions for special cases, such as the voluntary euthanasia of a terminally ill adult, killing in war, or judicial capital punishment):

1. The killing of an adult or a child is a serious wrong, and should accordingly be punished by law
2. The killing of a higher animal such as rabbit, though perhaps morally significant, is not a serious wrong, while the killing of a lower animal such as a mosquito is morally insignificant
3. The use of contraception, if wrong at all, is at most a minor wrong, while the killing of an unfertilised ovum or the removal of a tumour (at least if performed at the request of the "patient") is morally quite unproblematic

The arguments used by anti-abortionists accordingly attempt to show that abortion should be classed with the killing of an adult or child, whereas those used by pro-abortionists attempt to equate it instead with such things as the killing of an animal, the removal of a tumour, or the use of contraception. Let us look first at three very crude attempts to establish such equivalences.

"Hole-in-One" Arguments

The arguments below might be called "hole-in-one" arguments, because they purport to establish sweeping conclusions in a single logical stroke. They correspond to three extreme positions within the abortion debate, which we can for convenience name the "Conservative", "Feminist", and "Liberal" positions respectively (using capitals to signify these particular, polarised views).

"Conservative": *The Human Being Argument*
1. The fetus is a human being
2. Killing human beings is wrong
∴ Killing the fetus is wrong

"Feminist": *The Woman's Body Argument*
1. The fetus is part of a woman's body
2. A woman has a right to do whatever she wishes to any part of her body
∴ A woman has a right to kill her fetus

"Liberal": *The Person Argument*
1. The fetus is not a person
2. Only persons have any moral status
∴ The fetus has no moral status

All of these three arguments are manifestly valid – that is, anyone who accepts their premises is rationally committed to accepting their conclusion. But precisely for this reason no opponents who have their wits about them are the least bit likely to accept the premises. Imagine, for example, a dispute between a Feminist and a Conservative which revolves around the Woman's Body Argument. Initially, I would guess, many Conservatives will be likely to accept the second premise, that a woman has a right to do what she wishes with her body, but will resist the argument by rejecting the first premise, that the fetus is part of her body. Now let us suppose that the Feminist is able to support this premise, at least as regards the very early pre-embryo, by persuading the Conservative that the ovum is part of a woman's body, and that fertilisation leaves this status unaffected. This may be unlikely, but suppose he is convinced. What then? Will he give up and renounce his position on abortion? Of course not! He will simply conclude that his initial acceptance of the plausible second premise was too hasty, that although in most cases a woman has a right to do what she wishes with her body, there is after all at least one very important part of her body to which this principle does not apply – namely the fetus. And he is not being manifestly unreasonable in taking this position, for even if it is agreed that the fetus is part of its mother's body, it is clearly a very unusual and untypical part, with certain unique properties which may well be morally relevant (for example, it is arguably the only part of her body that has future interests distinct from her own). Hence it is surely dubious to assume that its "moral status" can simply be extrapolated from this sort of general principle, whose apparent obviousness clearly derives from parts of the body which do not share these unique properties.

An exactly parallel problem arises with the other two arguments. It may be possible for the Conservative to convince the Liberal that the fetus is a human being, for it is apparently a living being and is certainly of the species *Homo sapiens* rather than any other, but if the Liberal is persuaded of this then he can simply deny that killing human beings is always wrong, on the grounds that there are important exceptions to this rule, namely fetuses! (not to mention sperm and unfertilised ova, which by the Conservative's reasoning seem also to be "human beings"). And again this denial is not manifestly unreasonable, for even if the early fetus is indeed a human being, it is so strikingly different from other human beings (e.g. in its lack of activity and sentience) that there must be some legitimate doubt as to whether the conventional absolute prohibition on killing humans should be understood as applying equally to it. As for the Person Argument, the Conservative is likely to accept the first premise, that the fetus is not a person (at least if "person" is defined in what seems to be a fashionable way,[15] as a self-conscious being), but if he does so he is sure to reject the second premise, since he presumably does not believe that only persons have moral status – after all, according to him fetuses have moral status even if they are not "persons". If the Liberal then responds by claiming that "person" is a moral notion, and that persons are *by definition* those beings which have moral status, then perhaps the Conservative could be forced to accept the second premise, but he will now of course immediately deny the first instead, on the grounds that its meaning has changed: if "person" means not a self-conscious being but one with moral status, then the fetus, since it indeed has moral status, is, after all, a person.[16]

The lesson to be drawn from all of this is similar in some ways to one which we drew from our consideration of religion. There we saw that a valid argument which yields moral conclusions from religious premises, for example:

1. Christian principles are true
2. Christian principles imply that genocide is sometimes permissible
∴   Genocide is sometimes permissible

can always be turned on its head by someone who denies the moral conclusion. Such a person will either conclude that (some) Christian principles are false, or alternatively, will deny that Christian principles condone genocide. Likewise in the case of the three "hole-in-one" arguments above: it is simply naive to suppose that they can ever persuade anyone of the truth of their conclusion, for someone who starts out denying that conclusion is overwhelmingly unlikely to accept the premises which so obviously entail it. Even if persuaded by the first (apparently factual) premise, the opponent in each case will be able to resist the conclusion simply by rejecting the second (moral) premise, and because it is a moral premise which he rejects, no purely factual investigation will be able to show him to be mistaken – we have a straightforward clash of moral opinions, and no progress whatever.

Hume's Law indicates that the same will be true of any such simple moral argument: if it is valid then at least one of its premises must be morally loaded, and someone who begins from a contrary moral position, even if persuaded to accept all the purely factual premises of the argument, can always consistently reject that moral premise, and with it, the conclusion. In any "hole-in-one" argument the relation between moral premise and moral conclusion will inevitably be very straightforward, so that anyone who denies the conclusion will indeed almost certainly be happy to deny the premise. To make any progress in moral debate, therefore, we must look to arguments which probe much more deeply into our moral concepts, and which, rather than crudely appealing to a single explicit principle, instead either aim to tease out the more subtle implications of our general moral framework, or else try to show how some of the plausible moral principles to which the opponent already feels committed are in fact conflicting, so that his moral position must be revised. Perhaps the best examples of such arguments within the abortion debate are the liberal "Argument from Speciesism" (which is of the first type), and the conservative "Argument from Potentiality" (which is of the second).[17]

The Argument from Speciesism: the Fetus as an Animal

The Argument from Speciesism is intended to show that the standard conservative appeal to the moral significance of the fetus' humanity, as manifested for example in the Human Being Argument, is morally repugnant (the term "speciesism" was coined to suggest an analogy with racism and sexism). Those who advance this argument typically go on to provide an account of moral status based on "personhood" rather than species membership, so it is often used as a prelude to the Person Argument sketched earlier. As presented below, the argument starts from the principle of universalisability – that any basic moral principle must employ only "universal" terms, in other words, terms which can be completely defined without any mention of particular individuals (or of particular groups of individuals).[18] This gives the argument a theoretical basis but a rather more technical feel than it usually has in popular accounts: most frequently, the first two steps are omitted,[19] and readers unaccustomed to such philosophical niceties are welcome to omit them here.

1. A being's moral status can only depend on its morally relevant "universal" properties, and not, for example, on its colour (which is universal but not morally relevant) nor on its individual identity (which is not a universal property and therefore *cannot* be morally relevant)

2. Membership of the species *Homo sapiens* is not, in itself, a universal property[20]

3. Hence membership of the human race is not morally relevant, any more than membership of the Caucasian race is morally relevant

4. Therefore the moral status of any human being cannot depend just on the fact that it is human – it must as an individual have whatever properties (perhaps feelings and desires, rationality, self-consciousness, capacity for action and for relationships) endow something with that status

5. The morally relevant universal properties (feelings and desires, rationality etc.) of the mature members of other species of mammals greatly exceed those of a human fetus

∴ The moral status of a human fetus cannot be greater than the moral status of an animal such as a mature rabbit and so since we do not consider a rabbit to have a serious right to life, neither should we attribute such a right to the human fetus

Such an argument is very powerful, since it is based so immediately on the fundamental and widely respected principle of universalisability (or less technically, on obvious considerations of fairness between species). At the very least it presents a serious challenge to anyone who would accord humanity a favoured moral status, to justify that status in terms which are themselves morally respectable. Here, then, we are not left with a crude moral standoff between the two sides, for if the conservative fails to meet the challenge of the Argument from Speciesism, then he must apparently reject a principle which is widely thought to be constitutive of our whole moral framework.

The Argument from Potentiality: The Fetus as a Child

The Argument from Potentiality can be seen as an attempt to meet the challenge of alleged speciesism, by highlighting a morally relevant difference between the human fetus and other animals, a difference which depends not on their current properties, but on their future possibilities. A simple version of this argument is as follows:

1. Although the human fetus may currently have none of the *actual* properties (feelings and desires, rationality etc.) that confer moral status, nevertheless it has the *potential* to acquire them, in that it will naturally develop into a mature human possessing all of these properties to a high degree

2. No non-human animal has the potential to develop into a being whose morally relevant actual properties are of a similar degree to those of a mature human

3. If any property is morally relevant, then the potential to acquire it is also morally relevant

∴ A human fetus has some morally relevant universal properties (namely, its potentialities) which would justify conferring on it a greater moral status than that of any non-human animal

Here we reach the heart of the abortion debate. For it seems fairly clear that the Argument from Speciesism is correct to claim that the early human fetus, on the basis merely of its existing observable properties, cannot possibly merit the special moral status which the conservative wishes to ascribe to it. So the only non-speciesist and non-religious ground which can be given for its claimed intrinsic special status is that of its potential: it may not *currently* have the properties which we take to be of supreme moral significance, and which mark our species out from all others, but in the course of time, if the fetus is allowed to develop normally, it *will* have them – it therefore has now the *potential* to become a mature human being with all that this implies.

The crucial premise in this argument is the third, which we might call the "potentiality principle", and the argument's power will depend greatly on the interpretation and justification of this premise. The conservative's usual strategy here is to argue that a commitment to this principle is already implicit in the generally accepted "moral baseline" beliefs from which the abortion debate starts – in particular, our almost universal belief in the serious wrongness of killing young children.[21] If the conservative is successful in showing that the only way of making sense of this belief is in terms of a child's potentiality, then the consistent liberal will be faced with a dilemma – either to give up his belief in the serious wrongness of killing infants, or else to acknowledge that he is, after all, implicitly committed to the serious wrongness of abortion.

Potentiality Criticised: Abortion as Contraception

Liberal critics of the potentiality principle have generally tried to refute it directly by showing its implausible consequences rather than attempting to undermine it by proposing an alternative account of the high moral status of infants. Some, indeed, have seen no need of such an alternative account, and have accordingly been prepared to countenance the moral acceptability of infanticide.[22]

The standard liberal "refutation" of the potentiality principle can be set out as follows:[23]

1. According to the conservative, killing the fetus is seriously wrong not because of its actual properties (feelings and desires, rationality etc.), but solely because it has the potential to develop into a mature human being

2. However the unfertilised ovum and the sperm, taken as a pair, also have the potential to develop into a mature human being

3. Hence, on the conservative's potentiality principle, the unfertilised ovum and sperm have a similar moral status to that of the fetus, and it is therefore seriously wrong to kill them

4. If it is seriously wrong to kill the unfertilised ovum and sperm, then contraception is a morally serious offence

5. But contraception is not a morally serious offence

∴ The conservative's potentiality principle is false

It may be that the fourth step here could be disputed, on the grounds that
contraception often merely allows the ovum and sperm to die rather than killing
them, but even if it were plausible this objection would hardly matter, since
the third step by itself is damaging enough to the conservative. And since this
step seems to be directly implied by the first two premises, the conservative
who bases his case on the Argument from Potentiality has no alternative but to
challenge the symmetry which these premises allege, between the potentiality
of the fetus and that of the unfertilised ovum and sperm.

The usual conservative response at this point is to draw a distinction between
a strong sense of potentiality (which applies only to the fetus) and a weak sense
(which applies to the ovum and sperm).[24] One basis for drawing such a
distinction is the claim that the fetus, unlike the ovum and sperm, not only has
the potential to *bring about* the existence of a future adult human being, but
also, if it does so, will be *one and the same individual* as that adult. So the
ovum and sperm may have the potential to *produce* an adult human being, but
only the fetus has the potential to *become* one.[25]

Again the liberal can reply, maintaining the equivalence of ovum and fetus.
He might, for example, appeal to the possibility of parthenogenesis (whereby a
single ovum can develop without fertilisation) to ascribe to the unfertilised ovum
precisely that strong potentiality which the conservative ascribes to the fetus.
And again the conservative can respond, by adding to his strong notion of
potentiality the requirement that the individual concerned must have the capacity
not only to become an adult, but to do so under its own, natural, internal
genetic control, without the sort of artificial external manipulation which
successful parthenogenesis would presumably require. Yet again the liberal can
come back, pointing out that the development of the fetus is not itself entirely
under internal genetic control (and not at all initially), but like that of the
parthenogenetic ovum is crucially dependent on a number of "epigenetic"
influences.[26] And so the debate goes on, with the conservative repeatedly
attempting to establish a moral asymmetry between the fetus and the ovum/sperm
pair, and the liberal continuing to dispute it.

The Shape of the Debate

Although we have briefly examined only a few of the many arguments within
the abortion debate, we can already see clearly the pattern which characterises
that debate as a whole. For on the one hand, the pro-abortionist will aim to
undermine the special claims of the fetus which supposedly derive from the fact
of its humanity, and will thus attempt to steer our moral intuitions towards
seeing the fetus as like a lower animal, or an unfertilised ovum, rather than like
a child; while on the other hand, the anti-abortionist will try to justify the fetus'
disputed special status, by showing how our ordinary moral beliefs require us
to see it as like a child or adult rather than like an animal. In both cases,
however, the arguments will appeal to the baseline of our generally shared moral
beliefs about children, animals, contraception and so on. The central question
of the debate, therefore, is whether these "commonsense" moral beliefs indeed
commit us, on pain of inconsistency, to a position for, or against, abortion.

The "Polarisation Paradox"

There is a conspicuous feature of the abortion debate which, in the light of what has been said above, may seem highly paradoxical. We have seen that moral argument in general must start from a baseline of mutually accepted moral beliefs, and typically proceeds by attempting to uncover the (sometimes deeply hidden) implications of those baseline beliefs. Furthermore it is clear that the principal arguments within the abortion debate fit comfortably into this pattern: both the pro- and anti-abortionist arguments fundamentally appeal to commonsense moral principles (such as the serious wrongness of killing children), or to more subtle general features of the commonsense moral framework (such as universalisability or fairness). It is very surprising, therefore, that most of the participants in this debate appear to be drawn by these arguments towards highly polarised positions which seem to square very badly with the baseline of commonsense morality from which they supposedly begin. Let us call this the "polarisation paradox". It is perhaps best illustrated by spelling out some of the logical consequences of the three extreme views outlined earlier, all of which have what would surely seem to the uncommitted to be implausible and indeed quite unacceptable moral implications.

Unacceptable Implications of the "Conservative" Position

On the "Conservative" view, abortion is as bad as the deliberate killing of an adult, at no matter what stage in pregnancy it is carried out, and it is therefore wrong even where the mother is an eleven-year-old girl, and even where her pregnancy is only a few hours advanced, and is moreover a result of rape. Abortion may possibly be justifiable where it is necessary to save the mother's life, but even in this case the doctor who performs it is in the dubious position of murdering one individual to save another (*the doctor* cannot plead self-defence, even if the mother could). Conservatives are typically also opposed to euthanasia, and if so they will reject abortion even in cases of diagnosed genetic disease, and even where the disease is so serious that others might be inclined to kill the fetus out of mercy, to save it from a life which will inevitably and foreseeably be nasty, painful and short (e.g., Tay-Sachs disease or Duchenne muscular dystrophy).

Not surprisingly, however, some of the most implausible consequences of the Conservative view are associated with very early pregnancy, where an ascription to the fetus of the same moral status as an adult seems particularly hard to take seriously. First, it implies that the intra-uterine device, and any variety of drug that similarly acts partly by preventing implantation, is a potential murder weapon rather than a mere contraceptive, whose knowing use presumably warrants suitable punishment: at a time when the burgeoning population is already putting the planet's resources under considerable stress, the effect of prohibiting so many of the Third World's most effective contraceptives can only be imagined. A second consequence of the Conservative position is that countless morally significant lives (estimated at 50% of fertilised ova)[27] are being regularly lost in early pregnancy, through spontaneous abortion – surely the consistent Conservative should support attempts to avoid this appalling loss of life, by promoting research on methods to help bring these unfortunate fetuses to term. No matter that it seems likely that a high proportion of them are chromosomally abnormal, and aborted for that very reason: if they have the same status as an adult human, then we should presumably make serious efforts to help them survive.[28] Consistent Conservatism, therefore, would not only seriously hamper efforts to control Third World population growth, but would also apparently entail spending an ever-increasing proportion of the developed world's budget on coping with its own population boom which, if spontaneous abortion were significantly reduced, would be made up very largely of a massive increase in the proportion of severely handicapped infants.[29]

Unacceptable Implications of the "Liberal" and "Feminist" Positions

Just as the extreme Conservative view seems particularly implausible at the beginning of pregnancy, so the extreme "Liberal" and "Feminist" views seem equally implausible at the end of pregnancy and beyond. For according to the Liberal who bases his position entirely on the Person argument given earlier (and who, typically, understands a "person" to be a being whose mental life significantly exceeds that of a newborn baby), even the eight- or nine-month fetus, and even the young baby after its birth, have no moral status whatever, and could therefore be killed (or, say, donated for scientific experimentation) without compunction and for any reason however trivial: because the fetus moves or the baby cries too much, because it is the "wrong" sex, or even perhaps for entertainment. The extreme Feminist position shares these implications in so far as they affect the unborn fetus, for this is supposedly a part of the mother's body and can accordingly be removed, with no more thought than would accompany a haircut, should the mother so choose – for example if a termination at seven months will save her the nuisance of having to postpone a trip abroad.[30] Surely most would consider these to be conclusions almost as evidently objectionable as the sanctioning of genocide: if the Liberal and Feminist arguments really have these implications, then so far from justifying their conclusions, they only succeed in revealing the unacceptability of their premises.

Diagnosis of the Paradox

It seems unlikely that many people would be initially attracted by the extreme implications of the "Conservative", "Liberal", or "Feminist" views. Certainly many would accept them, but most of these would do so, I suggest, reluctantly rather than enthusiastically, because they feel committed to accepting them on the basis of whatever fundamental principles seem to them to be required to support their immediate moral "intuitions" about abortion in general. Thus a Conservative, for example, will not typically *start* from a firm view about the case of a just-pregnant eleven-year-old rape victim – his moral intuitions are far more likely to get a grip on cases that are less obviously problematic for him, where pregnancy is the result of carelessness rather than rape, where the mother is an adult, and where the fetus concerned is sufficiently advanced to be "visibly" human. Seeking a means of justifying such "intuitions", he may then be drawn towards some principle such as the Sanctity of Human Life, and hence endorse the Human Being Argument outlined earlier. Having reached this point, he will now feel forced to pronounce a negative judgement on the child rape case, but this judgement will be based not on immediate moral intuition, but on the demands of consistency and the apparent logical force of the Human Being Argument.

Likewise most pro-abortionists will not, I suggest, usually begin with clear "intuitions" about the case of a healthy, eight-month viable fetus, but are far more likely to focus on the relative insignificance of the early pre-embryo, the tragic results of congenital disease, the sometimes devastating effects of unwanted pregnancy, and the serious dangers of back-street abortions.[31] Some may also see evidence of sexism in the Conservative's disapproving attitude towards the unwilling mother,[32] and understandably react by adopting a Feminist line. Others may be shocked by the striking contrast between the Conservative's anxious concern for a mere "bundle of cells" which happens to be human, and his relative disregard for the far more highly advanced members of other species: this will probably incline such people towards a Liberal position. At this point, again, the search for a theoretical justification takes over, with the Feminist appealing to the Woman's Body Argument and the Liberal to the Person Argument. The demands of consistency then propel them both down the slippery slope towards a blanket endorsement of universal abortion on demand.

If these speculations are at all correct, then it may be that what is responsible for the polarisation of the abortion debate is not the extremism of the protagonists' basic moral "intuitions", but rather an over-enthusiasm for simple, all-encompassing rules (and corresponding hole-in-one arguments) that leads them to generalise far too quickly from a limited range of examples. This diagnosis would explain why all of the extreme positions conflict with "commonsense" morality on one particular point: they all claim that abortion at any stage has much the same moral status, whereas the commonsense consensus surely endorses what I earlier dubbed the "developmental view", that whatever the final judgement on late abortion may be, it is, at any rate, morally a significantly more serious matter than very early abortion. The failure of the extreme positions to accommodate this compelling belief is a clear indication that the spurious demands of over-simple systematisation, and the straitjacket of absolute "principles", have here gained the upper hand over moral common sense.

Escaping from the Trap

The diagnosis just given suggests a possible means of escape from the polarisation trap. For if it is true that polarisation is an artefact of the assumption of moral simplicity rather than a genuine reflection of the various protagonists' basic moral "intuitions", then it may be possible to undermine the extreme positions by challenging that assumption, and by showing how a more subtle and sophisticated treatment of the issue can reasonably accommodate the most fundamental intuitions of all concerned. Moreover if, as I have suggested, the arguments for the extreme positions ultimately derive their strength from those parts of the "commonsense" moral consensus to which they so conspicuously appeal, then there is no way that they can legitimately be used to retaliate against a position which more faithfully reflects the overall nature of that consensus. If the *a priori* assumption of a single-dimensional solution is rejected, then there will be no basis on which they can challenge a more sophisticated position which better fits the varied contours of our commonsense moral landscape. It seems, then, that the polarisation paradox may contain the seeds of its own dissolution.

How can we attack this pervasive assumption of the moral simplicity of abortion? Presumably the most direct method would be to provide a complete alternative account of the issue, which while being more complex and heterogenous than the popular extreme positions, would be both internally coherent and morally compelling. I shall soon attempt to sketch what might be a small contribution towards such an account, but before doing so I shall try briefly to undermine the "simplicity assumption" in another way, by explaining how such an assumption, though entirely false, might nevertheless have become so deeply entrenched. At least three factors seem likely to have played a part. First, widespread traditional attitudes to the ethics of homicide, which (no doubt for obvious sociological reasons) generally treat it as an area where simple and absolute rules hold sway. Secondly, the influence of the Judaeo-Christian moral tradition, with its powerful emphasis on straightforward, categorical, God-given laws. Thirdly, Christian teaching on the soul and the nature of man, which has generally been taken to imply that human status is an all-or-nothing matter: one either has a rational, immortal soul (in which case one merits full moral respect as a being "made in the image of God"), or one does not (in which case one is, by comparison, morally irrelevant).

None of these three considerations now seems at all persuasive: the first merely begs the question, the second we have already dismissed, while the third relies on a concept which (quite apart from any other difficulties it may have) has been rendered wildly problematic by the development of evolutionary theory. If man indeed evolved gradually from the animals, then it is hard to see any place for a uniquely human rational soul, or indeed for any other kind of soul which might radically distinguish our metaphysical status from that of the animals. And if, as seems reasonable, our "moral status" too developed gradually, in tandem with our bodies and brains, then this provides excellent reason for denying that moral status in general, and in particular that of the fetus, must be an all-or-nothing matter rather than one of degree.[33]

It may be that a fourth influence, no doubt itself a hangover from the other three, has been largely responsible for maintaining the popularity of the simplicity assumption, namely the language in which the abortion debate is usually conducted, and which can all too easily cast its spell over the unwary participant. Take, for example, the common tendency to present the central issue in terms of "rights", which already seems to presuppose a clear-cut answer, given that the possession of a right is paradigmatically an all-or-nothing affair and also morally overriding: the fetus either has the right to life or it doesn't, and if it does, then that is the end of the matter. It is also often assumed, though it does not follow, that if the fetus lacks the right to life then that too settles the matter: to make such an assumption is to presuppose that abortion can only be wrong if it involves the infringement of a fetal right. Rights are obviously very precious on this view, and only to be accorded to those of appropriate status. Thus we arrive at the hackneyed question of the "moral status of the fetus", a question whose very phrasing seems to suggest not only a crude division of the moral universe into rights-bearers ("persons") and others, but also a similarly crude picture of morality itself, with individuals as independent bearers of objective moral value, governed entirely when their interests conflict by those rights and obligations which appropriately correspond to their varying "status".

We must be careful not to be bewitched by such language. For we may wish to conclude that the claims of the fetus are not after all a matter of absolute "rights", but we need not thereby be committed to seeing abortion as permissible or unproblematic.[34] Likewise, as I have suggested, we may wish to view the status of the fetus as a matter of degree. Finally, as we shall see, we may wish to reject the whole individualistic picture of morality, by considering the problem of abortion not only with regard to the fetus and mother, but also with regard to the other members of their moral community.

Defending the Middle Ground

Let us pause for a moment to take stock. We have seen that the arguments of both the liberal and conservative start from a baseline of generally accepted moral beliefs, for example beliefs in the serious wrongness of killing a child and the relative inconsequentiality of killing an animal such as a rabbit. The liberal then seeks to show that certain fundamental principles that are implicit in our moral baseline, notably the principle of universalisability (and its corollary, the "principle of non-speciesism"), inevitably commit us to placing the fetus at the inconsequential end of this spectrum, along with the rabbit. The conservative aims to counter this move by appealing to a potentiality principle, supposedly also implicit in our moral baseline, which while respecting the constraint of universalisability, forces us to place the fetus at the other end of the spectrum, along with the child. Meanwhile, I have suggested, the entirely consistent and eminently defensible preference of "commonsense morality", uncorrupted by the polarised language and spurious oversimplifications that so bedevil the abortion debate, would be to place the fetus somewhere in the middle of this moral spectrum, its position depending very largely on its particular degree of development. I shall now try briefly to substantiate this suggestion.

My strategy for defending the middle ground will be as follows. First, I shall show that even without appealing to any principle of potentiality, it is quite easy to defend in a non-speciesist way the commonsense claim that the killing of a developed human fetus is far more serious than the killing of a rabbit. This result may seem to be damaging only to the liberal's case, but we shall see that it also has the more subtle consequence of significantly undermining the conservative's claim that his strong principle of potentiality is indeed implicit in the baseline of commonsense morality. I shall then go on to consider the issue of potentiality in a little more detail, with the aim of showing that even if a potentiality principle were implicit in commonsense morality, it could only very questionably be extended to cover the case of the early fetus, while even if it could be so extended, it still would not vindicate any extreme conservative position, but would on the contrary support the commonsense developmental view, that the moral significance of the human fetus is at least to some extent proportional to its development.

Speciesism and Human Concern

The principle of universalisability, as the liberal insists, implies the unacceptability of a certain kind of preference for our own species – the conservative cannot consistently claim that the "intrinsic moral status" of an early human fetus is greater than that of an animal such as a rabbit (let us call this the "intrinsic superiority claim"), simply on the ground that the fetus is human and for no other reason. An appeal to potentiality then seems to be the conservative's only plausible way of defending his claim, but it is important to see that even if this appeal were ultimately to fail, and his intrinsic superiority claim to be rejected, this would not immediately imply the conclusion which the radical liberal wants, namely, that we should treat the human fetus with no more respect than the rabbit. Such a conclusion would follow only if our moral obligations to others depended entirely on their "intrinsic moral status", but this assumption, once stated, can easily be seen to be questionable for at least two reasons.

The first reason is that our obligations may depend not only on the intrinsic properties (moral or otherwise) of those with whom we deal, but also on their relationship to ourselves. For example I consider myself to have far greater obligations towards my wife and children than I have towards anybody else, but I do not need to pretend that their intrinsic moral status is greater than that of all other wives and children in order to justify these special obligations.

The second reason, which is a generalisation of the first, is that our obligations towards someone (or something) can depend not only on their intrinsic properties, and their relationship to ourselves, but also on their relationship to others. Suppose, for example, that my young son David has a pet slug, Slimy, which he values very dearly. I personally dislike slugs, and would not normally hesitate to kill one if I saw it in our garden, but in the circumstances described I would certainly not kill Slimy. However my sense of obligation towards "him" does not in any way indicate a change of heart about his intrinsic moral status compared with others of his species – on the contrary, I stay my hand out of consideration for David, not for Slimy.

It should be noted that neither of these examples of preferential treatment, for my family and for Slimy respectively, is in any way a violation of the principle of universalisability. For I can happily endorse the corresponding universal rules, first, that everyone has special obligations towards the members of his own family, and secondly, that any animal (or indeed thing) which is valued by any member of any species should in general be treated with some corresponding respect. The availability of such universal rules substantially reduces the impact of the Argument from Speciesism, for it shows that it is in principle possible to justify giving more respect to the human fetus than to a rabbit without infringing against universalisability, and without having to rely on controversial claims about the fetus' superior intrinsic moral status. This can be done in a variety of ways, for example by endorsing universal principles of the following kinds:[35]

> *Principle of Special Obligation*
> Any member of any species has a special obligation to protect any other member (fetus or otherwise) of its own species
>
> *Principle of Sympathetic Respect*
> Any member of any species, if it is an object of love and concern to others (of

any species), should be accorded additional respect in proportion to the magnitude of that love and concern

Though perhaps plausible enough, I shall not here put any weight on the first of these two principles, for it may appear to be no more than a cover for pernicious speciesism, given that we are easily the most powerful species on earth and depend on no others for protection.[36] It also seems to be suspiciously *ad hoc*, for at least three reasons. First, we are presumably the only terrestrial species with moral obligations; secondly, our special obligation to the mature members of our own species can be perfectly well explained in a number of familiar ways without invoking any such principle; thirdly, there is no obvious independent reason why the principle should include fetuses within its scope (or indeed immature organisms of any species, terrestrial or otherwise, which have as yet no morally relevant actual properties).

The principle of sympathetic respect, however, is open to no such objection, and indeed seems fairly persuasive. For we do tend to give some additional respect to those people and animals (and even objects, especially works of art) which we know to be dear to others, and this cannot be just out of consideration for those others' feelings, for it can even apply after their death. One qualification of the principle may, however, be appropriate, for the respect which we sympathetically extend to the objects of others' concern may well depend on our approval (or at least non-disapproval) of that concern: if for example a friend is captivated by some charismatic Nazi, then his uncritical admiration is unlikely to increase my regard for that Nazi, but may on the contrary make my disgust all the stronger. Fortunately, however, such considerations have little impact on the argument regarding abortion, where as we shall see the relevant sentiments are clearly worthy of our approval.

The argument, then, is that just as a slug can merit some respect, however minimal, because of the affection of a small boy, so a human fetus, or a child, can also merit respect, and in much greater measure, because of the affection and concern of its parents and their community. And of course the same will apply to the young of any other species which values its offspring (though some may wish to restrict this to cases where the mature animals' own "moral status" is sufficient to confer respect on those they value). However several factors then combine to provide a powerful case for viewing the human fetus and child more generally with special respect. First, there are obvious evolutionary reasons, in view of the human child's unusually long period of total dependency, for expecting human parental affection to be almost universal and extremely powerful. Secondly, it can be expected that human parents, given even the most primitive understanding of the processes of reproduction, will imaginatively extend this affection from the anticipated child to the fetus, at least once the fetus can be easily thought of as a child (e.g., when they are aware that it looks human), and especially once its activity becomes physically apparent (at "quickening"). Thirdly, it is inevitable that the parental experience of this affection, of valuing offspring so highly, will stretch beyond the immediate family, and colour the view that parents take of other children and other fetuses.[37] Finally, these widely shared attitudes to children and fetuses are likely to mould the moral language and thought of any human society, so that even those who have never themselves experienced parental or personal affection for children will nevertheless come to share, to some extent, the attitudes of those who have.

This account is not merely a sociological sketch of how a certain moral attitude is likely to develop. It is also, if on the right track, and if the principle of sympathetic respect is legitimate, a vindication of that attitude. For it serves to show that the human fetus and child are in a unique social situation which vastly inflates their perceived moral status quite independently of their intrinsic qualities, and in a manner which cannot apply to the young of any other existing (terrestrial) species, simply because the members of those species lack the biological, social and intellectual characteristics which bring it about. Having once explained why we should be so strongly and universally partial towards our own young, the principle of sympathetic respect can then be invoked to provide what might seem to be a "bootstrap" justification of that very partiality. But there is no circularity here, and no appeal to speciesist assumptions – merely a commitment to value those beings (whatever they may be) that others (of any species) value.

We have now seen that an account can be given of why we do, and should, accord special respect to human infants and fetuses, even if their morally relevant intrinsic properties are no more advanced than those of, say, a rabbit. No doubt other accounts could also be given, based for example on the principle of special obligation above, and I make no claim for the unique correctness of that which I have sketched. But if that sketch is at all in the right direction, then it seems to have a number of significant implications for the abortion debate. For first, it shows against the liberal that it is possible to justify a special respect for the human fetus and child without infringing against the principle of universalisability, and without embracing speciesism. Secondly, it provides a reason for supposing that this special respect should increase with age, so that the child should be accorded more respect than the baby, the baby than the late fetus, the late fetus than the embryo, and so on. Finally, it somewhat undermines the conservative's claim that the potentiality principle is an essential, though implicit, part of commonsense morality. For if the special respect that we owe to children can be perfectly well explained and justified without recourse to that principle, then a major part of the conservative's case, namely his claim that only potentiality can account for our attitude to children, is demolished.

The Implications of the Potentiality Principle

Any account of the special moral status of children which does not appeal to the conservative's potentiality principle (such as that given above) *ipso facto* undermines the credentials of that principle, by casting doubt on its alleged indispensability to the justification of that particular commonsense moral belief. But this by itself cannot prove that the potentiality principle has no role whatever within commonsense morality, and since so many have considered it to have such a role, it is worth investigating just what implications this would have for our position on abortion. Suppose that it were to ·be conclusively established that our commonsense moral attitudes towards adults and children, and even towards animals, in fact depend significantly on their perceived potential: would this then imply that the commonsense moral framework is implicitly committed to a conservative position on abortion? There are at least two strong reasons for denying any such implication, the first of which is concerned with the power of the potentiality principle, and the second with its scope.

The first reason is based on the natural and compelling assumption that the moral value of potential personhood, for example, is less than that of actual personhood, just as the honour due to a potential monarch (president, saint, grandmaster, professor) is less than that due to an actual monarch (president etc.). If the moral status of a fertilised ovum is solely derived from the possibility of its future enjoyment of morally significant capacities (such as feelings and desires, rationality, self-consciousness etc.), then surely this status must at least be somewhat diminished by comparison with that of an actual person, who already enjoys those capacities, and whose erstwhile mere moral possibilities have now become solid realities.[38] But this assumption can then be powerfully combined with the observation that a fertilised ovum is a potential person only *in virtue of* its potential to become an embryo: developing into an embryo is an absolutely essential stage on its long journey to personhood. The fertilised ovum, therefore, has moral value only in so far as it is a potential embryo, and given our stated assumption, it follows that the moral status of a fertilised ovum must be less than that of an embryo. Likewise the embryo is a potential person only in virtue of its potential to become a fetus: therefore, by the same reasoning, the moral status of an embryo is less than that of a fetus. And this same argument can, of course, be repeated for all the intermediate stages of embryonic and fetal development, showing that so far from supporting a strict conservative position, the potentiality principle would instead lead much more naturally to some sort of developmental view.

The second reason for doubt about the conservative's appeal to the potentiality principle concerns the principle's range of application rather than its force. Let us use the term "moral universe" for all those individuals (notably humans and many animals, but perhaps not slugs and mosquitos!) which have moral significance, that is, whose "status" is sufficient to require that their interests should be taken into account, however minimally, in relevant moral decisions. Then the crucial question is this: does the potentiality principle apply to any individual whatever, including those which would otherwise have absolutely no moral significance, or does it apply only to those which are already members of the moral universe? This question is crucial because the early fetus, whose brain has not yet developed sufficiently to achieve consciousness,[39] seems to have little claim to a place within the moral universe *except* on the alleged basis of its potentiality – we would not normally consider a being to be worthy of moral consideration if it were quite incapable of having even the most primitive of experiences (and indeed it is far from clear that the notion of "moral consideration" makes any sense as applied to such a being). So if the potentiality principle were to apply only to those already independently within the moral universe, then it could get no purchase in the case of an early fetus, and hence could not endow such a fetus with any moral significance at all.

An analogy might help to bring out the genuine plausibility of this restricted interpretation of the principle. Suppose that a company decides to adopt a pay policy which determines any individual's salary partly on the basis of his potential for advancement within the firm, so that a potential managing director will, other things being equal, be paid more than a potential head of accounts, a potential head of accounts more than a potential chief clerk, and so on. Then the question arises: should this policy extend to those who are not yet employed by the company but who might be in the future, including those potential directors who may just have submitted their job applications (not to mention those who are currently at school or college)? Presumably not: a company that pays its employees according to their potential is not thereby committed to paying its potential employees as well, however promising they may be – one has already to be on the payroll in order to qualify for the potentiality bonus! And likewise, on the restricted interpretation of the potentiality principle, one must already count morally, at least to some extent, before the consideration of one's potential can carry any moral weight.

So we have two different interpretations of the potentiality principle, one of which applies only to already-qualified members of the moral universe, and one of which applies also to potential members. Only the latter interpretation will ascribe any moral value to a fetus whose present capacities are in themselves morally worthless: this broader interpretation, therefore, seems to be required by the conservative if the potentiality principle is to be of any use to him in opposing the abortion of an early fetus which is not yet capable of consciousness. And naturally the conservative's opponents, for that very reason, will in contrast prefer the former, more narrow interpretation. But how are we rationally to decide between the two? Obviously we cannot appeal to pre-established assumptions about the moral status of, say, a ten-week fetus, since any such appeal will immediately beg the very question at issue, and in any case the nature of the abortion debate suggests that on the status of such a fetus there is absolutely no pre-established commonsense consensus. What we require, therefore, is a generally accepted *independent* moral belief, whose truth or falsity crucially depends on the interpretation of the potentiality principle, and which can thus be used to adjudicate between the two rival interpretations.

Unfortunately, however, no such belief is likely to be found, not merely because (as I argued earlier) the place of the potentiality principle within commonsense morality is anyway extremely uncertain, but also for a more interesting and particular reason. This is that the two interpretations of the potentiality principle differ only with respect to those individuals which on the one hand currently have no "actualised" moral significance, but which on the other hand have the potential to acquire such moral significance in the course of their future development. But the only beings that we know which develop in this way are, of course, the reproductive precursors of animals and humans: fetuses, embryos, pre-embryos and (arguably) gametes. And it is precisely the moral status of these very entities which we are trying to discover. So there is no realistic possibility of finding any independent and relatively uncontroversial moral belief from which we might hope to extrapolate a solution to this singular problem. The problem of the status of the early fetus, in so far as it depends on the potentiality principle, is entirely unique![40]

The Middle Ground

We have now looked again at the key arguments of the liberal and conservative camps, namely, the Arguments from Speciesism and from Potentiality, and we have found good reason to doubt the extreme conclusions which are commonly thought to follow from them. The Argument from Speciesism can be opposed in a number of ways, in particular by appeal to a plausible "principle of sympathetic respect" which, without being arbitrarily speciesist, provides a reason for ascribing to the developed human fetus a far higher moral status than that which we ascribe to an animal such as a rabbit. The protection afforded to the fetus by this principle, however, is greatly dependent on its stage of development, and the principle thus not only undermines the most objectionable consequences of the extreme liberal position, but also provides us with a plausible rationale for the commonsense developmental view.

Our assessment of the Argument from Potentiality is less clear-cut. First, we have found some reason to doubt that the potentiality principle is indeed implicit in commonsense morality as the conservative claims, given that the high moral status of infants can be explained perfectly well without it using instead the principle of sympathetic respect. But even if the conservative is in fact correct to claim that it is thus implicit, we have seen that it too will lead naturally to the developmental view, and can only very dubiously provide any protection at all for the early embryo which is not yet conscious. The conservative will no doubt wish to interpret it as providing such protection, but significantly it appears that he will in principle be quite unable to give any independent grounds for doing so.

It seems, then, that the way may now be clear for a developmental position on abortion, which sides with the liberal at the beginning of pregnancy, and with the conservative at the end. Exploration of the details of such a position, however, must wait for another occasion.

Conclusion: The Complex Problem of Abortion

In this paper I have attempted to provide the outline of a case for a "moderate" position on the morality of abortion, though most of my arguments have had the immediate purpose of undermining the familiar extreme positions rather than directly securing the middle ground. One reason for this indirect strategy has been what I take to be the manifest plausibility of the "developmental view": it is, I believe, so overwhelmingly natural to see a massive moral distinction between the microscopic blob which is the early pre-embryo, and the fully-formed sentient and active individual which is the nine-month fetus, that only the spurious demands of religious dogma or of simplistic theoretical systematisation could ever lead anyone to deny it. I have therefore sought primarily to show that neither religion nor moral theory has the power rationally to depose the developmental view – if I have here been successful, then the moderate position should win by default as long as it is internally coherent. Hence I have also tried to illustrate, by arguing from the "principle of sympathetic respect", how it is indeed possible to give a plausible account of the developmental view which is consistent with the structure of our "commonsense" moral framework. Many different such accounts could perhaps be given, and I do not claim that this particular one is the best available: its main purpose is to illustrate a possibility rather than to demonstrate a necessity.

The key to my argument against the extreme positions has been the identification of a "polarisation paradox", which arises from the combination of two claims: first, that the arguments used to support these extreme views do, and must, essentially appeal to elements of our "commonsense" morality, and thence derive their force; secondly, that the moral implications of the positions thus supported are wildly at odds with that same commonsense morality. If these claims are correct, then it does indeed seem to follow that a coherent alternative which better matches our overall commonsense framework will be immune to rational attack from either of the extreme positions which it displaces. This still leaves the possibility of an appeal to religious authority, but I have attempted in advance to spike the guns of any such appeal by showing some of the theoretical obstacles which stand in its way, particularly when it is used to support a position which again seems, on purely moral grounds, highly implausible.

All this, of course, leaves much to be done. The developmental view is consistent with a great variety of moral positions, and I have not attempted to clarify exactly where I would myself be inclined to draw the moral line (or, more probably, range of lines) between a fetus which can unproblematically be aborted on demand (as can, I believe, a pre-embryo), and one for whom the protection conferred by the principle of sympathetic respect (and probably a variety of other considerations) amounts in effect to an absolute prohibition (as it does, I believe, in the case of a healthy and viable fetus). Far more discussion is needed of this fiendishly complicated issue, not least to establish what force remains in the standard liberal and conservative arguments which have been criticised here. For although I have tried to show that they have insufficient power to overthrow the commonsense developmental view, this does not imply that they have no force whatever, and indeed we have seen already that the potentiality principle can easily combine with the developmental view, and may, if accepted, have significant implications for its detailed working out. This paper can claim, then, only to have added some substance to the natural observation that certain extreme positions in the abortion debate are too one-sided and remote from common sense to be credible. But this mere ruling out of the extremes does not get us very far: most of the hard work remains to be done![41]

Notes

1. For simplicity, I shall generally use the single word "fetus" indiscriminately to refer to the conceptus, zygote, pre-embryo, embryo, and fetus, so that the word will carry no implications concerning stage of development.

2. I shall often speak, apparently uncritically, of such things as the "commonsense moral framework" and even of commonsense moral "intuitions". Such language should not be taken to indicate any particular meta-ethical view, or any naïve illusions about the existence of a unified and coherent moral consensus – it is simply a way of referring concisely to those widely shared "intuitive" moral beliefs (such as that it is wrong to kill children but permissible to kill mosquitos) to which any moral theory which hopes to gain general acceptance must ultimately be answerable. To keep the paper reasonably accessible, I have tried to make my arguments entirely independent of meta-ethics, and have generally framed them using the standard terms ("moral status" etc.) of the popular debate, even though the moral ontology which such terms suggest seems highly problematic. I am confident, however, that a more critical meta-ethical approach would lend further support to my overall position (for example, in providing additional theoretical justification for my appeal to the "principle of sympathetic respect" on pages 178–180).

3. In philosophical contexts it is hard to avoid "sexist" language grammatically but without clumsiness, and I have therefore conformed to the traditional policy of using masculine pronouns to include both sexes. I sincerely hope that this policy will cause no offence to the reader, even if he happens to be female.

4. For a discussion of precisely this issue see Lee (1986) chapter 2.

5. For my own view on the rationality of the belief in a supremely good God, whose will is therefore morally authoritative, see Millican (1989).

6. For references to the work of these theologians, and for further details on the historical points that follow, see Dunstan (1984, 1988), Engelhardt (1974), and especially Noonan (1971).

7. See Dunstan (1988) for evidence of this influence.

8. An appeal to what is "natural" is still very common amongst both religious and non-religious anti-abortionists, but unfortunately tends to beg the question. For clearly much medical treatment that would be enthusiastically defended by them (e.g., the use of incubators and life-saving drugs) is "unnatural" in the obvious sense, while many manifest evils (such as earthquakes, floods, drought, and pestilence) have been entirely due to natural causes, so it is hard to draw the distinction which they require without relying on other controversial moral or religious considerations.

9. For a sober assessment of the various biblical passages that have been thought relevant to the abortion debate, see Wilkinson (1988) pp 232, 252–8.

10. Aristotelianism was by no means the only major philosophical influence here – Stoicism for example significantly moulded the early Christian attitude to sex.

11. Including those concerned with immortality and infant baptism.

12. Such a person might do well to read the classic and trenchant attack on the doctrine of infallibility provided by Salmon (1888).

13. I explore the implications of this last possibility in Millican (1989). In particular, I begin by attempting to refute the suggestion that "what the Supreme Being wills" is good by definition (a suggestion famously attacked in Plato's *Euthyphro*) by showing not only the moral, but also the epistemological and religious unacceptability of understanding His "goodness" in a way that would make it entirely different from human goodness.

14. Strictly this is somewhat oversimplified, since a persuasive moral argument can have an indirect form, in which for example a moral premise is shown to lead to an unacceptable conclusion, the point of the argument being not so much to deduce anything from that premise, but rather to demonstrate its own falsity. Likewise, much moral investigation takes the form of an attempt to find a "best fit" between theory and "intuition", rather than merely involving deductions from a pre-established baseline. It obviously remains true even here, however, that such moral discussion can only get started on the basis of at least some antecedent moral agreement.

15. Discussions of abortion which invoke this kind of criterion of personhood and moral significance include Harris (1985) chapter 1; Tooley (1983) especially chapter 5; Warren (1973) pp 54–7.

16. A similar ambiguity, between a purely descriptive and a moral notion, is possible in connection with the term "human being". Warren (1973 p 53) suggests that the Human Being Argument derives its superficial plausibility from such an ambiguity.

17. The most notable "feminist" contribution to the debate is probably that of Thomson (1971), though she does not endorse the extreme Feminist position presented above. Her "Famous Violinist Argument" would certainly need to be taken into account in any comprehensive treatment of abortion, but I do not discuss it here because it does not, like the other arguments we are discussing, address the question of the status of the fetus. For useful criticism, with which I am broadly in sympathy, see Hursthouse (1987) chapter 5.

18. Thus would-be basic moral principles such as "everybody should obey *me*", or "all foreigners should be deferential to the English" would be not only morally absurd but even logically unacceptable.

19. Many liberals apparently take it to be *obvious* that a being's species is in itself morally irrelevant (for example Glover 1977 pp 50–51; Harris 1990 pp 69–70), and therefore see no need for a theoretical argument to that conclusion (Tooley 1983 pp 61–77 is the most notable exception). Singer (1979) presents an explicit two-stage argument from universalisability in which he first (pp 10–12, 18–19) uses it to derive a principle of "equal consideration of interests", and then (pp 48–54) goes on to deploy this derived principle against speciesism.

20. The point here is that to be human is not just to have those general properties which are common to humans: a synthetic copy of a man made by an advanced alien civilisation might have these properties, but would not be a member of our species, because it would not be related to the common stock of humanity. Thus any definition of what it is to be human must inevitably mention particular individuals or particular groups, and this is what violates the principle of universalisability. It may seem surprising that Kant himself, considered by many the apostle of universalisability, states that we should "always treat humanity . . . as an end" in one of his formulations of the Categorical Imperative, often quoted by conservative moralists (Kant 1785, p 91). But it is clear from the context that Kant is no speciesist, since his rule is intended to apply to any *rational* being – he simply knows of no others.

21. See for example Stone (1987) pp 820–3. Devine (1978 chapters II and III) appeals to the wrongness of both infanticide and the killing of the reversibly comatose to reject what he calls the "present enjoyment principle" (that a being's rights depend only on its present qualities) in favour of a potentiality principle.

22. Most notably Kuhse and Singer (1985) chapter 6; Singer (1979) pp 122–6; Tooley (1983) chapter 11.

23. For example Glover (1977) p 122; Harris (1990) pp 70–71; Kuhse and Singer (1982) pp 61–62; Tooley (1983) pp 182–3. Singer and Dawson (1988) extend this standard objection, with added force, to the case of human embryos *in vitro*.

24. See for example Buckle (1988) pp 93–96 (though Buckle is no conservative); Johnstone (1982) pp 49–50; Stone (1987) p 818.

25. Very difficult and controversial issues arise here concerning identity and individuation in the pre-embryo stage. See for example Dawson (1988); Holland (1991); Kuhse and Singer (1990).

26. For details see Johnson (1989) pp 2–4.

27. The estimate that 50% of fertilised ova might be lost through spontaneous abortion is quoted by Potts et al. (1977) p 60: the figure is very uncertain, since most spontaneous abortions probably occur before the mother is aware that she is pregnant. Of those pregnancies which survive long enough to be recognised clinically, only about 15% abort spontaneously (Bieber and Driscoll 1989 p 59).

28. It seems that between 30% and 60% of spontaneously aborted fetuses have chromosomal abnormalities (Bieber and Driscoll 1989 p 63). The Conservative might try to salvage a plausible policy here by appealing to the distinction between acts and omissions, so that killing early embryos will be wrong, but allowing them to abort permissible. However a complementary problem could arise in the case of an embryo with cleavage arrest, incapable of progressing beyond the early stages of cell division. Suppose that such an embryo were able to implant and survive indefinitely *without* intervention – how could the strict Conservative, who endorses the Human Being Argument, justify its (surely desirable) termination, since on his own principles it is apparently a human being?

29. Even without an appeal to the distinction between acts and omissions, the Conservative need not be committed to the prevention of as many spontaneous abortions as is medically possible (just as he need not be committed to maintaining large numbers of elderly patients indefinitely on life-support systems), since available resources will obviously impose some limit. However, it remains true that he must view this limitation on prevented spontaneous abortions, even in the first few days of pregnancy and even in the case of severely abnormal fetuses, as *gravely* regrettable, and this in itself seems implausible enough.

30. This example, which Thomson (1971 pp 65–66) calls "indecent", is considered morally unproblematic by Warren (1973 p 59).

31. For impressive evidence of the dangers posed by back-street abortions, see Chapter 14.

32. Radcliffe Richards (1980 pp 221–6) argues that the exception which conservatives commonly make for abortion in the case of rape can only make sense on the assumption that their prohibition in other cases is based on the disapproval of women who have "indulged willingly in sex without being willing to bear a child" (p 223).

33. The assumption that moral status must be all-or-nothing seems to lie behind the popular conservative "Argument from Continuity", according to which the gradual and continuous development of the fetus from conception to birth implies that it has the same moral status throughout. Clearly such an argument is hopeless if moral status, like the fetus' physical dimensions, can increase by gradual degrees.

34. Generally in legal contexts, anything that is not forbidden is permitted, but we should not be seduced by quasi-legal talk of "rights" into assuming that the same is true of morality. For even some acts which are characterised by a strict observance of "rights" can nevertheless be morally objectionable, for example if they are grudging, heartless, mean, or even legalistic.

35. Two other possibilities are made use of by Devine (1978). First, he proposes a "modified species principle" (pp 53–4) which ascribes personhood to *all* members of any sufficiently intelligent species (even to those members which are not themselves intelligent). Secondly, he endorses an "overflow principle" (p 101), according to which "the principle of respect for persons extends . . . to things closely associated with persons". He takes the latter to indicate both that "corpses ought not to be treated as ordinary garbage", and that "a modicum of reverence should be accorded to processes by which persons come to be" (and hence presumably to human fetuses).

36. Something like this principle of special obligation was apparently the basis for the Warnock Committee's ascription of a "special status" to the human embryo (Warnock 1987 p 10). Warnock hints at an argument founded on our natural "preference" for our own species, but such a biased preference would only justify a *moral* conclusion here on the strength of the sort of argument which I give below, which presupposes the principle of sympathetic respect.

37. This point helps to explain the widely felt relevance of viability to the moral status of the fetus. For a fetus which is viable will be at the same developmental stage as some infants who have already been born alive, making a sympathetic extension of concern almost irresistible since, as Zaichik (1980 p 21) puts it, "it is only due to this fetus' bad luck" that it is not already born.

38. Thus we would rightly be outraged by a mother who, while in hospital awaiting *in vitro* fertilisation treatment, elected to save from a fire a test-tube containing her newly fertilised ovum rather than her existing child.

39. For a recent discussion of the concept of "brain birth" which reviews some of the neurological data, see Jones (1989).

40. This need not imply that the problem is insoluble, but does suggest that illumination must be sought not from the extrapolation of moral conclusions from analogous real-life situations, but rather from the consideration of imaginary "thought-experiments" such as the following. Suppose that fertilisation in a humanlike species of alien were to occur not through genetic combination of the gametes, but rather through selective "activation" of some of the (vast number of) genes already present in the ovum – instead of itself contributing genetic material, the sperm would simply activate whatever genes within the ovum correspond most closely to its own. Thus the unfertilised ovum would be manifestly *one and the same individual* as the fertilised ovum, and would plausibly therefore be just as much a potential person. But it is hard to believe that this makes a significant difference to its "moral status" when it is so far from achieving any "actualised" moral significance: for example, would we really change our mind about contraception if it turned out that our own reproduction functioned in this way? I suspect, but cannot prove, that all such thought-experiments which relate to the status of the pre-embryo will similarly favour a liberal rather than a conservative position at that stage.

41. For help and useful criticism I am very grateful to Nina Collins, Christopher Coope, Gordon Dunstan, Chris Megone, Jim Parry, Roger White, and especially Jennifer Jackson.

References

Bieber FR, Driscoll SG (1989) Evaluation of spontaneous abortion and of the malformed fetus. In: Reed GB, Claireaux AE, Bain AD (eds) Diseases of the fetus and newborn. Chapman and Hall, London, pp 59–74

Buckle S (1988) Arguing from potential. Bioethics 2: 227–53 and reprinted in Singer et al. (1990) pp 90–108

Dawson K (1988) Segmentation and moral status. Bioethics 2: 1–14 and reprinted in Singer et al. (1990) pp 53–64

Devine PE (1978) The ethics of homicide. Cornell University Press, Ithaca

Dunstan GR (1984) The moral status of the human embryo: a tradition recalled. J Med Ethics 1: 38–44

Dunstan GR (1988) The human embryo in the Western moral tradition. In: Dunstan GR, Seller MJ (eds) The status of the human embryo: perspectives from moral tradition. King Edward's Hospital Fund for London, London, pp 39–57

Engelhardt HT Jr (1974) The ontology of abortion. Ethics 84: 217–34

Glover J (1977) Causing death and saving lives. Penguin, Harmondsworth

Harris J (1985) The value of life. Routledge & Kegan Paul, London

Harris J (1990) Embryos and hedgehogs: on the moral status of the embryo. In: Dyson A, Harris J (eds) Experiments on embryos. Routledge, London, pp 65–81

Holland A (1991) A fortnight of my life is missing: a discussion of the status of the human "pre-embryo". In: Almond B, Hill D (eds) Applied philosophy. Routledge, London, pp 299–311

Hume D (1740) A treatise of human nature. Selby-Bigge LA, Nidditch PH (eds) 2nd edn. (1978) Clarendon Press, Oxford

Hursthouse R (1987) Beginning lives. Basil Blackwell, Oxford

Johnson MH (1989) The onset of human identity and its relationship to legislation concerning research on human embryos. In: Bromham D, Forsythe E, Dalton M (eds) Ethical problems in reproductive medicine. Leeds University, Leeds, pp 2–7

Johnstone B (1982) The moral status of the embryo. In: Walters W, Singer P (eds) Test-tube babies. Oxford University Press, Melbourne, pp 49–56

Jones DG (1989) Brain birth and personal identity. J Med Ethics 15: 173–8

Kant I (1785) Grundlegung zur Metaphysik der Sitten. Translated by Paton HJ as The moral law (1948) Hutchinson, London

Kuhse H, Singer P (1982) The moral status of the embryo. In: Walters W, Singer P (eds) Test-tube babies. Oxford University Press, Melbourne, pp 57–63

Kuhse H, Singer P (1985) Should the baby live? Oxford University Press, Oxford

Kuhse H, Singer P (1990) Individuals, humans and persons. In: Singer et al. (1990), pp 65–75

Lee S (1986) Law and morals. Oxford University Press, Oxford

Millican PJR (1989) The Devil's advocate. Cogito 3: 193–207

Noonan JT Jr (1971) An almost absolute value in history. In: Noonan JT Jr (ed) The morality of abortion. Harvard University Press, Cambridge, Massachusetts, pp 1–59

Potts M, Diggory P, Peel J (1977) Abortion. Cambridge University Press, Cambridge, England

Radcliffe Richards J (1980) The sceptical feminist. RKP, London

Salmon G (1888) The infallibility of the church, 4th edn. (1914). John Murray, London

Singer P (1979) Practical ethics. Cambridge University Press, Cambridge, England

Singer P, Dawson K (1988) IVF technology and the argument from potential. Philosophy and public affairs 17: 87–104 and reprinted in Singer et al. (1990) pp 76–89

Singer P, Kuhse H, Buckle S, Dawson K, Kasimba P (eds) (1990) Embryo experimentation. Cambridge University Press, Cambridge, England

Stone J (1987) Why potentiality matters. Canad J Philos 17: 815–29

Thomson JJ (1971) A defense of abortion. Philosophy and public affairs 1: 47–66

Tooley M (1983) Abortion and infanticide. Clarendon Press, Oxford

Warnock M (1987) Do human cells have rights? Bioethics 1: 1–14

Warren MA (1973) On the moral and legal status of abortion. Monist 57: 43–61

Wilkinson J (1988) Christian ethics in health care. Handsel Press, Edinburgh

Zaichik A (1980) Viability and the morality of abortion. Philosophy and public affairs 10: 18–26

CHAPTER 16

Toleration in the Abortion Debate

Jennifer C. Jackson

What methods, what strategies, is it defensible for us to employ when campaigning on a contentious moral issue? What kinds of intolerance may we legitimately manifest towards the opposition in our endeavour to win converts and influence opinion? Could we be justified in refusing on principle even to engage with the opposition in public debate? And what of the legitimacy of "playing" on people's emotions, or of not correcting misinformation put about by some of our supporters which helps our cause? Or, in making use of premises in argument that our opponents accept but we do not or, of appealing to arguments that we know to be invalid but by which the opposition may be taken in?

I propose to explore the rights and responsibilities of campaigners in regard to one particular contentious moral issue: abortion, and, for the sake of simplicity, I will construe the debate on this issue as one between pro-lifers and pro-choicers. As this enquiry is concerned only to establish whether certain campaign strategies are indefensible even if those using them are in the right on the issue, we need not for present purposes address the substantial issue as to which side (if either) on the abortion debate is in the right – and I therefore avoid expressing an opinion on this issue.

An Asymmetry Between Pro-life and Pro-choice

We should not be surprised if we find that those on one side of this debate seem disposed to conduct their campaign in a less tolerant vein than the opposition. There appears to be an asymmetry between the opposing stances which, if unexamined, may excite understandable but perhaps unjustified resentment. To the pro-choicers it may appear that whereas they themselves are prepared to agree to disagree about the moral acceptability of abortion, and to endorse a policy which is neutral or even-handed on the issue, the pro-lifers do not reciprocate with a similar show of respect and tolerance.

Does not a policy which is permissive on the issue count as neutral and even-handed – as is appropriate where an issue is morally contentious? The permissive policy does not compel any of us to act against our consciences. Furthermore, pro-choicers demonstrate their readiness to take seriously the minority pro-life view, by their supporting safeguards being built into medical practice to ensure that doctors and nurses who share the minority view are not required or pressured into actively assisting in the practice. A permissive policy on abortion, then, enables all of us to act as our consciences dictate – or does it?

When one considers how the abortion issue is perceived by the pro-lifers it becomes apparent why they can in conscience show intolerance towards the pro-choicers. When pro-choicers tolerate the pro-lifers' rejection of abortion and even show some willingness to accommodate what they will doubtless call pro-lifers' "sensibilities" by enabling medical staff to choose (where feasible) not to be involved, they are not thereby condoning deeds which they regard as unjust: pro-choicers accept that anti-abortionists are within their rights in declining to undergo or assist in abortion. Pro-lifers, on the other hand, were they to condone the practices the pro-choicers wish to defend would be condoning what they believe to be unjust.

It is hardly surprising, then, that the pro-lifers do not adopt a "live and let live" attitude towards the opposition who in their view are not "letting live". Being just after all involves not merely avoiding acting unjustly oneself, it also involves caring that justice be done to and by others as well as to and by oneself. Being just is not merely a matter of minding one's own business – or rather, preventing and checking injustice is or should be everyone's business. (We can, of course, delegate some of our responsibilities to special officers, for example, to constables, inspectors or guards.) Pro-lifers, then, ought not in conscience to be complacent about the attitude of the opposition.

Compare the seeming evenhanded neutrality of a shop which displays cosmetics for sale which have been tested on animals alongside alternative cosmetics which have not: "let the customers choose as their consciences dictate". But of course evenhandedness towards the just and the unjust cannot be condoned by those who care about justice. It is understandable, therefore, that those who regard animal testing as a grave injustice are not prepared to agree to disagree nor to regard this kind of evenhandedness from merchants as a demonstration of neutrality on the issue. Thus, the permissive policy on abortion is not really evenhanded since, although it does not compel any of us to act against our consciences, its existence does understandably cause moral affront to one side and not to the other. We can expect the pro-life side which suffers the affront to be intolerant of it.

Pro-lifers' Intolerance

Now granted that the pro-lifers have a duty to be intolerant of what they perceive (rightly or wrongly) to be injustice, what form should their intolerance take? How ought they to manifest it? Their duty, I would suggest, is qualified in three ways.

Firstly, since this duty of intolerance derives from the just person's concern to prevent injustice, pro-lifers are obliged to manifest intolerance only where they are in a position to do so effectively, i.e., in a way that is likely to end or reduce the injustice being done: not, therefore, where their opposition is likely to be ineffective or even counter-productive. Failure to manifest intolerance in such circumstances would not be evidence of a lack of concern on their part.

Secondly, assuming that we must not do evil so that good may come, must not therefore commit one kind of injustice in order to prevent or check another, we are under a duty to manifest intolerance only where we can do so without significantly infringing other people's rights. I say "significantly" to leave open the possibility that some incidents and kinds of injustice might arguably be defensible as the "lesser evils": certainly not fire-bombing an abortion clinic in a way that put lives at risk but possibly defensible if adequate precautions were taken to make sure that only equipment and premises would be damaged.

Thirdly, our duty to manifest intolerance towards injustice allows us a certain discrimination over how and when we act on it. It is what we may call an "unbounded" duty like e.g., the duties we are under to protect the weak, care for our families or educate ourselves and unlike such "bounded" duties we are under e.g., not to steal or cheat or lie. In the case of the latter bounded duties only, it makes sense to say: "I have acted in accordance with this duty", and "I have done precisely what this duty required of me". Unbounded duties impose in a way that is open-ended but also which allows the duty-bearer some discrimination in how or when one acts in accordance with them. In the case of bounded duties, one is obliged to conform strictly, precisely to their "dictates". You cannot excuse a theft today on the grounds that you stole nothing yesterday or the day before (or a lie to Jones on the grounds that you did not lie to Smith or Brown) whereas precisely what you must or must not do in view of your duty to prevent injustice is indeterminate both in that it is not clear how far you have to go: whether, e.g., as a pro-life gynaecologist it is enough that *you* do not perform abortions although you relieve your pro-choice colleagues of other work so as to enable them to shoulder "your share" so to speak, and in that you can defend your failure to lend any support to one worthy cause by citing another which you are supporting.

Thus, while we are under a bounded duty not to act unjustly ourselves, e.g., not to commit murder, our duty to prevent injustice from occurring in the world at large e.g., by preventing murder, is unbounded. There being many injustices perpetrated in the world, our failure to manifest intolerance in any particular way even where we know that we could do so effectively and without thereby causing other injustice does not necessarily show a lack of concern for justice on our part. Thus pro-lifers are not obliged, though they are entitled, to manifest intolerance toward a permissive policy even where their opposition can reasonably be expected to be effective and is not itself causing other injustice.

Pro-choicers' Intolerance

We have seen that an attitude of intolerance of pro-lifers towards pro-choicers can be expected. What, though, of the attitude of pro-choicers to pro-lifers: is it not easy for the former to tolerate the latter? In fact so easy that, strictly speaking, "toleration" is not an issue since from the pro-choice point of view a pro-lifer who refuses to undergo an abortion does no wrong?

Toleration may, though, be an issue for pro-choicers on some occasions. "Toleration" implies putting up with something seen as "bad": not necessarily "morally bad" and even if seen as "morally bad", not necessarily as "unjust".

While all pro-choicers are committed to the view that pro-lifers are acting within their rights in refusing to undergo abortions (and hence are not making choices which are wrong in the sense, "unjust") some may still see such a choice in certain circumstances as morally indefensible on *other* grounds e.g., as reckless, inconsiderate or selfish (hence a wrong choice in the sense, "morally indefensible"). In such cases it is both intelligible that these pro-choicers need to exercise tolerance and that they do not necessarily find doing so altogether easy.

The Conscience Clause

Easy or not so easy, pro-choicers are committed to tolerating pro-lifers' rejection of abortion as an option for themselves. Can pro-choicers be expected to be equally tolerant towards pro-life doctors and nurses who refuse to assist other people who request an abortion? From the pro-choice standpoint a refusal by a gynaecologist to assist people in having what they are entitled to demand of their gynaecologist is itself unjust unless in refusing oneself to assist one is not denying them their right – as if alternative professional assistance is on hand. How far then are pro-lifers who are in medical practice entitled to have their consciences "respected" by their pro-choice colleagues?

The Abortion Act of 1967 upholds the right of doctors to refuse to participate in abortion on grounds of conscience. And it is only reasonable, is it not, that such a right should be recognised vis-à-vis those with whom we disagree on moral matters: provided at least that respecting their rights to follow the dictates of their conscience does not mean allowing them to act unjustly?

Now we might expect, if as it happens most doctors are pro-choice rather than pro-life, or at any rate have no conscientious objection to carrying out abortions within the terms of the Act, that accommodating the consciences of their few pro-life colleagues should pose no problem. But what if it did? What if the demand in an area for abortion were high and gynaecologists were in difficulties coping? Might it not become necessary to adopt a policy of employing only pro-choice doctors in that area lest women be denied their right under the Act?

David Alton protests over the Yellowlees letter from the Chief Medical Officer to the Area Health Authorities which laid down just this policy: not to employ pro-life doctors in gynaecological positions if there was a demand for abortion in the area. David Alton (1988) complains that the directive "thwarts" the protection offered by the 1967 Act: "Effectively", he observes, "the instruction ruled out promotion and a career for any doctor specialising in gynaecology who pleaded the conscience clause". (p. 41)

But assuming that the *intention* behind this instruction was not to put pressure on pro-life gynaecologists to participate in activities they deemed to be unjust but simply to protect the basic legal right (and moral, as perceived by pro-choicers) of women to abortions – as allowed under the Act, I do not think that David Alton's claim stands. The protection of consciences that is extended to dissenting minorities must always be qualified by the obligation to act justly: the Health Authorities have an obligation to provide for women's requirements in accordance with the Act. The right of pro-life gynaecologists to have their consciences respected is, I am saying, a qualified one and does not guarantee that they will in no way be disadvantaged in their careers on account of their unwillingness to participate in what in some districts may be a mundane part of gynaecological work.

Manifestations of Intolerance and Questionable Means

As we have noted, pro-choicers can be expected to manifest a degree of intolerance towards pro-lifers just where they believe that the stance of pro-lifers puts in jeopardy *other* people's rights. Thus we can expect, in the debate over abortion, both sides to manifest intolerance towards one another's positions. They are both entitled, given their views, to do so. However, what counts as "manifesting" intolerance is somewhat indeterminate and it would seem that there is a wide range of different actions and inactions, verbal and non-verbal, violent and non-violent, which in the appropriate context would count as manifestations of intolerance: from shouting to shooting. Some of these manifestations may be justified in a given case, others not. For the remainder of this paper we will examine the defensibility of some of the characteristic manifestations of intolerance which surfaced during the recent campaigns on the issue of abortion in the UK in 1988 and 1990.

Being on Speaking Terms

We may assume that injustice is a serious matter: not something to be complacent about. But possibly some types of injustice are more serious than others e.g., rape more serious than vandalism, and certainly some instances of injustice may be in themselves trivial e.g., the theft of a penny. But murder is a serious kind of injustice by anyone's reckoning and murder of those who are so obviously utterly at the mercy of others may seem especially villainous.

From the pro-life standpoint an assembly of obstetricians and gynaecologists most of whom may be presumed to defend abortions as permitted by the Act and do themselves regularly perform them, is an assembly of murderers with innocent blood on their hands. Granted the gravity of the charge, the question arises whether those who levy it can be expected even to associate, even to enter into public discussion or debate with those who defend the practice. For, even to participate in debate may be said to signify that the opposition is entitled to some respect.

Similarly, if we academics provide a platform for a debate to take place, we willy nilly lend a degree of respectability to the participants (who are wont to indicate as much in their opening address with such a phrase as "It is an honour to be invited . . . "). Because of the indeterminacy which we have already noted that there is over how actively we are obliged to oppose unjust practices, we may be uncertain as to how far we ought to go in manifesting our intolerance: whether merely by holding ourselves aloof from debate or by seeking to interfere with debates taking place. At the least, I want to suggest that these are views which if seriously advocated we would rightly consider to be so obviously villainous that we would see fit not only to decline to participate in even sober (as opposed to rabble-rousing) public discussion of them but would also feel entitled to oppose our universities providing any platform for their critical discussion.

Imagine, for example, that there is a revival of Nazism in Germany and you are invited to join in a public debate on the question whether the gassing of the Jews in the 1940s was not after all a morally defensible policy. Suppose, further, that the speakers with whom you are being invited to debate actively participated in the gassing of the Jews and are now arguing that the programme should be resumed to protect the legitimate interests of the German people (Jews, in their view, being not "persons", but only human beings with correspondingly lesser rights).

Let us suppose, moreover, that the speakers in question are genuinely willing to debate the issue soberly and civilly with you: their demeanour is not fanatical. They admit to "appalling" mistakes having been made: there were "excesses" and "abuses" in the 1940s and if the programme were resumed safeguards would need to be enforced and perpetrators of abuse brought to book. They assure you that they did not and would not carry out terminations lightly, that it is where permissible, or regretfully necessary, the "lesser of two evils" and that every care must be taken to make the procedure as painless as possible for the terminees.

Perhaps they argue that a nation, just as an individual, must be allowed to have a right of self-defence, and if a nation's survival is threatened by the uninvited presence in its midst of a populace "fathered" on it by circumstances not of its choosing, it is entitled to take whatever steps are necessary to rid itself of the burden. To be sure, back in the 1940s many dreadful things were done to the Jews that could not be justified on appeal to the principle of self-defence: many more Jews might have been deported so that fewer would have had to be killed, the conditions of the death camps and of transportation thereto were a disgrace.

If these neo-Nazis were to display such a willingness to discuss the question civilly and critically with you, would it be incumbent on you to reciprocate in the same civil mode? Or, might you be justified in point blank refusing to engage with them and in urging our universities to deny them a platform? Is not incivility and intemperance towards such a view justified in as much as the question does not deserve debate: there are not arguments to be weighed on both sides. Even so, you might for tactical reasons decide to engage e.g., lest your refusal be misinterpreted by the uncommitted as an acknowledgment of the weakness of your position. I merely claim that manifesting intolerance by refusing even to discuss can be justified in principle.

It by no means follows, of course, that pro-lifers are justified in manifesting this form of intolerance towards pro-choicers. I assume that the programme of gassing Jews is (to us) *obviously* unjust. If abortion is as the pro-lifers claim, murder, it is unjust. But it may not be obviously so to us; is not obviously so, if we know of people who are relevantly informed, of evident good will, and seriously reflective on the matter, who do not see it to be unjust. Here, it will be suggested, we are surrounded by people who are relevantly informed, of evident good will, seriously reflective and who are pro-choice. Their opposition therefore deserves to be taken seriously. They may be mistaken but there is a prima facie case pro-choice to be answered.

But what is it to be of evident good will? Is it to wear a suit, smile, act courteously, give away money to good causes, have generally liberal attitudes, read the *Guardian*? If only such features were reliable indicators of good will, we could each of us readily verify in the course of a week's participation in a conference the suggestion that we were surrounded there by people of evident good will. But such features are totally unreliable: neither necessary nor sufficient.

What do we mean then by "good will"? Is it simply a matter of meaning well and is meaning well simply a matter of having a clear conscience? For the purposes of determining whose views on moral matters deserve to be taken seriously surely a more positive account of good will is called for: not just absence of guilt or of malice but presence of the concerns that belong to those who are virtuous viz. concern for the welfare of others and concern for justice.

Thus, I suggest, we need not take seriously the opinion of someone on a controversial moral issue if it is apparent that however free from malice he is, he is quite indifferent to the suffering of others. Of course, for someone simply to pay no attention to the sufferings of others is hardly credible: in order to survive in this world we humans have no choice but to pay attention to the sufferings of (some) others. But we can do this for purely prudential reasons. The person of good will, I am saying, sympathises with the sufferings of others: he does not just give heed to sufferings in so far as doing so is convenient in view of his other concerns.

Now perhaps we can reasonably assume that doctors typically do have this concern: it seems to provide such an obvious motive for pursuing a medical career. But that a doctor, or anyone else, cares about justice is not so easily to be assumed or established. It is not even as if we are all agreed as to what justice is and, therefore, what caring about it involves.

Here I shall assume a particular view of justice, that the mark of having a concern for it is a certain fastidiousness about means, about how one pursues legitimate or even noble ends: a kind of firmness against the convenient setting aside of certain principles, a firmness that is only revealed when standing by these principles requires a resistance to pressures, a preparedness to swim against the tide.

So if I suggest that we are surrounded here by gynaecologists and obstetricians of good will I am hypothesizing that they have both these concerns. I cannot pretend on the basis of largely superficial acquaintance *qua* conference participant myself to have the evidence.

What bearing has the presence of good will on the question of whether we owe those who disagree with us on moral matters at least a polite hearing? The point I wish to establish is not that good will as I have defined it is any guarantor of sound opinion: one may have good will and yet not be relevantly informed, and even if one has good will and is relevantly informed one may still be thoroughly confused and hence not competent to advise: hence though doctors have good will they may *still* have innocent blood on their hands. My point is simply that unless one has good will as here defined as well as being relevantly informed and reflective on the issue under consideration, one's views do not even deserve a hearing. Proper humility should lead us to listen to the opposition – but not just to *any* opposing view.

Let us then define a controversial moral issue as one on which people of apparent good will, who appear to be relevantly informed and reflective, disagree. With any such issue, the opposition is entitled to a polite hearing: they have at least a prima facie case. Thus I would suggest; that we rightly refuse even to hear the case for gassing the Jews: it does not qualify nowadays at least by the above criteria: we cannot envisage such a policy now being seriously advocated by people of good will, relevantly informed and reflective. The issue of abortion, on the other hand, I submit, does qualify nowadays as controversial by the above criteria. I conclude, accordingly, that it is unreasonable for pro-lifers or pro-choicers to manifest the extreme form of passive intolerance of refusing on principle to share a platform with one another. Let us turn then to consider some of the questionable tactics that were used in recent campaigns on the abortion issue.

"Playing" on Emotion; Photographs and Replicas

In their campaigns against abortion pro-lifers have made use of photographs and plastic replicas of foetuses to put across their message. Since these tactics have drawn critical comment from the opposition, let us consider the legitimacy of their use.

That they can be persuasive, nobody denies. As David Alton (1988) says about the photograph, of which he made copious use, by Lennart Nilsson of a foetus which had miscarried at 18 weeks, "it was worth a thousand words" (p. 17). Alton observes that a photograph can show us simply what may be much more difficult to convey in words. But the value of the photograph in this context is not just that seeing is believing but that seeing may move us to care: consider, e.g., how charities make wide use of photographs as a form of persuasion, not just to convey information. David Alton (1988) says that "The Abortion lobby hates the sight of the Nilsson photograph. It shows what they would rather people did not see: the clear and unmistakeable humanity of the child" (p. 17). But are there legitimate grounds for complaint about the use of photos and replicas by pro-lifers: even if their photos and replicas faithfully portray the stage of foetal development in question? Certainly most vigorous protest was made. The tactic of posting these dolls to MPs was characterized in the press by such epithets as "gruesome", "macabre", "ghoulish", and "grotesque". Yet these dolls were in themselves no less appealing in appearance than babies. It was only in the context of their role in the abortion debate that such epithets could intelligibly have been thought appropriate.

Jo Richardson, Labour MP for Barking (in correspondence with me: 8th January 1991: 4th February 1991) has expressed her opposition on two counts about the posting by SPUC of life-size plastic replicas of 18-week-old foetuses to MPs: (1) that the secretaries who open MPs' post may include women who have recently undergone an abortion or had a miscarriage: they might well find the experience "very upsetting" and (2) that these replicas are in a way misleading in so far as they convey the impression that the foetus at 18 weeks is a "self-contained, separate being – in short, a baby" whereas in fact the foetus is still not viable and depends for its existence on its mother who, therefore, (in Jo Richardson's view) still has the ultimate right to withdraw consent to the continuation of a pregnancy.

Now we can hardly expect those who regard abortion as a form of murder to desist from an effective way of putting across this message lest people at the receiving end, whether they are the intended recipients or no, may be "very upset". To be sure, to cause *unnecessary* distress to the secretaries would be cruel. But if the only way of reaching the people at whom the message was aimed was via their secretaries, then the distress might be deemed to be an unfortunate foreseen but not intended consequence outweighed by the urgency of putting an end to the injustice at issue. Perhaps, though, this shock tactic was adopted by the pro-lifers not to inform, let alone convert, the MP recipients of the replicas (who might be expected to react adversely) but to rally the support of sympathisers to their own campaign for whom the replicas would be visible and poignant reminders of the urgency of their cause.

But what about Jo Richardson's other objection, that the replicas are in a way misleading? From the pro-life standpoint (and indeed from the standpoint of some pro-choicers, viz. those who claim the right to abort viable foetuses) the non-viability of 18 week old foetuses is an irrelevance. Hence pro-lifers cannot agree that if replicas mislead in *this* way, it matters in the slightest. But suppose, for the sake of argument, that Jo Richardson is right to attach the significance she does to viability, it does not follow that the pro-lifers' use of replicas is indefensible. If pro-lifers cause deception thereby, they may be doing so neither intentionally nor negligently. I conclude therefore that their use of replicas (and photos) may be defensible, even if they are mistaken on the issue.

Education and Balanced Presentation

The nature of materials supplied to schools by some sections of the pro-life movement has also been criticized by pro-choicers: teachers have been supplied with video materials and also with foetal replicas for use in class discussions on abortion. Education authorities are obliged to ensure that teachers' discussions of such contentious moral issues should be balanced. Does the use of materials likely to stir emotions undermine balanced presentations? Can balance be preserved by allowing the use of such materials provided they are forthcoming from partisans on either side?

Let us recognize at least that appealing to children's emotions for educational purposes is not as such reprehensible nor need recourse to such appeals be evidence that we are unable to make a *rational* case for accepting a conclusion. Even where a rational case is uncontroversially well-founded it may fail to convince. Consider, for instance, the case against children taking up cigarette smoking (or indeed drugs) as a habit. If it is evident that children are more likely to be persuaded to resist acquiring the habit if teachers make use of visual aids, e.g., of films which appeal to the emotions, in conveying the message, would we not all applaud their use even though it would be foreseeable that these materials might be very upsetting for some pupils e.g., for a child whose parent had died of lung cancer? We would say that such suffering "can't be helped" and is necessary if we are to prevent a great deal of suffering.

But then I assume that teachers do not have to present a balanced view on the pros and cons of smoking. It is not a controversial moral issue. Where there is a duty to maintain a balanced presentation, should teachers eschew materials that are likely to stir emotions? Or, does the commitment to balance require only that teachers allow both sides to appeal to the emotions or neither?

From the standpoint of partisans on such an issue, what matters most is that injustice be prevented and hence that people be persuaded of the injustice by whatever (legitimate) means. But from the standpoint of those who are undecided, the "floating voters" on the issue, what matters most is that the conclusion they arrive at is rationally grounded. Therefore, I suggest, while it is rational for partisans to appeal to the emotions of the floating voters it is also rational for the floating voters to beware of such appeals, to be on their guard lest these cloud their judgement.

Do appeals to emotions on such issues make rational deliberation more difficult? Imagine a teacher seeking to give a balanced presentation on the pros and cons of capital punishment. He is offered, let us suppose, as visual aids: (1) a film of victims dying from a terrorist's shooting and (2) a filmed hanging of a convicted terrorist. Would pupils be helped or hindered through exposure to such materials in forming a rational judgement on the issue? The duty to provide a balanced presentation is, after all, only one aspect of a more fundamental duty to foster rational reflection on the issue. Thus it is, perhaps, not enough that a teacher balances one intemperate presentation with an equally intemperate presentation from the other side. The result of such an approach may be more confused thinking on the issue, not less.

Misinformation and Scaremongering

We have already taken on the assumption that we may not do evil that good may come. If we may assume that lying is one such evil thereby ruled out, our participation in disseminating specific items of information which we know to be false must always be indefensible. But what if some of our fellow campaigners put about misinformation: have we a duty to correct it? We need not suppose that these campaigners themselves intend to deceive anybody. They are perhaps more credulous than we are. But if we (come to) know or even have good reason to suspect that what they say is in fact false, is it indefensible for us to be complacent about "putting the record straight"?

I believe it is. While we do not in general have a duty to correct other people's mistakes, where we are making *common* cause with certain others, must we not assume a responsibility for each other's actions? One of the pharmaceutical company, Roussel UK's, grouses about pro-life organizations is that their supporters are wont to put about scaremongering stories about the abortifacient RU 486 which Roussel disbelieves and yet when Roussel calls on these organizations either to provide the supporting evidence or repudiate the stories, they do neither. If such allegations against these organizations are true, is not their failure to respond in either way indefensible? Or is it not at least *prima facie* indefensible: an organization might reasonably plead that its limited resources made it impossible to check out every item or even follow up all challenges and queries it received?

"Hypocritical" Arguments

Another common grouse levied against the pro-lifers is that in their campaigning they appeal to arguments which in their own view are irrelevant but which may be expected to dent the opposition e.g., they argue that RU 486 is not safe for women, has not been adequately tested and will cause long-term psychological stresses in those who avail themselves of it. Now let us suppose that they are at least sincere in so far as they honestly believe that all this is true. Nevertheless, it is not the *real* reason why they oppose the use of RU 486. The real reason why they oppose it is that it is an abortifacient which it would still be, of course, if it were ever so safe and convenient. Is it hypocritical of pro-lifers to appeal in this way to considerations which they can expect to influence the opposition though from their own standpoint they are irrelevant?

Such *ad hominem* appeals surely need not be in the least hypocritical. The pro-life faction need make no pretence about the basis of their own opposition to RU 486. But if what is for them the crucial consideration does not move the opposition but other considerations do, why should they not avail themselves of these to dissuade the opposition from acting unjustly – as they see it? If a robber points his gun at me and I plead "Don't shoot me: there is a concealed camera on the premises by which you'll be identified" am I being hypocritical just because the real reason I don't want him to shoot is not that he will get caught and punished but that I don't want to die?

It is defensible, then, to make use of premises in arguments that our opponents accept although these same arguments do not explain our own position. But appealing to arguments which we know to be invalid but by which the opposition may be taken in, is another matter. Here, it seems to me, hypocrisy is unavoidable. How can we *present* such arguments but as if we take them seriously, that is, believe them to be valid? To do so would be dishonest just as much as if we were to deliberately disseminate misinformation.

Conclusion

I will now summarize our findings in regard to the intolerant stances and questionable tactics we have reviewed. It has been argued that the following stances or tactics are indefensible even if those who use them are in the right on the abortion issue: refusing in principle to engage in debate with the opposition, manifesting complacency toward misinformation being disseminated by fellow campaigners and arguing "hypocritically" where that is understood to mean only: the deployment of arguments which *we* know to be invalid.

Appealing to people's emotions to win them to our view on a controversial issue turns out to be a more problematic tactic. I have argued that our recourse to such a tactic does not of itself prove that we are unable to make a rational case. But I question whether those in particular who have a duty to present a balanced view, should incorporate any such appeals. It does not follow that partisans may not defensibly use them (outside the classroom). But they use them defensibly only if they have reason to believe that despite whatever distress their use causes to some, they may still be effective in winning converts or in rallying support. Perhaps that is something that is often difficult to gauge in advance: even where such appeals cause an immediate outcry, it is not obvious that they have misfired.

Neither pro-lifers nor pro-choicers in the UK are content with the *status quo* on the abortion issue. But the *status quo* which permits abortion under some circumstances ought to be more tolerable for pro-choicers than for pro-lifers. Thus we should expect the latter to be more vociferous on the subject and to be campaigning more aggressively to change the *status quo*.

With a morally controversial issue such as abortion a difficult balance needs to be struck between tolerance and intolerance. On the one hand, we may overdo the tolerance, become apathetic or hardened and therewith compromise our principles: our sense of outrage needs to be nurtured and sustained if the policies which we oppose are seriously unjust. On the other hand, we may overdo the intolerance and thereby wreck the very debate in society that might, if allowed to proceed, enable others to come to understand the injustice of the policies which we oppose. As Aristotle says, it is not easy to be virtuous: an exercise of judgement is involved in the particular choices we have to make as to what we tolerate, how we tolerate, towards whom we are tolerant and on what occasions.

References

Alton D (1988) Whose choice anyway? Marshall Pickering, Basingstoke

CHAPTER 17

Tolerance: Virtue or Vice?

D.W. Brown

It is a commonplace to remark that western democracies are pluralist societies; commonplace too to remark that this has implications for religion. Less frequently observed is the fact that the issue of pluralism and its implications also now raises itself with respect to medical ethics. In the religious case the answer given is mutual tolerance, but what this means is seldom carefully examined. Nor is this the case in medical ethics, where discussion typically proceeds on the assumption that rational argument could eventually result in agreement, rather than considering what should be done once an impasse is reached. But impasse situations are undoubtedly reached, and then various forms of coercive action are sometimes the result. An obvious example from the United States would be the way in which both sides in the continuing abortion debate have resorted to threatening or even violent forms of behaviour, for instance upon abortion clinics or elected officials' homes. Again, in this country we find advocates of animal rights resorting to various forms of violent protest against the use of animals in medical experiments.

In what follows I shall ignore the moral rights or wrongs of the position which the protesters are attempting to support by their coercive action. Rather, what interests me is what arguments might be used to persuade that tolerance is a virtue rather than a vice. In the process I hope to show not only the continuing relevance of the arguments which were originally used to justify religious tolerance but also the way in which the difficulties this created for religion have clear parallels in current confrontations over morality.

But before proceeding to that topic, we must first clarify what we mean by tolerance. Though some commentators deny that this is a legitimate use of the word, there is no doubt that in ordinary English there is a very weak sense according to which to tolerate something implies no more than that one is indifferent to it. Thus one may tolerate variety in religious belief or sexual practice simply because one thinks it a matter of no importance. But such a view is hardly compatible with respect for those whom one is tolerating, which surely must imply taking seriously their claim that great consequences hang upon such beliefs. This explains why minority religions are often infuriated by such tolerance. They want not just to be allowed to exist, but to be taken seriously, and so have access to the media and so forth. It is also an irritation which can sometimes afflict practitioners of the majority religion as well, as in T.S. Eliot's well-known remark that "the Christian does not want to be tolerated", meaning thereby that he does not want just to be "put up with" or "endured": he wants to be taken seriously.

Apart from the laziness implicit in such an attitude, the other obvious point of critique which may be made of such a tolerance of indifference is its intellectual arrogance. This is no doubt why a more morally acceptable form is seen to lie in a respectful recognition of disagreement. The alternative view is taken seriously as a legitimate option which though neither liked nor currently adopted as one's own, one can conceive of circumstances where this could be so. Such circumstances may be seen as further argument, or simply as some alternative scenario, for instance, different genes generating homosexual desires or a different homeland a different religion. In a number of national editorials[1] marking the retirement of Robert Runcie as Archbishop of Canterbury he was praised for displaying this kind of tolerance within a pluralistic Church of England, and indeed his final sermon was a plea for precisely this kind of tolerance. But the fact that his primacy was also marked by accusations of him "firmly nailing his colours to the fence"[2] well illustrates how easy it is for this kind of tolerance to degenerate into moral or religious relativism. It is this tendency which readily explains recent arguments over religious education in schools. It is one thing to insist that in a pluralist culture children should be made sympathetically aware of the variety of religions in their midst; another, that the expressing of preferences among them should be foreclosed. Hence the debate, on the one hand about the need to reflect the fact that we still live in a predominantly Christian culture, and on the other that explicitly religious schools should be made available for all faiths.

Runcie's successor, George Carey, is a very different kind of man. Already we find him using strong language of his opponents, for instance labelling as heretics those who oppose the ordination of women.[3] Whether tactically this is wise, I leave on one side, but there is no doubt that we expect religion and morality to generate such strong emotional commitment, and this is indeed well reflected in the two medical examples with which I began. For there would surely be no shortage among pro- and anti-abortionists and animal liberationists who would take the view that such tolerance of polite disagreement constituted a profound attack upon the seriousness of the issues upon which they are engaged, and the sense of moral outrage which their opponents' positions generate in them. The animal liberationist feels compelled to speak of cruelty, and the absolutists in the abortion debate on the one hand of murder of the unborn and on the other of a kind of rape, as the women's body is compelled to act in ways against her will.

On such a scenario it may seem hard to resist the conclusion that tolerance must become a vice. For, if without specifying the context we were to say that someone was prepared to tolerate fundamental interference with women's bodies, cruelty and murder, we would have little hesitation in regarding them as morally culpable for their inaction. Indeed if we were told in general terms of the typical tactics currently being employed to prevent these offences, such as verbal harassment of those about to perpetrate the evil deeds, we might well question whether they were going far enough. None the less it was in the face of such strongly opposed convictions that religious tolerance emerged. So what I want to do in the rest of this paper is examine some of those original arguments to see whether a third strong sense of tolerance is in fact feasible, one in which it is accompanied by strong moral disapproval of one's opponents' views and actions.

The first argument which I shall take is not historically the earliest but perhaps the one most likely to appeal to an academic community, that an open, tolerant society is the best way of ensuring the ultimate emergence of the truth. As one might expect from the author of *The Open Society and its Enemies*, Sir Karl Popper is a strong contemporary advocate of this argument[4] and indeed if comparison is being drawn with the former, closed societies of eastern Europe or other totalitarian nations, it is tempting to think the point self-evident. But at least two caveats need to be drawn.

The first is implicit in the phrase "the free market of ideas". For what free markets ensure is not necessarily the emergence of the truth but, as it were, the most saleable truth. Thus truth may be distorted by other interests in a number of ways, for instance by the class interests of the press barons or the unwillingness of society in general to hear some unpalatable truth, such as British misconduct in war. In an influential essay of 1965[5] Herbert Marcuse used the phrase "repressive tolerance" to characterise the way in which the appearance of tolerance can actually systematically divert people away from perception of the truth. It is a theme which was taken up by another, younger member of the Frankfurt School, Jürgen Habermas, in his *Knowledge and Human Interests* (1968). Subsequently in his *Theory of Communicative Action* (1981) he has worked out in elaborate detail his theory of how truth can only properly be pursued by making such interests explicit, so as to discount them.

Likewise, in the case of both abortion and animal liberation there surely are interests on both sides which inhibit easy perception of the truth. It would take considerable heart-searching for a doctor to admit that his present actions constitute cruelty or murder, just as it would be no easy matter for his critics to accept themselves as pure sentimentalists or so priest-ridden as to be incapable of independent judgment.

Of course one might argue that this points all the more to the need for an open society of ideas. But a second, even more powerful restraint on that ideal needs to be conceded, and that is the fact that though the impression of a shared dialogue is created and sometimes even real, more often than not no progress is made because what is at stake is not just one particular issue but an entire moral framework. For instance on the abortion issue it would be naïve to suppose that the two sides merely disagree about when human life or personhood begins. They also disagree about what makes adult human life valuable, for instance how important pleasure and pain are within it. The way in which the 1662 Prayer Book Litany enjoins prayer for the avoidance of "sudden" (i.e., painless) death as a great evil may be used to illustrate wider differences.[6] Concentrating on the narrower issue thus actually distorts the nature of what is at stake and fails to alert the two sides to further likely areas of disagreement. Even attempting to find some wider principle such as respect for life as a way of encapsulating the difference fails accurately to reflect the extent of the disagreement. The fact that the Church opposed the doctors' prolongation of life in the case of Karen Quinlan or General Franco shows that something rather different is at stake, entire rival frameworks for assessing the value of human life.

It was recognition of this fact which led Alasdair MacIntyre to write *After Virtue* (1981) with its pessimistic conclusion that ethics could only be done within rival ethical communities. Two subsequent books, *Whose Justice? Which Rationality?* (1988) and his Gifford Lectures *Three Rival Versions of Moral Enquiry* (1990) have sought to demonstrate that dialogue and comparison is after all possible, largely, he suggests, through attempting to answer the question: Which moral theory has the greatest explanatory power?

However, the process he envisages is such an intellectually arduous one that it is hard to see how the great mass of human beings could acquire the competence to take part in the discussion. Yet that should not generate pessimism on our part about the force of this argument for tolerance based on the pursuit of truth. For much the same might be said about the capacity of ordinary people to weigh definitively the truth claims of the rival religions, but this has not forced educationalists to retreat from giving school children a basic imaginative grasp and some of the tools for assessment.

Adults of an older generation continue to underestimate the differences between the religions and to speak misleadingly of "other faiths" or "other paths to salvation", as though all the major world religions share the same concepts and vocabulary. The rising generation is at least aware that no such simple direct comparisons are possible. Even something so apparently obvious as "holy book" means something quite different in Christianity, Islam and Hinduism – the Koran functioning more like the divinity of Christ than the Bible within Christianity, and Hinduism having no clear notion of written authorities.

In fact there would seem no reason why, in principle, a comparable education should not be offered in rival ethical frameworks. What stands in its way is the fact that whereas religions have a long tradition of making their underlying assumptions explicit, there is no similar tradition in respect of rival moral systems. But all this surely argues for is the need for hard, creative work in attempting to make these underlying assumptions explicit.

Take the case of abortion. Anti-abortionists sometimes speak of a right to life, as though all that was at stake was two competing rights within a shared framework of discourse, this and a woman's right over her body, but all this does is disguise a much deeper, underlying conflict. It is difficult to find satisfactory terminology, but if we speak of a conflict between life seen as a gift and life seen as a product that at least gets us nearer to the heart of the debate, and explains why the strong anti-abortionist is also likely to be opposed to, or at least suspicious of, a number of other recent innovations in reproductive medicine. By gift I do not wish to imply that all holding this view assume a religious perspective and thus a divine giver. Many do not; it is just that I cannot find another suitable word. The important point lying behind it is the conviction that the child should be seen as something over against oneself, not something subject to manipulation. That perhaps now makes it clearer why from the gift perspective the opposed view is seen as having a "product", manipulative attitude towards the possibility of a child, with choice of sex, intelligence and physical characteristics all, at least in principle, on offer and not just the avoidance of handicap. From such a perspective modern reproductive medicine opens up the unwelcome scenario of the child as "the perfect product", as an instrument for the fulfilment of the parents' wishes rather than a totally independent entity. Indeed, when the argument is put in this way, it is possible for the anti-abortionist to turn the tables on his critic, and insist that it is his opponent who is in the grip of religious prejudice rather than the reverse. For a desire for the child as perfect product sounds suspiciously similar to the primitive desire for immortality through one's posterity, with all the problems that raises with respect to appropriate attitudes towards one's children.

Likewise, to argue with animal liberationists about the degree of pain involved to the animals compared with the likely saving in human pain is in most cases to distort radically the basis of their objection. Many of them seem to hold a semi-mystical view of our fundamental identity with the natural order and our consequent need to respect this. If that then really is their wider moral framework, tolerance must surely involve a more sympathetic consideration of that wider perspective.

Popper sees Voltaire as anticipating him in this argument from truth, but, as might be expected from someone who was a deist in religion, there is not the same confidence about human ability to find the truth.[7] It is often asserted that the rise of religious tolerance corresponds with the rise of scepticism in religion, and this may seem confirmed by Voltaire's attitude, but, as Cranston[8] among others has pointed out, arguments not based on uncertainty about one's own possession of the truth were already widely accepted a full century earlier.

In England, the most influential was Locke's *Essay on Tolerance* of 1688. Though there are some pragmatic considerations in his case, his principal argument is one of principle, and indicates a deep Christian concern. But before turning to it, it will be helpful to examine briefly a more developed pragmatic argument from one of Locke's contemporaries, Pierre Bayle's reciprocity argument. Bayle, like Locke, was writing in exile in Holland but whereas Locke's hopes for England were soon to be fulfilled in the 1689 Act of Toleration, Bayle was facing a worsening situation in his native France where Louis XIV had just rescinded almost a hundred years of toleration with his revocation of the Edict of Nantes in 1685.

Part of Bayle's response is his reciprocity argument which has recently been developed by one of his modern admirers, John Kilcullen.[9] In essence it is the claim that tolerance pays since it prevents one's opponents from claiming that they have gained the moral right to reciprocate with intolerant behaviour. In the context of the history of religious wars in post-Reformation Europe the argument had much plausibility. Today, not only does it continue to be plausible, it may be strengthened by the observation that even without the fear of reciprocal action, coercive behaviour may itself be counter-productive. For instance, noisy protests at abortion clinics might well swing public opinion in favour of those women being harassed rather than the unborn children whom the protesters see themselves as defending.

This is not to say that the argument is of universal applicability. For it would be hard to deny some conspicuous cases of the success of violent protest. This may have to be conceded even with the IRA, especially if one accepts the view of a sensitive Roman Catholic politician like Lord Fitt that the creation of the Council of Ireland will only exacerbate Protestant fears of a united Ireland.[10] But perhaps more worrying than such rare exceptions is the way in which direct action and other forms of group pressure have become much more prominent in recent years and so not only compelled opponents to resort to similar methods but raised fundamental questions about the functioning of tolerance in a democracy of this kind. An interesting illustration of the way in which our society has changed without us always realising it is given by Lord Scarman who observes that demonstrations were so rare in the thirties when he was a student that his teachers were seriously canvassing the view that they were

illegal, on the grounds that the public highway exists solely for free access.[11]
While not denying the legitimacy of this and other forms of group pressure, it
surely must be conceded that they do raise difficult questions about whether
democracy functioning in this way has not become more like the balancing of
rival pressure groups, with the resultant danger of less vociferous or less
influential groups having their legitimate grievances overlooked. This is certainly
a major concern of the American philosopher R.P. Wolff, who, with what
justification I do not know, gives as one of his examples of unfair group pressure
that coming from the American Medical Association.[12]

As we have just seen, the two arguments considered so far, though of
considerable weight, are far from being water-tight. This is a consequence of
the fact that they seek to justify tolerance in terms of some further objective,
the pursuit of truth or the attainment of one's own objectives, since inevitably
there may be occasions when these could be more effectively pursued by other
means. That is why the third argument which makes tolerance a principle in
itself is of such importance. In Locke's version it amounts to the claim that
persecution and intolerance can never achieve the objective which a religion
seeks. For force can never produce that "faith and inward sincerity" which alone
can "procure acceptance with God".[13] We might put this in more modern
language by saying that tolerance is entailed by the principle of autonomy, that
religious and moral belief is only of worth in so far as it is freely chosen
according to one's conscience. Indeed one may legitimately claim that a person
has failed to assume a moral framework at all until he has accepted the principle
in this form. For it is arguable that one has not acknowledged the moral identity
of another human being until one has conceded both his separate access to moral
intuitions and his responsibility to form his own judgment on the basis of that
independent access.

So far as the toleration of opinions of which one strongly disapproves is
concerned, there seems in fact at the moment to be considerable muddle in the
public mind, as some of the comments which have been made in respect of the
Salman Rushdie affair well illustrate. The appeal on one side has tended to be
to the literary merits of the book and on the other to the blasphemy laws
protecting Christianity, but both types of appeal seem to me an irrelevance; in
the latter case because apart from one successful prosecution in the last 30
years[14] the blasphemy laws are in effect a dead letter; in the former, partly
because I doubt the literary merits of the work and partly because in any case
the same issue would have arisen had Rushdie presented the offending passages
simply as an oral skit.

While in no sense wishing to endorse the resultant *fatwa*, which as Malise
Ruthven has recently observed[15] seems in any case to have been largely the
result of political motives, I cannot share the laments expressed over the general
Muslim sense of outrage. It is tempting to suggest that tolerance is compatible
only with cool, rational debate but, if so, that would be to ignore many types
of morality and, I suspect, what is an element in almost everyone's morality:
that one cares deeply for something and is outraged when its integrity or dignity
is violated. Such is the Muslim attitude to the Koran, and I would not wish it
otherwise. Equally, I myself as a Christian was outraged when I was shown
the James Kirkup poem which led to the successful blasphemy prosecution. But
from that it need not follow that I must approve of the blasphemy laws or
would wish them extended to include other religions.

Of course it is difficult to hold together both a sense of outrage and tolerance, the conviction that there is a right that this should be said, but it does seem to me important morally that they should be able to co-exist. Yeats' famous lines about the best lacking all conviction do contain a salutary warning. It is very easy for tolerance to degenerate into indifference, as for instance in the way in which even some Christian clergy seem willing to use blasphemous expressions. Surely strength of conviction and a point beyond which a sense of outrage is generated must go together. And so, returning to our two medical examples, so far from it being a cause of worry if vituperative language is used on the two sides of the debate, there would be something wrong were this not so.

But what of satire and parody, as was the case with *Satanic Verses*? Once again I do not think that we should see this as a cause for regret. We could only think so were we to deem formal, rational argument as the only proper forum of discussion. Even philosophers can resort to various rhetorical devices in order to aid their arguments, as Martin Warner has recently illustrated in his study of Plato, Hume and Nietzsche among others.[16] Among rhetorical methods satire is one of the more powerful. Nor is its force necessarily illegitimate. It attacks its opponent where he is psychologically at his weakest, ruthlessly exposing apparent contradictions at the heart of his position, as in Rushdie's treatment of Muhammad. But that does not mean that he necessarily succeeds. Response to satire is often a strengthening of resolve, and indeed arguably this is what has happened to the Muslim community in Britain with it attempting to form, for the first time, national structures out of its disparate groups. Indeed the failure of the dominant culture to distinguish whether a particular pronouncement on the issue came from Barelwis or Deobandis, or Ahmadis or Maududis (to mention just two contrasting positions within our Muslim fellow citizens) indicates well how superficial is our tolerance of the minority cultures in our midst.

It may be worries on this score which led to the amending of the Public Order Act of 1936 into the Race Relations Acts of 1965 and 1976. The earlier law had a clear rationale, in that it required a probable breach of the peace to ensue from inflammatory words before police action was taken, whereas the 1976 Act makes offensive language itself punishable. One might draw a parallel with the blasphemy laws and indeed in some national codes, for example that of Germany and India, race and religion are covered under the same rubric, but, as we have already noted, the blasphemy law in Britain is effectively a dead letter. The most recent major work on the law of Free Speech suggests that even purely factual material, such as statistics suggesting lower intelligence among blacks, could contravene our present law.[17]

Yet, ignoring direct instigation to violence which there is good reason for banning, it is hard to see what could justify treating this form of offence with greater consideration than any other. Moreover, is it not the case that the legislation effectively suppresses a common moral perspective, namely that which gives central place to the equation of national with cultural identity? It is a major force in the modern world; one need only consider what is currently happening in eastern Europe. Yet in Britain it is very difficult to have a sustained discussion of the issues without offending the race laws. One suspects that this cannot but be harmful in the long term to the nation's health, since what could once be discussed publicly and challenged is now simply expressed privately without dissent among sympathisers.

But is it really wise, you may ask, to allow strong emotive or parodying language? Is violent confrontation not going to be the inevitable result? Here, again, education would seem to hold the key. As children grow up, they all become familiar with insult at the personal level, and learn how to cope with it without either resorting to violence or necessarily not taking offence. So why should it not be possible to train communities and groups in a similar kind of way? Insult is scarcely compatible with friendship, but it is not incompatible with co-existence. It is hard to see legislation as anything more than a temporary expedient until society has grown more accustomed to the expression of strongly incompatible views without resort being had to violence.

But, unfortunately, the abortion and animal liberation case is more complicated than this, as not only is the question of offensive language involved but also the claim that serious harm is being done to a third party. Significantly, in a move that anticipates John Stuart Mill's *Essay on Liberty* two centuries later, Locke did not extend toleration to the putting into practice of unacceptable views, since, he argued, the interests of others were then affected.

Initially, the best way forward might seem to be the suggestion that tolerance is the appropriate response where an issue is contentious within a particular society, even where third party harm is concerned. This is the position adopted by the controversial American Roman Catholic moral theologian, Charles Curran.[18] Though personally opposed to abortion he has argued not only against attempts by his fellow Catholics to overthrow the 1973 legalisation but also for the provision of facilities at public cost. His case seems based on the idea that the means should be made available to exercise one's conscience freely where an issue is contentious or doubtful. But that will not do for at least two reasons. First, the most committed on both sides of the two issues in question do not in fact see the matter as uncertain; they are already convinced in their own minds, and its seems an odd argument to suggest that, because some doubt, all should doubt. Secondly, as a general principle this would produce some clearly unacceptable consequences. For instance in Nazi Germany it would have meant toleration of the government's treatment of the Jews since this was seen as appropriate behaviour by a significant proportion of the people

A much more acceptable, though by no means foolproof, strategy would be to insist that motivation always be taken into account, and that if an altruistic good is the aim, even if harm to some third party is the result, this none-the-less constitutes prima facie grounds for tolerance. Once again this would be an important aspect of moral education, that children should be given the tools to be able to distinguish between the application of an alternative moral system and the stepping outside of morality altogether. That would still be to impose some limits on tolerance, since clearly abortion on demand or experiments on animals for improved cosmetics could not seriously claim to have such an altruistic purpose. In such cases I fail to see what argument could be given to pesuade their opponents towards tolerance. But in the more central cases there surely now is an argument: that the altruistic motive indicates a morally motivated exercise of the autonomy of conscience, even if it is believed to be misdirected.

Throughout this essay I have drawn a number of parallels between religious education in a pluralist society and moral education. Both require serious engagement with the fact that different frameworks are sometimes involved and not just occasional differences of principle, if a proper understanding is truly to be reached and truth sought. With both it is important that the notion of a sense of outrage at certain sorts of offence should not be abandoned; for that indicates a proper level of commitment. But with neither should this generate intolerance nor the need for legal restrictions provided our educational system takes serious account of the need to train groups and communities, as well as individuals, in the proper handling of insult. At its most basic there lies the parallel that tolerance is a sine qua non of both since the foundations of both are laid upon something which cannot be forced, in the one case a free commitment of belief and in the other the autonomous exercise of conscience.

Notes

1. *The Times*, 31 January 1991; *Church Times*, 1 February 1991.

2. *Crockford's Clerical Directory*, 1987/8: Preface, p 68.

3. "A very serious heresy" was the actual phrase used in the interview published in *The Reader's Digest*, 1990.

4. E.g., in "Toleration and intellectual responsibility". In: Mendus S, Edwards D (eds) (1987) *On Toleration*. Clarendon Press. Oxford, pp 17–34.

5. Marcuse H. (1969) Repressive tolerance. In: Wolff RP, Moore B, Marcuse H (eds) *A Critique of Pure Tolerance*. Jonathan Cape, London, pp 95–137.

6. A similar failure to take account of conflicting wider moral perspectives plagues treatment of the problem of evil in the philosophy of religion. Cf. Brown DW (1989) The problem of pain. In: Morgan R (ed) *The Religion of the Incarnation*. Bristol Classical Press, pp 46–59.

7. Voltaire's entry under "Tolerance" in his *Philosophical Dictionary* largely consists of a recitation of the enormous range of opposed positions which have been held in the history of Christianity.

8. Cranston M (1987) John Locke and the case for toleration. In: Mendus S, Edwards D (eds) *Toleration and Intellectual Responsibility*. Clarendon Press, Oxford, pp. 101–21, esp. p. 118. WK Jordan in his major work *The Development of Religious Toleration in England* (1940) took a rather different view. Cf. e.g., vol. 3, p 475, which speaks of "the contagious spread of indifference".

9. Kilkullen J (1988) *Sincerity and Truth*. Clarendon Press, Oxford, esp. pp 89–93, 106–135.

10. Cf. Mendus S, Edwards D (eds) (1987) *Toleration and Intellectual Responsibility*. Clarendon Press, Oxford, p 79.

11. Ibid. p 51.

12. Cf Wolff RP (1969) In: Wolff RP, Moore B, Marcuse H (eds) *A Critique of Pure Tolerance*. Jonathan Cape, London, pp 11–61, esp. pp 56–57.

13. *Works of John Locke* (1727), Vol. II, p 243.

14. The *Gay News* trial of 1979: R. *v.* Lemon.

15. Ruthven M (1991) *A Satanic Affair*. Hogarth Press, London, pp 108–116.

16. Warner M (1989) *Philosophical Finesse*. Clarendon Press, Oxford.

17. Barendt E (1985) *Freedom of Speech*. Clarendon Press, Oxford, pp 161–167, esp. p 164.

18. Curran CE (1979) *Transition and Tradition in Moral Theology*. University of Notre Dame Press, pp 230–250. It is interesting to find a philosopher making the same appeal to uncertainty, but using it to argue against public provision for abortion: cf. Sher G (1981) Subsidized abortion: moral rights and moral compromise. In: *Philosophy and Public Affairs*, pp 361–374.

CHAPTER 18

Are There Moral Authorities?

R. M. Hare

I have been struck, as many must have been, by the very small impact that philosophers have had on the current public debates in Britain on moral issues. This is partly because their help is not often sought; and partly because when it is sought the philosophers are not always helpful. There are now some good philosophers who work in applied philosophy. And there are also some philosophers who attempt this, but who, because of their faulty grasp of ethical theory, are not in a position to help very much. On the continent the position is much worse. I have also been struck on recent visits to Scandinavia and Germany first by the great public interest there is in moral questions, especially in medicine, but secondly by how uncommon it is for philosophers to be asked to serve on committees and working parties that study such questions. It is much more usual for clergymen and lawyers to have a place on them. That perhaps shows that clergymen and lawyers are regarded as some sort of authorities on moral questions, but philosophers are not.

I do not want to claim that philosophers are authorities in the sense in which some people think that clergymen and lawyers are; I shall be arguing later that in that sense there are *no* authorities on these questions: we have to decide them for ourselves, though some people, through a combination of practical experience and clear thinking, may have become better able than others to handle them. But nevertheless it is striking how often, when these questions are discussed in Parliament or in the media, palpable confusions and fallacies are made in the arguments, and repeated again and again – confusions and fallacies which any competent philosopher would at once spot. The role of the philosopher is not that of an authority, but of someone who is able to help avoid these blunders.

However, the position seems to be improving a little. I was much heartened to read my Oxford colleague Jonathan Glover's report to the European Commission, called *Fertility and the Family* (1989). This was prepared by a working party under his chairmanship, and deals with the same range of subjects, roughly, as the Warnock Report (1984). There is no comparison between the two reports. Lady Warnock came to some, on the whole, sensible conclusions; but, because the ethical theory she favours is of an intuitionist sort which is not strong on providing arguments, she did not afford much in the way of reasons for them which would stand up (Hare 1987). That is why the Report did not do much to help Parliament when recently it debated the Bill which deals with embryo experimentation. We are still not out of that wood, and will not be until we learn how to argue better. The members of Glover's working party were continentals from various related professions; I know only one of them, a very sensible and able German philosopher and medical doctor, Bettina Schöne-Seifert; but evidently Jonathan Glover, who wrote the Report, succeeded in a way that philosophers ought to be able to in getting his working party to be clear about the arguments and thus arrive at some helpful conclusions. It is a fine piece of work, and it is a great pity that it has not had so much attention in this country as the Warnock Report – partly, I think, because it was a Report to the European Commission and not to H. M. Government.

There is also excellent work coming out from the Centre for Human Bioethics at Monash University in Australia, whose Director Peter Singer has with his colleagues produced some very well-argued books. Their conclusions may not please everybody, but the quality of their reasoning is a model of its kind. They also have some skill in public relations, and in Australia are attended to. Peter Singer himself had a rough passage in Germany two summers ago; he was demonstrated against, and some of his talks had to be cancelled; the Germans have not yet, on the whole, caught up with ideas which are commonplace in countries such as the Netherlands and Denmark, for example. But from a recent visit I think that things are going to alter once the supply of clear-headed philosophers increases in Germany, and once these philosophers devote more of their attention to practical issues. Both of these things are starting to happen.

Let me now address the question in my title, and say why I think there are no authorities, in the strong sense that some people think is the only sense, on moral questions, but that, nevertheless, thought about them can be done well or badly, and that philosophers can help us to do it better. Obviously the first thing I must do is to sort out the different senses of "authority", and then examine the claims of various candidates to be authorities in these different senses. The first sense need not detain us, because it is really irrelevant to our concerns. This is the sense in which an authority is a person or body that *enforces* laws or moral requirements by imposing sanctions – in other words by punishing those who break them. I do not think that when people look for an authority on questions of morals they are looking for someone who will punish offenders against, for example, the rules of medical ethics. It may be important to have authorities in this sense, but I shall treat as prior the question of who should decide what the rules are or ought to be. Until we can answer the latter question it is too early to ask who should enforce the rules. (On the question of the justification of punishment, see Hare 1986.)

A sense of "authority" that we do need to discuss is the one in which I said that some people think there are moral authorities, and that is the sense in which "authority" means "source of unchallengeable answers to questions". In this sense we treat people as authorities on the content of their own experiences. Though some philosophers might dispute this, I think we can agree that if I say I am in pain, and mean it in the accepted sense of the words, nobody else can safely tell me that I am wrong, unless he can somehow show that I am speaking insincerely – that I do not really believe what I am saying. I shall not discuss in general what other questions can receive authoritative answers of this sort; that would be too big a topic. But we do need to ask whether moral questions can ever be answered authoritatively in this way. This would be the case if, sometimes, somebody could just pronounce that some act was wrong, and nobody could dispute this.

Let us then ask whether there is any person or body that can give answers to moral questions that simply cannot be disputed. Can judges, for example, fill this bill? If they are judges in the highest court in a jurisdiction they can certainly give to *legal* questions answers that cannot be challenged. But one of the important distinctions between law and morality is that judges cannot do for moral questions what they can do for legal ones. The reason is that what judges decide is what the law *is*, and not what it ought to be, or in general what ought to be done. When the House of Lords has pronounced that the law is such and such, I cannot then turn round and say that it is not (though I can, if I am a rebel, challenge the legality of the entire jurisdiction: see Hare 1967). But if the House of Lords says that something is morally wrong and I do not think that it is, I am entitled to my opinion. Perhaps, though the law is as the House of Lords says it is, it ought to be changed.

If judges are not moral authorities in this sense, are legislators in any stronger position? Parliament can decide, not just what the law is, but what it is to be. In the United States the situation is not so clear, because there is a written constitution, and the Supreme Court, a judicial body, can say that laws passed by Congress are unconstitutional and therefore of no effect. And jurists dispute at length on the extent to which judges can be said themselves to determine, not just what the law is, but what it is to be. Certainly it seems as if the Supreme Court in the United States, and even, though less commonly, the House of Lords here, do determine what the law is to be as well as determining what it is. But I shall not be expected to go into that tangled question here. It suffices to say that, when it comes to a question of morals, legislators are in no better position to decide than are judges. That something is morally wrong is never part of the content of a Bill before Parliament; but if it were, and Parliament voted that it *was* morally wrong, it would still be open to any of us to disagree, and we should be entitled to our opinions. So we may conclude that legislators are not moral authorities any more than judges are. MPs of course have, and should have, moral reasons for voting as they do, but their votes, however unanimous, do not *make* something morally wrong; nor do laws enacted by the Queen in Parliament determine what is to be morally wrong, but only what is to be illegal.

At this point it may be suggested, as it is by some modern intuitionists such as Ross, that moral authority does not reside in any particular office or station, but in the generally accepted opinion of all morally educated people. It would not do to go further and say "of all people"; for we cannot rely on a consensus for answers to questions on which obviously there *is* no consensus. But if we are to rely on the morally educated, how do we tell who is morally educated? On a question such as abortion, for example, or embryo experimentation, or surrogate motherhood, or euthanasia, we find different people, all of whom can claim to be morally very well educated even by Ross's standards, saying opposite things. Unless we argue that the people on the other side must be morally uneducated because they disagree with us, how else are we to determine whether they are? I shall come back later to the question of how to decide what counts as good or as bad moral thinking; this is obviously going to be the crucial issue. Neither "the many" nor "the wise", as Aristotle (1095a 18) might have put it, are to be relied on without our own independent scrutiny.

Having thus dismissed the State and other secular moral authorities, what about the Church? Here the matter is, initially, somewhat easier, because the

Church does not ever claim to determine *by its own authority* what is morally wrong. In the eyes of most churchmen, God is the authority on moral questions, and the Church is at most passing on his commands to the laity. And not all Churches claim to do even this with authority. The same is true of the hierarchies of other religions. The Roman Church may be the only church whose head claims to pronounce on moral questions *ex cathedra*; and even the Pope does not claim to *decide*, of himself, by his own authority, what is right or wrong. He claims only to be a mouthpiece for the divine commands.

So is God the ultimate moral authority? This question raises two further very difficult problems. The first is, "Even if we agreed that God is the ultimate determiner, by his commands, of what is right and wrong, how could we tell what in fact he does command?" The second is, "Even if we could determine this, would the fact that God forbade something necessarily, of itself, make it wrong?" I shall take these two questions in order.

There are various opinions on how God's will is to be known. The simplest one is the extreme Protestant doctrine, if I may call it that, that God, in the form of the Holy Spirit, speaks directly to the individual believer and tells him (or her) the answers to moral questions. To this Hobbes replied: "Though God Almighty can speak to a man, by Dreams, Visions, Voice and Inspiration, yet he obliges no man to believe he hath so done to him that pretends it; who (being a man) may erre, and (which is more) may lie" (Hobbes 1651, chap. 32; cf. Hare 1984). Even if we allowed that God speaks to men directly, the problem remains of when we can be sure that this has happened. The difficulty of "discerning the spirits" already troubled the early Church, and St. Paul's way out of it is not very helpful (I Corinthians 12:3). It is significant that substantially the same difficulty arises whether we ask who is an authority on moral questions or who is a reliable mouthpiece of God's will. As we shall see, the only way out of the difficulty is to do some moral thinking ourselves.

It was, no doubt, in order to avoid the chaos that ensues if individuals claim direct access to God's will, that the Church took on the office of declaring it. But the Church (even the Roman Church whose head speaks *ex cathedra*) is in no better position than individuals are. After all, the Pope too is an individual; and he, also, "may erre, and (which is more) may lie". In order to decide whether a particular Pope has erred, or lied, we have to study the content of his pronouncements, and see whether it stands up.

Those Protestants (the great majority) who reject direct access to God by individuals, or at least desire some confirmation of what they claim God has said, are less likely to appeal to the Church as authority than to the Bible. Notoriously, different people find support in the Bible for very diverse opinions:

> Hic liber est, in quo quaerit sua dogmata quisque,
> Invenietque in eo dogmata quisque sua.

Nevertheless, nobody should deny that much wisdom is to be found in the Bible, and it is worth digressing a little to look for some of it on the question of morality. Morality is a very large part of religion, and Christian morality of the Christian religion; and since Popes and prelates are very apt to take for granted that Christian morality forbids this and that, without thinking that they need to substantiate their claims, it is worth while asking what is the central foundation of Christian and biblical teaching on moral questions. The answer, I am quite sure, lies in the doctrine of *agapê*.

According to St. Matthew 22:39 we are commanded to love God, and this entails, according to St. John 14:15, keeping his commandments. Of the two commandments on which hang all the law and the prophets, the second is to love our neighbour as ourselves (St. Matthew, *loc. cit.*). This is put in other words in St. Matthew 7:12 as "All things whatsoever ye would that men should do to you, do ye even so to them; for this is the law and the prophets." The law that we should love our neighbour as ourselves is found in the Old Testament too (Leviticus 19:18); it is Jewish as well as Christian, and is indeed a constituent of the moral teaching of all the great religions. Joseph Butler, the great eighteenth-century moral philosopher and theologian, writes

> From hence it is manifest that the common virtues, and the common vices of mankind, may be traced up to benevolence, or the want of it. And this entitles the precept, *Thou shalt love thy neighbour as thyself*, to the pre-eminence given to it; and is a justification of the Apostle's assertion, that all other commandments are comprehended in it; whatever cautions and restrictions there are, which might require to be considered, if we were to state particularly and at length, what is virtue and right behaviour in mankind. (1726, sermon 12)

And he later says forthrightly:

> Thus morality and religion, virtue and piety, will at last necessarily coincide, run up into one and the same point, and *love* will be in all senses *the end of the commandment* (*loc. cit.*)

However, he heavily qualifies this claim in a footnote, and in the *Dissertation on Virtue*, admitting duties and virtues not based directly on benevolence, in opposition to the utilitarianism of Hutcheson. Both his main claim and the qualifications greatly influenced me when I was developing my two-level account of moral thinking (Hare 1976, 1981). In my view we can at the critical level base morality on love or benevolence and hence on doing our best to satisfy the preferences of all impartially, but this very benevolence will make us cultivate virtues and acknowledge duties which on the face of it owe nothing to benevolence. To this problem we shall return.

I shall be claiming later that the same commandment of love, or a more general and clearer version of it, can be arrived at by reason, as Kant saw. If someone, using reason, concluded that this was the commandment that it was his duty to keep, he could go on to reason that since God is good this must be what he commands. But this at once takes us on to the second, and more fundamental, difficulty in basing morality on the will of God. In a famous passage (1785, BA92 = 443), Kant repeats an idea which appeared in a more rudimentary form in Plato (*Euthyphro* 10a):

> ... we cannot intuit God's perfection and can only derive it from our own concepts, among which that of morality is the most eminent: but ... if we do not do this (and to do so would be to give a crudely circular explanation), the concept of God's will still remaining to us – one drawn from such characteristics as lust for glory and domination and bound up with frightful ideas of power and vengefulness – would inevitably form the basis for a moral system which would be in direct opposition to morality.

The argument is, in other words, that if we assume the premiss that God is good, we can infer that it is our duty to conform to his will; but that if we do not, there is no such implication. But in order to be assured that he is good, we have to make at least this one moral judgement on our own account; so although, once this judgement is made, we can make all the rest of our moral judgements on the basis of God's will, it would be arguing in a circle to base our belief in his goodness on the goodness of what he wills, and the goodness of what he wills on his goodness.

I think that Kant's argument is in substance correct. We have now come to the end of the list of possible moral authorities, in the sense of "sources of unchallengeable answers to moral questions"; and none of them, whether human or divine, will do. In both cases the trouble is the same; if the "authority" is once assumed to be wise and good, then we can thereafter get all the rest of our moral judgements from the "authority"; but we cannot assume this without making a moral judgement on our own part which is independent of the pronouncements of the "authority". It is easier to see this in the case of human authorities. For example, if we ask, concerning a supposed Platonic philosopher king, "Is he really a philosopher king, or is he a tyrant masquerading as one?", we can only answer the question by ourselves assessing his moral worth and wisdom (Hare 1955). Kant argues that the same is true even of God.

If there are no moral authorities in the sense we have been using, how *are* we to settle moral questions? The answer is, by ourselves doing some moral thinking. But this raises a further question: "Can this moral thinking be done well or badly? Can some do it better than others?" Plato certainly thought so, and so did Kant. Although the candidates we considered cannot, any of them, claim to be authorities in the sense discussed, they might claim to be authorities in a different sense: they might claim to be better at doing moral thinking, that is wiser, than the rest of us. But before we can assess these claims we have to ask what it is to be good at moral thinking. And this in turn depends on what makes moral thinking good moral thinking.

Whether any kind of thinking is good thinking is in part, but only in part, a question of logic. We have to ask, therefore, whether there is a logic that applies to moral thinking. Let us assume that, at any rate, whatever additional logical restrictions there are on moral thinking, the same ordinary logic which governs thinking in general applies to moral thinking too; at least, in thinking morally, we have to avoid contradicting ourselves. But what is or is not a self-contradiction depends on what in particular we are saying. For example, it is self-contradictory to say "It is red and it is not red" (in the same sense of "red"). But it would not be self-contradictory to say "it is red and it is not blue". The alteration in the wording – the fact that we are saying something different – affects the logic. By substituting "blue" for the second occurrence of "red" we alter what is said, and this makes what is said no longer self-contradictory. Of course, if "blue" and "red" meant the same, the statement would still be self-contradictory; but they do not.

This illustrates the dependence of logic on language. There are a lot of complicated disputes among logicians about the nature of this dependence; but I hope that what I have said so far would meet with general agreement. We have seen that the meanings of the words "red" and "blue" can affect the logical restrictions on what is said. We have to ask, therefore, whether, and in what ways, the introduction of words such as "ought", "right" and "wrong", as they are used in making moral statements, affects the logic. In the example I have just given the change from "red" to "blue" affected it. But it would have affected it just as much if we had changed "and" to "or". "It is red or it is not red" is not self-contradictory; indeed, it logically must be true. "And" and "or" are what are called logical words or logical constants; other logical words are the so-called modal operators such as "must". They too affect the logic. If I say "He is out, but it is not the case that he must be out", that is not self-contradictory; but if I say "He must be out, but it is not the case that he is out", that *is* self-contradictory. I have argued elsewhere (Hare 1981, pp. 2 and 10) that words such as "ought" resemble these modal operators, in particular in the fact that, unlike "red" and "blue", they owe their meanings entirely to their logical properties. And we determine what these logical properties are (what the rules are for their consistent use) by seeing what statements containing them correct speakers of the language treat as self-contradictory or inconsistent. This gives us a way of testing a piece of moral thinking to see whether it is logically in order.

What then are the logical restrictions on the use of these moral words, if we are to avoid self-contradiction? There are more than one; but the one that should interest us here is the so-called requirement of universalizability (I apologize for this long word). This says that you contradict yourself if you make moral judgements about two situations which you agree to be identical in their non-moral properties, and these judgements ascribe to one of the situations moral properties which they deny of the other. For example, if I say "He did wrong, but there might be another situation just like this one, with people in it just like these, with the same characters, motivations, etc., but in that other situation the corresponding person would not be doing wrong", then I am contradicting myself. I think that most moral philosophers would agree that "wrong" has this feature, though some hold that it is not logic alone that gives it the feature, but a substantial *moral* principle. I shall not argue about this here. Nor shall I argue with those few who claim that it is not a feature of moral words at all; they only claim this because they have not fully understood the thesis of universalizability. I have argued elsewhere that moral words do have this feature, and that it is a logical feature (Hare 1963, pp. 30ff.). But I hope it will be agreed at least for the sake of argument that they do have the feature.

This feature is closely connected with the *agapê* doctrine that I mentioned earlier. Indeed, though I cannot substantiate this as a matter of history, I think it likely that the reason why we have in our language moral words with this feature is that the requirement to love our neighbour as ourselves has got built into the language as a result of the growth of Christian moral ideas and similar ideas in other religions. This often happens with words. For example, it was not until recently that scientists discovered that water is composed of two parts of hydrogen to one of oxygen; but now you may find in the dictionary that in one (but only one) of the senses of "water" it is true *by definition* that water is H_2O. What has happened is that a thesis which was a substantial thesis about water has got written into the language as an analytic truth, true in virtue of the meanings of the words. I think the same has happened with "ought" and universalizability. But this is not the place to argue that this is so.

If it is so, then we could free ourselves from this logical requirement just by stopping speaking in moral terms – that is, by giving up the moral language; but there would be a penalty for this: we should no longer be able to say the things, and in particular to ask the questions, that we now ask using the moral words. I shall assume that actually people will want to go on asking these questions and trying to find answers to them. And if we do go on asking them, we are bound, in thinking about possible answers, to follow the requirements of logic, and in particular the requirement of universalizability, which is the linguistic embodiment of the command to love our neighbour. We shall see later where this leads us.

So then, one necessary ingredient of good moral thinking is logic. But, as I said, it is not the only ingredient. Someone whose logic was faultless, but who paid absolutely no attention to the facts of the situations he was thinking about, could not be said to be doing his moral thinking well. These two ingredients, logic and the facts, are what determine the goodness of a piece of moral thinking. Richard Brandt has expressed this well: he says "I shall preempt the term 'rational' to refer to actions, desires or moral systems which survive maximal criticism by facts and logic" (1979, p. 10). But what facts do we have to attend to if we are to do our moral thinking well?

What we have to attend to are facts about what we should be doing if we did one or other of the things open to us to do. But what we should be doing is affecting the course of events in some way. For example, if I give somebody a drug which kills him, what I am doing is (among other things) *bringing about* his death. It is the consequences of my actions (for example the action of administering the drug to him) that make it *that* action, the action of killing him. There are some confused philosophers who think that it is wrong to consider the consequences of actions when judging their rightness or wrongness; but if they were less confused they would see that the sense in which the consequences of actions determine what the actions are, and thus their morality, is a different sense from that in which they are using the word. Everybody must agree that, in the sense of which *I* have been using it, facts about consequences affect the morality of actions, because they determine what the actions are.

But what facts about what consequences do we have to consider? Some consequences, no doubt, are irrelevant to morality. For example, the fact that in giving a person a drug, which involves moving my hands in certain directions, I displace molecules in the air which otherwise would have gone elsewhere, is almost always morally irrelevant. So we are unlikely to say that all the physical consequences of an action are relevant to the moral assessment of it. But some are, and we have to say which, and why. For example, many would say that if a drug would kill the patient if administered, that is a morally relevant consequence. About some consequences, though, people are likely to disagree. If what is killed is a one-week-old embryo, some would say that killing it just does not matter morally, but others would strongly dissent.

The consequences that we think morally relevant are going to be those which are mentioned in whatever moral principles we apply to the situation. For example, if we think that one ought not to kill any human being after conception, then we shall think it morally relevant that to administer a certain drug would kill an embryo. But if we do not accept such a principle, we shall not think it relevant. So the question of relevance boils down to the question of what moral principles we should accept.

If we take the command to love our neighbour as "the law and the prophets", and accordingly accept the principle that we should do to others as we wish them to do to us, the question becomes a bit easier. We have to ask what in particular we wish should be done to us if we were in exactly the position of the person whom our action will affect. This means that what we have to consider is the effect on that person's preferences. If we were in exactly his (or her) position, we should have his preferences; for if the preferences were different the position would be different. If this is right, it is very important. It means, for example, that if, as is certainly the case, embryos have no preferences, we shall not mind what happens to us if we are embryos. But, I hasten to add, we shall mind what would happen to us if we were the person that an embryo would turn into if not killed. It matters very much to me that the embryo that turned into me was not killed. This is the basis of the so-called argument from potentiality that is much used by anti-abortionists. But we are not in any case going to bring to birth all the children that we in theory could bring to birth. The clearest example of this is where we have two embryos but can only implant one of them. But the same applies where a family has, for good moral reasons, decided not to have more than one more child and to abstain thereafter; it will be this child now or another child later, but not both. So the potentiality argument, as I have interpreted it, does not compel us to increase the population without limit, or indeed more than a justified population and family planning policy allows (Hare 1975, 1988, 1989a).

Normally, in doing something to one person we are also doing things to a lot of others. For example saving the life of one drowning person may mean leaving another to drown. To the question "Who is my neighbour?" we might answer "Whoever is affected by my actions"; but in most cases many people will be affected, and this raises the difficult question of how the interests of these various people (or what we wish should be done to us if we were each one of them) should be balanced. We wish that if we were either of the drowning people we should be saved; but how do we decide which we ought to save if we cannot save both? I can think of no better answer than that provided by a further application of the requirement to universalize (which, I said, was the embodiment of the *agapê* doctrine). We have got to find universal principles that we can accept for all situations, whatever role we ourselves occupy in them. I have to do what I wish should be done to me in each of these situations in which I occupy different roles; but when I have to balance the wishes I have for all these roles, I am likely to give greater weight to the stronger preferences. So, in our example, if I know that one of the drowning people is drowning because he was trying to commit suicide and wants to die, and the other is a well-meaning person but a poor swimmer who is, perhaps mistakenly, trying to rescue him, but himself very much wants to live, then I shall think I ought to save the latter.

Such cases raise many problems which have been discussed, often helpfully, by philosophers; but there is no space to go into them now. Let us return to the main point, which is that good moral thinking demands attention to logic and to the facts. The logic of the moral words requires us to prescribe as if *we* might be any one of the people affected, that is impartially, loving them all as ourselves. The facts of a situation determine what we should be doing to each of them if we acted in each of the alternative ways open to us. These two requirements will make us consider the interests, which are a function of the present and future preferences, of all the people affected, and to try to maximize the furtherance of these interests. This is substantially the view of a typical utilitarian. Kant would have put the same point in a different way; he would have said that we have to make the ends of the others our own ends (1785, BA69 = 430). Kant and the utilitarians, far from being diametrically opposed as most people think, have a great deal in common, and indeed almost everything in common when we are speaking of our duties to other people. And both, as J.S. Mill (1861, chap. 2) and Kant (1785, BA13 = 399) saw, have an affinity with the Christian doctrine of love.

So then, who are the authorities on moral questions? We saw that there are none in the strong sense of "authority" in which it means "source of unchallengeable answers". But in the weaker sense of "people to whom we would be right to go for advice, because they are good at moral thinking", there are indeed authorities. I said that to do good moral thinking requires an understanding of the logic of the questions we are asking, and a knowledge of the facts. This neatly divides up the class of moral authorities in this weaker sense. For some people will be better at the logic, and others will be better at the facts. Philosophers *ought* to be better at the logic, though not all of them are. And practitioners of the disciplines concerned (doctors for example) are likely to be better at the facts. To attend to the really important facts, however, they have to have more than medical knowledge, and more even than the knowledge that other disciplines could give of the consequences of actions; they have to have the sensitivity, the empathy, to know what it is like to be in the situation of the others affected, for example their patients.

Since these two kinds of authority, on the facts and on the logic, are not likely to be possessed to the same high degree by one person, there is everything to be said for teamwork. That is why I have got furthest towards an understanding of vexed questions such as abortion and euthanasia when I have been in working parties and seminars which include both sorts of people. We help one another. What then about the lawyers and the clergymen? They can help too, and have done so on the working parties I have taken part in. But they have done so only in so far as they have been able to play one or both of the roles I have distinguished: either that of sorting out the arguments by a clear understanding of their logic, or that of making us acquainted with facts that we did not know about before, especially facts about the impact on people of what we do. So anybody can play a useful part who knows what he is up to, and does not claim to be any kind of pontiff.

I have left myself room to add some comments, not on all the papers in the conference, but on those on which my own paper has a particular bearing. First, Peter Singer's handling in Germany in 1989, which I mentioned briefly, is relevant to Jennifer Jackson's views on toleration. He was to have spoken on the question of euthanasia for severely defective neonates. In the event there were street demonstrations by organisations of cripples, Protestant and Catholic religious groups, and the Greens (though nobody could be greener than Singer). One entire conference at which he was to have spoken had to be cancelled; so was his lecture at another university, and those who had invited him were threatened with dismissal. He was able to speak only at one place, to a small audience which had followed him from the hall that had been booked to a smaller room. Euthanasia is widely discussed elsewhere; but in Germany, for obvious historical reasons, it is taboo. This is good example to illustrate Jennifer Jackson's problem. (Since I wrote this, another entire conference on applied philosophy at Kirchberg in Austria, has been cancelled because the organisers refused to withdraw invitations to certain named individuals whom higher authority wished to ban for fear of similar agitation. These included Singer and myself. The conference was to have been one of the well known series of Wittgenstein Symposia.)

Secondly, it surprised me that Peter Byrne should have used the term "liberal" in such a narrow sense that liberals fall victim to his strictures. I call myself a liberal, like J.S. Mill, and it seems to me that neither liberals nor even utilitarians need have any difficulty in condemning promiscuity. This is because of the harmful consequences it has for the partners, their children and indeed the stability of marriage in general, which most people think is an institution to be preserved. Nor have they any difficulty in condemning slavery. I hope that what I have already said both here and in Hare (1979, 1981) makes clear how this can be done. The key move is to show that acts which impair respect for good principles may be vicious from a utilitarian point of view, even though their present consequences may not, apart from this, be harmful.

I have never, I think, been at a conference on practical issues at which there was a higher proportion of good to bad arguments; and of course the good ones could all be supported by a Kantian utilitarian like me. I was especially pleased to hear Jim Thornton and Torbjörn Tännsjö discussing our duties to possible future people on lines which I find congenial (see Hare 1974, 1988).

I come lastly to Mary Warnock's paper. I find it hard to say whether I was the target of her first two paragraphs. This is certainly suggested by their wording; she says, of the bad old days, "the task of philosophy was held to be the analysis of the language of morals, such words as 'duty', 'ought' and 'right'. My first book was called *The Language of Morals*, and in it I did indeed analyse these words, as well as "good".

But I hope she does not think that I was one of those who needed to be drawn "willy nilly" into practical ethics by American students of the Vietnam period. Indeed, I was often in America in those days and I found that my theoretical and applied ethical work had already put me in a position to say to them some things that I hope they found helpful (see, e.g., Hare 1989b, ch. 3, written 1968, and 1966 for my views at that time on war and civil disobedience). I had been tormented by the problem "What could be counted as a just war?" (one of the issues she mentions) at least since 1936, a generation earlier, and had indeed first taken to philosophy in an attempt to answer it, and many other troubling questions raised by the Second World War. My first published paper on practical ethics was Hare (1955) (lectures given in Germany a year earlier), and since then I have written a lot about practical, especially on medical, issues, and have served on many working parties about them (though not on such exalted ones as those which Mary Warnock has chaired). I have written on them more as my confidence in my understanding of the logic of moral argument has grown, until now I devote about half of my time to them. Of four books of collected essays I am currently publishing, three are on practical issues. It was not the Vietnam War but the Second World War (indeed the aftermath of the First, in which Mary Warnock and I grew up) that got me going on them.

I can agree with many of the things that she says, and have said them myself. The difference is that I have thought it necessary to give reasons for them. This entails studying the logic of moral argument, which in turn entails studying the logical analysis of the language of morals. It is significant that at present analytical philosophers, who study this, are under heavy attack in Germany precisely because they do address practical issues. Analytical philosophy is "viewed as the intellectual foundation of bioethics", considered by their attackers to be a pernicious discipline with which no right-thinking philosopher would have anything to do (Schöne-Seifert and Rippe, 1991). In her paper (p. 27) she passes from a position with which nearly everybody (Kantians, utilitarians, the lot) would agree, viz. that in making moral judgements one has to put one's own interests temporarily on one side, to the position that one must not even put them on an exactly equal footing with those of others. This is certainly contrary to the Kantian, and the utilitarian, and the Christian doctrines which I have defended in this paper, yet she gives no reason for the abrupt transition. But at least she now declares herself a utilitarian in matters of public policy.

References and Bibliography

References in the text are to the date and page-number, unless otherwise indicated.

Writings of R. M. Hare

(1955) Can I be blamed for obeying orders? *The Listener* [Oct.]. Reprinted in Hare (1972)

(1963) *Freedom and Reason.* Oxford University Press

(1966) Peace. RSA lecture, Australian National University, Canberra, Reprinted in Hare (1972)

(1967) The lawful government. In: Laslett P, Runciman WG (eds) *Philosophy, Politics and Society* vol. 3. Basil Blackwell, Oxford. Reprinted in Hare (1972)

(1974) The abnormal child: moral dilemmas of doctors and parents. *Documentation in Medical Ethics* 3. Reprinted as "Survival of the weakest" in Gorovitz S (ed) *Moral Problems in Medicine,* 1st edn. Prentice-Hall (1976)

(1972) *Applications of Moral Philosophy.* Macmillan, London

(1975) Abortion and the golden rule. *Philosophy and Public Affairs* 4.

(1976) Ethical theory and utilitarianism. In: Lewis HD (ed) *Contemporary British Philosophy* vol. 4. Reprinted in Sen AK, Williams BAO (eds) *Utilitarianism and Beyond,* Cambridge University Press (1982), and in Hare (1989b)

(1979) What is wrong with slavery. *Philosophy and Public Affairs* 8. Reprinted in Hare (1989b)

(1981) *Moral Thinking.* Oxford University Press

(1984) Rights, utility and universalization. In: Frey R (ed) *Utility and Rights.* University of Minnesota Press. Reprinted in Hare (1989b)

(1986) Punishment and retributive justice. In: Adler J, Lee RN (eds) *Philosophical Topics* vol. 14. University of Arkansas Press. Reprinted in Hare (1989b)

(1987) In vitro fertilization and the Warnock Report. In: Chadwick R (ed) *Ethics, Reproduction and Genetic Control.* Routledge

(1988) Possible people. *Bioethics* 2.

(1989a) A Kantian approach to abortion. In: Bayles MD, Henley K (eds) *Right Conduct,* 2nd edn. Random House. Reprinted in *Social Theory and Practice* 15 (1989)

(1989b) *Essays on Political Morality.* Oxford University Press

Other Writings

Aristotle *Nicomachean Ethics.* References are to pages in the Bekker edition

Brandt RB (1979) *A Theory of the Good and the Right*. Oxford University Press
Butler J (1726) *Fifteen Sermons* and *Dissertation on Virtue*. Selections in Raphael DD (ed) *British Moralists* vol 1. Oxford University Press, 1969
Glover JCB et al. (1989) *Fertility and the Family*. Fourth Estate, London
Hobbes T (1651) *Leviathan*
Kant (1785) *Grundlegung zur Metaphysik der Sitten*. References are to pages of earliest editions and of the Royal Prussian Academy edition, as given in the margin of the translation by HJ Paton (*The Moral Law*, Hutchinson, 1948)
Mill JS (1861) *Utilitarianism*
Plato *Euthyphro*
Schöne-Seifert B, Rippe K-P (1991) Silencing the singer. *Hastings Center Report* 21
Warnock, Baroness M (chmn) (1984) *Report of the Committee of Inquiry into Human Fertilisation and Embryology* (HMSO cmnd. 9214). Reprinted with additions as *A Question of Life* by Basil Blackwell, Oxford, 1985

Subject Index